Politics and the Scottish Language

and other collected essays in literature, culture and politics

Macdonald Daly

New Ventures
Seattle and London
2020

Politics and the Scottish Language and other collected essays in literature, culture and politics
by Macdonald Daly

The right of Macdonald Daly to be identified as author of this work has been asserted by him in accordance with the Copyright, Designs and Patents Act, 1988.

First published in the USA and the UK by New Ventures, 2020.

Cover design by The Ever-Shifting Subject.

ISBN 9781602719910

CONTENTS

This book is for Bernard McGuirk,
With whom it was joyful to work.
For twenty-five years
He made me laugh tears
And he never once called me a jerk.

The essays in this book are the collectable pieces on literature and cultural studies I wrote, from a theoretical perspective which can accurately if generally be termed Marxist, over a period of twenty-five years in which I taught at the University of Nottingham.

While it is an understandable assumption that intellectual work and political engagement are closely intertwined in a Marxist world-view, it is something of an irony to come to understand that many of the advances in Marxist criticism were made by those who had temporarily or permanently turned away from engagement in direct political activity. Trotsky's composition of *Literature and Revolution* has often been considered a grotesque political irresponsibility, a cultural distraction which, among others, prevented him from properly ensuring that he became Lenin's successor, in which case the nightmare of Stalinism might not have followed. Because of that very nightmare, Lukács turned from political activism to the "safer" arena of literary criticism, and the best remembered "political" novels of the twentieth century are devastating satires on the Soviet system and its self-declared identity with Marxism (Zamyatin's *We*, Koestler's *Darkness at Noon*, Orwell's *Animal Farm*, and Nabokov's *Bend Sinister*). Gramsci, incarcerated by Mussolini, could no longer agitate in the factory movement of Turin, and instead penned his prison notebooks, in which he adumbrated his theory of "cultural hegemony". Benjamin, exiled in Paris and unable to return to Hitler's Germany, wrote his important texts on the city's nineteenth century culture, literary and otherwise. His Frankfurt School colleagues Bloch, Adorno and Horkheimer, similarly relocated to New York, where they concentrated entirely on academic research which attempted to keep utopian and "high" cultural dreams alive. In the period of the Cold War, the only Marxist writer and critic of international repute who seemed to find the Eastern bloc congenial was Brecht. Otherwise, the main centre of gravity of Marxist cultural work shifted, paradoxically, to the capitalist West, where it has become mainly the preserve of critics and theorists, and only infrequently the resort of creative writers.

The paradox is not new within Marxism: Marx himself, after the political disappointments of 1848, retreated to the British Library to write *Capital*. Likewise, the post-war period of "ideological" criticism was marked by tremendous theoretical advance and elaboration, especially in France, in the hands of expressly or implicitly Marxist theorists such as Jean-Paul Sartre, Lucien Goldmann, Louis Althusser, Pierre Macherey, Roland Barthes, Etienne Balibar and Pierre Bourdieu. The "price" paid was an increasing academisation (and thus neutralisation of the political effectiveness) of the field, aided by a correspondingly intensifying rebarbativeness and obfuscation in the discourse many of these scholars employed. The experience of reading any of the critics named above can hardly be said to be easy or straightforward. The level of education and degree of wider philosophical and theoretical knowledge required for their understanding are taxing. These factors served to widen the gulf between both this scholarly and analytic Marxist aesthetics and that to which Marxist artists might actively subscribe (the chances of another Brecht appearing who might convincingly combine theory and creative practice became more and more remote) and the remnants of the committed "political" criticism which persisted (cheerfully untheoretical British texts like John Berger's *Ways of Seeing* [1972] or Paul O'Flinn's *Them and Us in Literature* [1975]) now seem vulgar and populist by comparison. Ever-fiercer internecine debates consequently erupted from time to time. The growing influence of Althusser in particular drew a rhetorically memorable but overweeningly hostile reaction from the English humanist Marxist historian E. P. Thompson in *The Poverty of Theory* (1978), and in a less fêted critique, Terry Lovell's *Pictures of Reality: Aesthetics, Politics and Pleasure* (1980), which calmly excoriated Althusserianism, but only to prescribe a return to a largely Brechtian aesthetics which by now seemed entirely of its moment and unresurrectable in the dawning of a period to be dominated by the "New Right". French Marxism had itself already been thrown into disarray by the political downturn following May 1968, shortly after which Althusser, in his most famous (or notorious) essay, "Ideology and Ideological State Apparatuses", implicitly abandoned the hope of any significant social change coming from within the ideological sphere.[1] Indeed, it was not

---

[1] Louis Althusser, "Ideology and Ideological State Apparatuses (Notes towards an Investigation)", *Lenin and Philosophy and Other Essays* (London: New Left

even that literature was no longer envisaged to have much potential for socialist radicalism: as Macherey and Balibar were to argue at greater length after him (in 1978),[2] Althusser now envisaged the teaching of literature by the modern state within its educational institutions as a powerfully reactionary force to which all-too-optimistic Marxists had been blind. It was one of the many hegemonic ideological means whereby the state persuaded its citizens to adopt a value system which ensured resignation to the world-as-it-is rather than agitation to create the world-as-it-could-be.

Nonetheless, theses, anthologies and monographs in Marxist aesthetics continued to pile up with impressive plenitude throughout the Cold War and Thatcher/Reagan periods in the liberal democracies in which the actualisation of Marxism, or even its slightest demonstrable effect on official political policy, seemed something on which one would have been foolhardy to have gambled. One can certainly trace its influence in every other theoretical trend, especially those with an implied or explicit political agenda, such as postcolonialism and feminism, which could eclectically adopt Marxist ideas and strategies without having to face, as Marxism itself did, the political embarrassment of something known as "actually existing socialism". The critique of the education system under capitalism, and of the specific rôle of literature within that system, was variously embellished, most often in relation to the literary classics, and frequently (especially in Britain) under the rubric of "cultural materialism", a term recommended by Raymond Williams in *Marxism and Literature* (1977) in a bid to advance Marxist aesthetics beyond the limiting concepts of "reflection" and "mediation" which Engels had long before sponsored.

But Marxist theory itself seemed paradoxically to have less direct political impact the more intellectually redistributed and reformulated it became. In the absence of any evident political use value, it nonetheless did acquire an obvious exchange value within the academic publishing and employment markets. In certain situations it seemed unperturbed that it could take a detour around political questions entirely. Fredric

Books, 1971), pp. 127-86.
[2] Etienne Balibar and Pierre Macherey, "On Literature as an Ideological Form", in Francis Mulhern (ed.), *Contemporary Marxist Literary Criticism* (Harlow: Longman, 1992), pp. 34-54.

Jameson's *Marxism and Form* (1971), the first of his many volumes which eloquently reconfigured Marxist aesthetic thinking, declared itself to be a "general introduction" to "a relatively Hegelian kind of Marxism", and he was thus able to bypass entirely the distractions of "vulgar" Marxist political positions, which had never made any serious impression on American intellectual life in the first place.[3] Jameson's work, whose main themes changed little in over fifty years, is perhaps the most supple, elegant and influential contribution made to Marxist aesthetics yet, but again at serious cost, for it has arguably refined and adjusted the intellectual methods of Marxism in its application to the arts in an exclusively contemplative mode, all the while neglecting to address the issue of what this means for actual political practice.

But this is a standard which Marxism, uniquely among critical theories, has exacted from itself, ever since the enunciation of the eleventh and most famous of Marx's "Theses on Feuerbach" concerning philosophers before him who only *interpreted* the world: "the point, however, is to *change* it". It remains the case, however, if the resourcefulness and survivability of capitalism is a touchstone, that Marxist intellectual theory has more evidently allowed us to interpret the world anew rather than manifestly changed the relations of production – and this truth seemed ineluctable when the "actually existing socialism" of the Eastern bloc crumbled in the late 1980s and the historic changes made in the name (if not the spirit) of Marxism went into dramatically rapid reversal.

One other truth seems to be that Marxism has consistently been more potent as a critique than as a programme. During the international oil crisis of the 1970s, capitalism entered one of the periodic slumps which Marx diagnosed as the inevitably recurring outcome of its systemic contradictions. One might have expected, in these circumstances, a widespread turn to Marxist explanatory models and political action. Instead, Jean Baudrillard's *The Mirror of Production* (1975) simultaneously threw down the postmodernist gauntlet to most fundamental Marxist tenets. Baudrillard was swiftly followed by Jean-François Lyotard, who attacked all "grand narratives" (including Marxism) in *The*

---

[3] Fredric Jameson, *Marxism and Form: Twentieth Century Dialectical Theories of Literature* (Princeton: Princeton University Press, 1971), pp. ix, x.

Postmodern Condition (1979). It is undeniably true that, over the next quarter century, postmodernism became the philosophy in the ascendant in the aesthetic sphere. While one struggles to name significant contemporary writers one can unequivocally designate as Marxist, a simple perambulation around any literary bookstore will now yield dozens who are undeniably postmodernist. In the critical sphere, attempts to integrate postmodernism (and/or poststructuralism) with traditional Marxism resulted in the oddly termed (and contestably conceived) "post-Marxism",[4] but mainstream Marxism has proved generally more resilient than other "grand narratives" to such incursions and, in books like David Harvey's *The Condition of Postmodernity* (1980) and Jameson's *Postmodernism, or, The Cultural Logic of Late Capitalism* (1991), produced the finest intellectual responses to the postmodernist challenge. The last read postmodernism, not as a school of thought, but as an intellectual apology for the changed nature of capitalism. Thus Jameson brought Marxism thudding back onto the table, in the intellectual sphere at least, with a classically Marxist argument, engaging with contemporary thought and society, and demonstrating the rôle of ideology, art, and immanent critique to the preservation of, developments within, and challenges to the economic order. The enterprise convinced many that, whatever emerges from the post-post-everything epoch within which all cultural discourse seems now to be conducted, the waning flame of Marxism, under whatever name and in whatever form, is unlikely to be extinguished, and will have much more to say about art and the social processes which engender it and which it, in turn, modulates.

The present book, although I hope the reader finds it more eclectic and less methodically purist than the label "Marxist" may suggest, gathers together my modest and scattered contributions to this general field. Some of these essays (like those towards the end of the volume on the 1992 UK General Election, and academic freedom) bear the mark of particular debates which occurred at particular times, and in the last instance in a very particular place. A couple (the essay on Fredric Jameson and on "The Critical Audience?") are published here for the first time, excess from projects which never ultimately saw the light of day or which could not, for one reason or another, finally contain them. The

---

4 See, for example, Tony Bennett, *Outside Literature* (London: Routledge, 1990).

remainder were self-evidently commissioned by publishers or editors as introductions or contributions to journals or anthologies of academic essays on prescribed themes. In each essay I have retained the particular forms of annotation/ bibliography of the original as published.

My thanks go to all the colleagues and collaborators who encouraged me to put my thinking onto paper, and in particular to Sean Matthews for allowing me to reprint the final item, which we wrote together. The essays do not appear in chronological order of composition or publication, but in a thematically associative sequence, insofar as that is possible with a disparate and in some respects miscellaneous body of work. I have appended dates of composition at the end of each essay. I have tinkered with the original texts little or not at all, apart from small contextual adjustments and interpolations made silently here and there, and so any intellectual deficiencies which remain are to be seen as the consequences of my failure to get wiser as I get older.

1 February 2020

In 1971, Fredric Jameson, possibly the most influential Marxist critic of the late twentieth century, recommended "a relatively Hegelian kind of Marxism" to the literary critical world. Those only partly acquainted with Marxism might have been forgiven for wondering why a political and philosophical doctrine which had so long prided itself on "overcoming" Hegel, on having turned Hegel on his head, on having morphed Hegel's idealist dialectic into the apparently quite contrasting doctrine of historical materialism, was itself seemingly being cast back into the politically conservative swamp from which it usually claimed to have rescued not only German philosophy but the entire modern world. Jameson dated the emergence of Hegelian Marxism to a short period of about fifteen years, the pertinent milestones being, in the German speaking world, "Lukács' *History and Class Consciousness* in 1923, along with the rediscovery of Marx's *Economic and Philosophical Manuscripts of 1844*"(first published, incompletely, in Russian in 1927, and completely, in German, in 1932) and, in France, "the Hegel revival there during the late thirties".[1] He did not need to be explicit that this was also the definitive period of developing anti-Stalinist revulsion in Western Europe. Our speculative reader may legitimately have surmised from Jameson that the fledgling Marxist criticism of the late nineteenth and early twentieth centuries, which had taken its stand on Marx's own oft-repeated sense that Hegelianism was a political dead end, was now itself ironically considered to have been a grand tour down a most disappointing methodological *cul-de-sac*.

Indeed, Jameson has seldom had anything to say on most of the neglected figures who will make an appearance in this essay, like Franz Mehring, William Morris, Antonio Labriola, and Georgi Plekhanov.[2] But the reader more familiar with Marxist modes of argumentation would have little

[1] Fredric Jameson, *Marxism and Form: Twentieth-Century Dialectical Theories of Literature* (Princeton, N.J.: Princeton University Press, 1971), p. ix.
[2] All of them are likewise ignored by as influential and as recent a selection as Terry Eagleton and Drew Milne (eds.), *Marxist Literary Theory: a Reader* (Oxford: Blackwell, 1996), which presents selections from Marx and Engels and thence leaps boldly ahead to Lenin without even a further nod at the nineteenth century.

problem with the proposition that a thing can turn into its opposite, or that a negation can be negated, without any return to the *status quo ante* being effected. Dialectical deftness is the stock-in-trade of Hegelianism and Marxism alike. The young pre-Marxist Marx, in a note appended to his doctoral thesis of 1841, in which he clearly had Hegel in mind, already had a definite grasp of the method:

> It is conceivable that a philosopher should be guilty of this or that inconsistency because of this or that compromise; he may himself be conscious of it. But what he is not conscious of is that in the last analysis this apparent compromise is made possible by the deficiency of his principles or an inadequate grasp of them. So if a philosopher really has compromised it is the job of his followers to use the inner core of his thought to illuminate his own superficial expressions of it. In this way, what is a progress in conscience is also a progress in knowledge. This does not involve putting the conscience of a philosopher under suspicion, but rather construing the essential characteristics of his views, giving them a definite form and meaning, and thus at the same time going beyond them.[3]

It is with reference to this description of the proper relation between a philosopher and his followers that this essay will ultimately offer an assessment of nineteenth-century literary critics who attempted to elaborate and/or practise a Marxist aesthetics. Did they, as Marx put it, "use the inner core of his thought to illuminate his own superficial expressions of it" in the aesthetic field? Or, as the relative silence concerning them of Jameson and many other commentators perhaps suggests, did they fail in this task? And if they failed, did any do so less ingloriously than others?

We must first of all, then, uncover the "inner core" of Marx's thinking with respect to art and literature, a task which virtually all who are fit to comment have acknowledged as difficult on account of the very "superficial expressions" of it which Marx left, not to mention the scattered textual locations in which they arise. There is, to be sure, the ultimate gift horse

---

[3] David McLellan (ed.), *Karl Marx: Selected Writings* (Oxford: Oxford University Press, 1977), p. 13.

Marx gave us, namely his "Preface" to *A Contribution to the Critique of Political Economy* (1859), in which he explicitly includes the "aesthetic" in his list of examples of "ideological forms" comprising the "superstructure" of society:

In the social production of their life, men enter into definite relations that are indispensable and independent of their will, relations of production which correspond to a definite stage of development of their material productive forces. The sum total of these relations of production constitutes the economic structure of society, the real foundation, on which rises a legal and political superstructure and to which correspond definite forms of social consciousness. The mode of production of material life conditions the social, political and intellectual life process in general. It is not the consciousness of men that determines their being, but, on the contrary, their social being that determines their consciousness. At a certain stage of their development, the material productive forces of society come in conflict with the existing relations of production, or – what is but a legal expression for the same thing – with the property relations within which they have been at work hitherto. From forms of development of the productive forces these relations turn into their fetters. Then begins an epoch of social revolution. With the change of the economic foundation the entire immense superstructure is more or less rapidly transformed. In considering such transformations a distinction should always be made between the material transformation of the economic conditions of production, which can be determined with the precision of natural science, and the legal, political, religious, aesthetic or philosophic – in short, ideological forms in which men become conscious of this conflict and fight it out. Just as our opinion of an individual is not based on what he thinks of himself, so can we not judge of such a period of transformation by its own consciousness; on the contrary, this consciousness must be explained rather from the contradictions of material life, from the existing conflict between the social productive forces and the relations of production.[4]

---

[4] Karl Marx and Frederick Engels, *On Literature and Art* (Moscow: Progress Publishers, 1976), p. 41.

It has seldom been noted how repetitious this passage is. Marx hardly builds an elaborate or complex argument here: rather, he reiterates a central idea in varied phrasing in a manner typical of someone intent on persuading a reader of a novel (for Hegelians an heretical) notion. The same three-element relation, actually quite simple subject-verb-object expressions, is simply described in three different ways: (1) [subject] the *economic structure of society* or *the mode of production of material life* or *social being* (2) [verb] *gives rise to, conditions* or *determines* (3) [object] the *legal and political superstructure*, the *social, political and intellectual life process in general*, or *consciousness*, respectively. In the English translation quoted, the three different formulations depict almost the same relation, being hardly at semantic variance with one another except in the verbs. But it is in the hazards of those verbs that markedly variant and incompatible versions of the relations between "base" and "superstructure" (and consequently between Marxism and art) have taken root.

The crucial three sentences read, in Marx's original, "Die Gesamtheit dieser Produktionsverhältnisse bildet die ökonomische Struktur der Gesellschaft, die reale Basis, worauf sich ein juristischer und politischer Überbau erhebt, und welcher bestimmte gesellschaftliche Bewusst-seinformen entsprechen. Die Produktionsweise des materiellen Lebens bedingt den sozialen, politischen und geistigen Lebenzsprozess überhaupt. Es is nicht das Bewusstsein der Menschen, das ihr Sein, sondern umgekehrt ihr gesellschaftliches Sein, das ihr Bewusstsein bestimmt."[5] The German verb "bedingen" in the second sentence is delicately nuanced: "bedingt" here could justifiably have been Englished (in ascending order of strength) as "presupposes", "conditions", "causes", "necessitates", or "determines", although many would argue that if Marx had the last in mind he would probably have reached for a stronger verb. The verb so translated, which he does use in the following sentence, is "bestimmen", which is even more varied in application: thus "bestimmt" could mean any of "modifies", "influences", "conditions", "decides", "defines", "designates", "fixes", "determines" or "predetermines". Now, there are clear differences of interconnectedness indicated by the causative

[5] Fritz J. Raddatz (ed.), *Marxismus und literatur: eine dokumentation in drei bänden* (Hamburg, Rowohlt, 1969), Vol. I, p. 152. I would like to thank Dr Svenja Adolphs for confirming some particulars of the original German.

verbs "gives rise to", "conditions" and "determines". The first defines a weak relation in which (a) simply creates the preconditions for (b); the second implies a stronger causative relation in which (a) influences or sets limits to the form of (b); the third might imply that (a) is the thoroughly controlling and moving force behind or within (b). If, for heuristic purposes, one leaves aside the complex social phenomena which Marx is actually describing, and replaces them with simpler correlates, as Marx himself does with the example of (a) "an individual" and (b) "what he thinks of himself", then the differences of interconnectedness are easier to appreciate. Take the alternative example of (a) a person's body and (b) a person's character. In this case, the first proposition is surely a universally acceptable one: it amounts to little more than a statement of the obvious, namely that to have a character one must possess a body. The second proposition would also probably pass without major disagreement: all that would be questioned is the degree to which character is affected by physiology. The third proposition, that character is controlled thoroughly and at all times by the operations of bodily reflexes, organs, genetic programming and so on, might gain the assent of certain neuroscientists and behaviourists, but is unlikely to meet with the approval of too many others, scientists included, not least because it seems to render the very concept of "character" (if it is merely an epiphenomenon) worthless: all talk of character can simply be reduced to physical terms in such a case.

The passage is evidently an example of what the soon-to-be Dr Marx had already diagnosed as a "deficiency of [...] principles or an inadequate grasp of them" because the three propositions are not mutually compatible: to leave all of them open as possibilities is precisely a "compromise", here no doubt made for the sake of the non-idealist, anti-Hegelian emphasis which Marx felt was required at the moment. Marx himself never went "beyond" them, although the early Marx demonstrably believed the opposite. It is worth recalling that the man who wrote, "It is not the consciousness of men that determines their being, but, on the contrary, their social being that determines their consciousness" had two decades earlier "criticised Democritus' strict determinism and came out in favour of Epicurus' position of freedom of man's consciousness to change his surroundings".[6] The sheer number and extent of Marx's casual and

---

[6] David McLellan, *The Thought of Karl Marx*, 2nd ed. (Basingstoke: Macmillan,

formal comments on art and literature, the pleasure he took in them and the value they obviously possessed for him, give the lie to any charge of philistine dismissal of the aesthetic or its importance. But only a decade previously, in *The Manifesto of the Communist Party* (1848), he could write, "Does it require deep intuition to comprehend that man's ideas, views and conceptions, in one word, man's consciousness, changes with every change in the conditions of his material existence, in his social relations and in his social life? What else does the history of ideas prove, than that intellectual production changes its character in proportion as material production is changed?"[7] Earlier still, *The German Ideology* (1846), a text written jointly with Engels which from the very first page is a bold, lacerating and unrelenting attack on Hegel and his contemporary followers, is replete with formulations which seem to vacillate between the uncompromisingly "deterministic" and pliably "conditional" versions of base/superstructure relations, but ultimately veer towards the former: "The phantoms formed in the brains of men are also, necessarily, sublimates of their material life-process, which is empirically verifiable and bound to material premises. Morality, religion, metaphysics, and all the rest of ideology as well as the forms of consciousness corresponding to these, thus no longer retain the semblance of independence."

But the same text also continually stresses that this is not how humans *live* their relation to the world: on the contrary, they seem always and everywhere to have acted as if the reverse were true, imagining that the moving principle of the world really is thought: "If in all ideology men and their relations appear upside-down as in a *camera obscura*, this phenomenon arises just as much from their historical life-process as the inversion of objects on the retina does from their physical life process."[8] Writing in 1852, in *The Eighteenth Brumaire of Louis Napoleon*, he could still say, "Upon the different forms of property, upon the social conditions of existence, rises an entire superstructure of distinct and peculiarly formed sentiments, illusions, modes of thought, and views of life. The entire class creates and forms them out of its material foundations and out of the corresponding social relations."[9] But it did not fail to dawn on

1979), p. 7.

[7] Marx and Engels, *On Literature and Art,* p. 73.

[8] Marx and Engels, *On Literature and Art,* p. 43.

[9] Karl Marx and Frederick Engels, *Collected Works* (London: Lawrence and

Marx that these apparent illusions were *socially produced* (always a key concept for him) and socially potent. "Production not only provides the material to satisfy a need," he wrote in the late 1850s, "it also provides the need for the material. [...] An *objet d'art* creates a public that has artistic taste and is able to enjoy beauty".[10] But if the appetite for beauty can become a *need*, akin to appetites more traditionally conceived of as physical, where does the material end and the non-material begin? There is no linear development in these sometimes contradictory, sometimes complementary thoughts. Variations on these themes, unpredictably inflected towards or between the various versions of the base/superstructure motif, can emerge at different points in Marx's *oeuvre* with something approaching randomness. As early as 1844 he could ferociously satirise capitalism's denial of the enjoyment of luxury, its imperative to save rather than spend, as one of its morally worst features, and in doing so he notably made no distinction between "material" and "non-material" activities: "The less you eat, drink and buy books; the less you go to the theatre, the dance hall, the public house; the less you think, love, theorise, sing, paint, fence, etc., the more you *save* – the *greater* becomes your treasure which neither moths nor rust will devour – your *capital*."[11]

It is important to note that the few texts in which we find Marx attempting to work out the implications of his theory of determination for specific forms of art show that he was in difficulty. Above all, there is the famous (or notorious) 1857 draft "Introduction" to *A Contribution to a Critique of Political Economy* (which was not published until 1903), in which he embarks upon a disquisition concerning the long-lasting appeal of ancient art stimulated by questions such as, "Is the conception of nature and of social relations which underlies Greek imagination and therefore Greek [art] possible when there are self-acting mules, railways, locomotives and electric telegraphs?" His answer to the conundrum of the ongoing social value of Greek art was, "Does not the child in every epoch represent the character of the period in its natural veracity? Why should not the historic childhood of humanity, where it attained its most beautiful form, exert an eternal charm because it is a stage that will never

Wishart, 1979), vol. XI, p. 128.
[10] Marx and Engels, *On Literature and Art*, p. 129.
[11] Marx and Engels, *On Literature and Art*, p. 133.

recur?"[12] This was a desperately bad stab at answering a good question, but more important than its bathos is the fact that Marx's response reverts to categories which are entirely non-Marxist. This may be one reason why he chose not to publish the draft.

However, the least satisfactory response to the shortcomings of Marx's thinking on these matters is to wave aside his inadequately worked out positions as merely nugatory. Marx was too influential a thinker for the tradition of aesthetic criticism he inspired to be ignored in this way. He himself, as we have already seen, described a more intellectually effective procedure. Did his followers attempt to construe "the essential characteristics of his views, giving them a definite form and meaning, and thus at the same time going beyond them"? It is certainly possible, at this distance, to identify the "inner core" of Marx's thought with respect to aesthetics. This essentially posits the truth that the human capacity to produce art is dependent on an economic system in which such production (and its consumption) is made possible, that art itself is a "secondary" phenomenon which bears the ineradicable traces or marks of its economic dependency (and is thus highly historically variable), but that it also creates new needs which themselves lead to the diversification of the product and thus (logically) would seem capable of intervening in the "primary" economic system. One might paraphrase Marx's thinking along these lines as prompting a number of questions which he himself is unable to answer but which provided a working agenda for his followers. Among these questions might be the following: *in what specific ways* do economic conditions "influence" the production of art in concrete cases?; *how much* is art influenced by economic conditions?; is there any way in which art can be said to be *relatively free* of such influence?; if so, can some arts, or some aesthetic texts, be said to be *more or less free* than others?; if not, is art, in the final analysis, *reducible to* economic categories?; or is it possible that the influence might also work *in reverse*, art precipitating modifications in economic life?

Some of these questions were tackled while Marx himself was still alive, but not by Marx. It is too little acknowledged that, in the aesthetic field at least, Engels, *pace* his own self-characterisation, did not simply play second fiddle to Marx as the latter's populariser. He not only supplemented

Marx's general reflections on art, but considerably enlarged upon them, and even introduced quite new emphases and lines of thought. This is nowhere more patent than in his espousal of Realism as his preferred aesthetic form. According to Stefan Morawski, "The word 'realism' does not appear in any text by Marx." [13] Later Marxist aestheticians' preoccupation with Realism, which can be found as late as Lukács and Raymond Williams, is almost entirely due to Engels. In its earliest emergence in his writing, this concern seems driven by the fact that the "reality" depicted by certain works of art coincides happily with Marx's historical materialist theory of "the real foundation", or, even more pedestrianly, with the mere practical necessities of spreading the socialist message. In 1844, for example, Engels articulated his enthusiasm for a contemporary painting by Karl Hubner, "The Silesian Weavers", which he praised in terms that referred to little other than its politically emotive content and its consequent efficacy as a piece of propaganda: it "made a more effectual Socialist agitation than a hundred pamphlets might have done".[14] But the very fact that Engels even saw fit to hail a painting as a notable contribution to the early progress of the Socialist movement is eloquent testimony to his sense of art's social importance.

Engels soon overcame (if indeed he ever held) the simple belief that the merit of a work of art is merely an index of the effectiveness with which it encapsulates a socialist politics, and this is why it would be unfair to lay the responsibility for the later Stalinist grotesqueness of the doctrine of "Socialist Realism" at his door. It is in his correspondence, not Marx's, that we first encounter a perspective on Realism which acknowledges it both as a set of aesthetic conventions and as a social form with especial resonance for Marxism. In April 1888, in a draft letter to responding to the author of a novel of working-class life, he famously announced, "Realism, to my mind, implies, besides truth of detail, the truthful reproduction of typical characters under typical circumstances", and criticised the work because it had failed to meet the criteria of

---

[13] Lee Baxandall and Stefan Morawski (eds.), *Karl Marx and Frederick Engels on Literature and Art* (New York: International General, 1973), p. 30.

[14] Baxandall and Morawski, p. 105. The painting is in the Kunstmuseum, Düsseldorf. A monochrome reproduction can be found in Margaret A. Rose, *Marx's Lost Aesthetic: Karl Marx and the Visual Arts* (Cambridge: Cambridge University Press, 1984), p. 105.

circumstantial typicality, in that it omitted to depict the working class as much more than a passive mass.[15]

It would be easy to dismiss this seemingly sweeping criticism of a large corpus of fiction as a product of Engels' highly politicised disposition, but to do so would fail to attend to its remarkable originality. We may now be used to authorial class allegiance, ideological tendency, and unconscious motivation as they can be found to operate in literary texts, but no one, before Engels, was prepared to articulate their putative effect *and* simultaneously establish a political dimension for evaluation of the aesthetic results. Moreover, Balzac's work is here appropriated for Marxism in a way that vitally undermines the vulgar Marxist notion that art be produced to a political prescription and its evaluation firmly subordinated to socialist ends. We may distinguish four implicit, associated points: first, literary writing is not an "opinionated" discourse and cannot be evaluated by the same standards as, for example, a political polemic; second, this is not to say that art is non-ideological, but that it is not (or should not be) *expressly* so; third, the ideological nature of an art work cannot be equated with the (conscious) ideology of the artist, and indeed may be in conflict with it; and, fourth, it therefore follows that classical or bourgeois art cannot simply be dismissed on the assumption that it is ideologically reactionary.

The fact that these points raise further questions which are not answered by Engels only demonstrates how they enlarge the scope of Marxist enquiry into art, its evaluation, and its functions. What stance should a Marxist critic take on classical or bourgeois works of art that cannot be read "against the grain" in the way that he reads Balzac? If analysis shows that the work is indeed reactionary, in however subtly tangential and aesthetically pleasing a manner, should Marxist critics thereafter simply wash their hands of it? Or should they embark on a critique of its content while praising its form? In short, how much is Marxist theory willing to separate the aesthetic value of a work of art from its ideological outlook? Just as Engels' comments on Balzac initiated a search for solutions to these problems, so too did they encourage

---

[15] Marx and Engels, *On Literature and Art,* pp. 91-2. On "tendency writing", see further Engels' letter to Minna Kautsky, 26 November 1885, quoted in Marx and Engels, *On Literature and Art,* pp. 87-9.

speculation as to the issue of Realism and its relation to Marxist "reality". It is clear from his closing remarks that Engels is praising the Realist mode in which he chose to write as much as he is praising Balzac himself. One cannot imagine, for example, a symbolist or a surrealist method being used to produce a "chronicle-fashion" history of society of a kind which might attract equivalent approbation from Engels. But does this amount to the proposition that Marxism privileges Realism above other artistic modes? Is aesthetic verisimilitude the inevitable correlative of Marx's conceptualisation of "reality"? Is it thus inherently "progressive" and other representational modes inherently conservative?

Marx had died in 1883. It is arguable that, in the twelve years remaining to him, Engels did considerably more than popularise the pre-existing conceptual and textual legacy Marx had bequeathed. As the surviving member of the partnership and keeper of the flame Engels was increasingly looked to by increasing numbers of younger Marxist intellectuals as the greatest living authority on the doctrine, and this gave him the privilege of being permitted to amplify its silences and smooth its rough edges. This did not occur when he and Marx worked alongside each other. A unique moment in intellectual history occurred in 1859, when, within a month, Marx and Engels both wrote separate letters to Ferdinand Lassalle, each adversely criticising with identically insincere courtesy Lassalle's recently published drama, *Franz von Sickingen*.[16] The two letters represent the closest reading of a single literary text Marx and Engels seem ever to have committed to paper, but their content and tone are so similar that it is hard to distinguish one from the other. Marx wrote several times to Engels in the intervening month, during which one suspects Engels became aware of and consciously echoed what he knew Marx already to have written.[17]

How different things were when Engels found himself by default to be the intestate Marx's intellectual heir. Called upon to act as Marx's editor, executor and exegete, he did not hesitate to reconfigure Marx's concepts in the light of new political and economic circumstances, most important of all the rise of social democracy in Germany. His most profound

---

[16] Marx and Engels, *On Literature and Art,* pp. 98-107.
[17] Karl Marx and Frederick Engels, *Collected Works* (London: Lawrence and Wishart, 1983), vol. XL, pp. 418-46.

innovation was the concept of mediation, promulgated in a letter to Franz Mehring in July 1893:

> The ideologist who deals with history (history is here simply meant to comprise all the spheres – political, juridical, philosophical, theological – belonging to society and not only to nature) thus possesses in every sphere of science material which has formed itself independently out of the thought of previous generations and has gone through its own independent process of development in the brains of these successive generations. True, external facts belonging to one or another sphere may have exercised a codetermining influence on this development, but the tacit presupposition is that these facts themselves are also only the fruit of a process of thought, and so we still remain within that realm of mere thought, which apparently has successfully digested even the hardest facts.[18]

An analysis which demonstrates "mediation", then, is one which traces "false" ideological consciousness to its "true" source in material interests, but does so without denying the social effectivity of ideology. With regard to art, the case has since regularly been made that aesthetic productions are important purveyors of ideological concepts and values. Marx himself was fond of showing that Shakespeare was radically insightful with regard to the relations between material interests and ideology, famously citing in *Economic and Philosophical Manuscripts of 1844* the "Gold? Yellow, glittering, precious gold?" soliloquy from *Timon of Athens* to show how "Shakespeare excellently depicts the real nature of *money*",[19] its ability to make real what can otherwise only be imagined, but also its capacity to transform, dictate or determine ideological consciousness. Engels' outline theory of mediation, then, would seem similarly to encourage analysis (or critiques) of conservative artistic works as ideological constructions producing "false consciousness". The analysis or critique would presumably show how this "false consciousness" is a mediation of "true" material interests, and demonstrate and evaluate (perhaps condemn) the

---

[18] Robert C. Tucker (ed.), *The Marx-Engels Reader*, 2nd ed. (New York: W. W. Norton, 1978), p. 766.
[19] Marx and Engels, *On Literature and Art*, p. 136.

degree of historical effectiveness of such works. Conversely, "radical" art would by implication tend to expose the material sources in which all ideological consciousness is rooted, thus producing a "true" (in Marxist terms, non-ideological or scientific) picture of the world. This proposed application of Engels' sketchy theory is obviously tendentious, not least in its suggestion that not all art, but only conservative art, is ideological. But it is a significant advance from a fairly rudimentary "reflection" theory (in which art [in the superstructure] merely *reflects* history [the base]) to a more sophisticated "mediation" theory (in which art *both reflects and has the capacity to alter* history). However limited or crude such nascent insights may seem now, they give Engels an important place in Marxist literary critical thought: in the aesthetic field at least, it was he who rendered the Marxist analytic method dialectical. "Mediation" was to remain a key concept for Marxists until as recently as Louis Althusser.

The recipient of Engels' letter, Mehring, has the distinction of writing what is acknowledged to be the first sustained volume-length study in Marxist aesthetics, *The Lessing Legend* (1893). Originally a series of journal articles, this began as a rebuttal to a particularly tendentious study of Lessing by the bourgeois critic Eric Schmidt, but grew into a spirited attack against an entire phalanx of German literary historians who linked the German literary renaissance of the eighteenth century to the rise of Prussia, thus associating the reign of the absolutist Frederick II and the birth of classical German literature. Engels' letter was primarily written to thank Mehring for having sent the book, which he had already told Karl Kautsky he considered "first-rate", [20] but as Engels' compliments to Mehring demonstrate, he considered the book's value to lie in its historical rather than its aesthetic analysis, as have most other commentators. To this day *The Lessing Legend* has been translated into English only in a radically abbreviated form, which has itself been long out of print, and consequently Mehring remains a literary critic whose reputation has made little impact on the anglophone world. [21] This is a sad fact, given his prodigious,

---

[20] Marx and Engels, *On Literature and Art*, p. 64.

[21] Franz Mehring, *The Lessing Legend*, trans. A. S. Grogan (New York: Critics Group Press, 1938). Very little of Mehring's work (other than his epoch-making biography of Marx, published in English in 1936) is available in English. This may be the appropriate point to note that Marxist writers of this period have, however, been astonishingly well-served in the internet era: Mehring is only one of the

incessant and highly scholarly activity. As we shall see, Mehring's association with Rosa Luxemburg proved to be his historical undoing at the hands of Stalin.

Mehring came to Marxism later than most, in his forties, with his aesthetic perspective already somewhat fully formed and fully Kantian, which, to say the least, would seem *prima facie* to pose a considerable idealist problem for a Marxist. (Indeed, there is a history of Marxist aesthetics waiting to be written along the lines that the principal advances in the field came from those, from Benjamin to Sartre to Williams, who came to Marxism from an idealist humanist background which they stubbornly refused fully to renounce.) Far from recanting his Kantian past, Mehring set about adroitly attempting to fuse the Marxist theory of ideology with Kantian (and Schillerian) aesthetics. For example, in one of the best known of his "Aesthetic Ramblings" (a regular column he contributed to the journal *Die Neue Zeit*, edited by Kautsky, in 1898-99), he resynthesised the Kantian theory of aesthetic judgment from a materialist point of view.[22] In so doing, he was the first to imply that Marxism had inherited a great deal from classical German aesthetics in particular as well as classical German philosophy in general. It took half a century for this emphasis to be taken up again by Herbert Marcuse and, ironically, the man who was to do Mehring's reputation most damage, Lukács.

It is surprising, given the fact that Marx and Engels spent most of the later parts of their lives in London, that only William Morris, in this period and from this part of the world, made a noteworthy and lasting contribution to Marxist aesthetics. (The temptation to include in this survey that even more famous frequenter of London Marxist circles – George Bernard Shaw – has been resisted. Shaw's early commitment to Marxism is indisputable, but it was decidedly on the wane from 1884, when he joined the Fabians and, predictably, took a socialist path that was, by definition, rather lukewarm towards Marxism. Most of his creative and critical work postdated this conversion and did not appreciably contribute

many Marxist writers rescued from almost complete oblivion, for example, by the extraordinary site **www.marxists.org**.

[22] The discussion can be found in Maynard Solomon (ed.), *Marxism and Art: Essays Classic and Contemporary* (Detroit: Wayne State University Press), pp. 102-106.

to Marxist aesthetics strictly conceived.) [23] Yet many of Morris's voluminous essays on art, literature and aesthetics were for long as hard to get hold of as they are difficult to do justice to in the restricted scope of the present essay. [24] More importantly, his unique utopian concerns and emphases take us back, as no other critic of the period does, to the influence on the early Marx of Fourier and Feuerbach. The following passage, for example, from the text of a lecture, "Art Under Plutocracy", originally delivered in the University of Oxford in November 1883, seems to bear all the marks of a writer who is familiar with Marx's *Economic and Philosophical Manuscripts of 1844*:

> [...] art is founded on what I feel quite sure is a truth, and an important one, namely that all art, even the highest, is influenced by the conditions of labour of the mass of mankind, and that any pretensions which may be made for even the highest intellectual art to be independent of these general conditions are futile and vain; that is to say, that any art which professes to be founded on the special education or refinement of a limited body or class must of necessity be unreal and short-lived. Art is man's expression of his joy in labour.[25]

But Morris could not possibly have known Marx's writings of 1844, which did not see the light of day in any form until 1927, and were not published

---

[23] Readers interested in pursuing Shaw's politics and its place in his work are referred to Gareth Griffith, *Socialism and Superior Brains: The Political Thought of George Bernard Shaw* (London: Routledge, 1993). For the same reason a number of European initiatives which took place under the sign of anarchist socialism are not accounted for here: see, for example, Eugenia W. Herbert, *The Artist and Social Reform: France and Belgium 1885-1898* (New Haven: Yale University Press, 1961).

[24] Even today most readers can assemble Morris's critical *oeuvre* only mosaic-like from a number of rather obsolete selections: see William Morris, *Stories in Prose, Stories in Verse, Shorter Poems, Essays and Lectures*, ed. G. D. H. Cole (Bloomsbury: Nonesuch Press, 1934) (particularly the section "Letters and Essays"); Eugene D. Lamire (ed.), *The Unpublished Lectures of William Morris* (Detroit: Wayne State University Press, 1969); A. H. R. Ball (ed.), *Selections from the Prose Works of William Morris* (Cambridge: Cambridge University Press, 1931) (especially the section "Art and Social Reform"); and A. L. Morton (ed.), *Political Writings of William Morris* (London: Lawrence and Wishart, 1979).

[25] Morton, pp. 66-7.

in full until 1932. His Marxist textual influences seem principally to have been Marx's *Capital* and Engels' *Socialism: Utopian and Scientific* (the pamphlet which laid bare to a larger than usual audience the utopian influences on the early formation of Marxism), both of which he read in French translation in the 1880s. Morris probably arrived at this Marxist juncture via non-Marxist sources such as Ruskin (who chaired the meeting at which the words above were first spoken) and that great influence on Ruskin, Carlyle, who was in the main responsible for plugging the British of the nineteenth century into classical German aesthetics of the eighteenth.

It is difficult to imagine how novel it must have seemed, in the industrial English Midlands of January 1884, to attend a lecture at the Leicester Secular Society (later published as "Art and Socialism", Morris's best known essay), and hear Morris open with the words, "My friends, I want you to look into the relations of Art to Commerce": note the "you", which turns what would otherwise be a statement of intent into an exhortation.[26] Morris's preference for addressing and encouraging his audiences to action, appearing in person before them, was a form of *praxis* all its own, and rather different from the mode of address of Marx, who usually preferred, when addressing popular audiences, to remain behind the screen of the printed journalistic word. But what "Art and Socialism" does have in common with Marx, although seemingly worked out semi-independently, or by extrapolation from certain sections of *Capital*, is a sure grasp of the "alienated labour" thesis. What Morris does that is new is quite specifically to relate two apparently disparate practices, art and labour, in defence of the proposition that "the world of modern civilization in its haste to gain a very inequitably divided material prosperity has entirely suppressed popular Art":

> [...] the cause of this famine of Art is that whilst people work throughout the civilized world as laboriously as ever they did, they have lost – in losing an Art which was done by and for the people – the natural solace of that labour; a solace which they once had, and always should have, the opportunity of expressing their own thoughts to their fellows by means of that very labour, by means of that daily work which nature or

---

[26] Morton, p. 109.

long custom, a second nature, does indeed require of them, but without meaning that it should be an unrewarded and repulsive burden.[27]

Of course, there is something quite idiosyncratic about this: Marx only very occasionally looked back to the Middle Ages as benignly as Morris habitually did, and Morris seemed incapable of explaining convincingly how the process of the eradication of popular art by commerce was to be reversed. In these respects, Morris bumped into and did not go beyond the limits of the utopianism which Marx had had to leave behind long before. In his own diverse artistic practice, for which he is rightly better known than his essays on art, Morris often seemed simply to be trying to revive the practices of the feudal past. But the fact that he was not practised in the ways of the historical materialist dialectic is not sufficient reason for such a rich body of work to have such a limited audience today.

Morris's plentiful writings on art and its problematics within capitalism are one indication that, by the *fin de siècle*, Marxism, even in the aesthetic field, had started to spread far beyond German borders. Engels' initiative on "mediation", for example, was almost immediately taken up, probably in acknowledgment of Engels' direct encouragement of him, by Antonio Labriola, a Professor of Philosophy at the University of Rome, in *La concezione materialistica della storia* (*Essays on the Materialistic Conception of History*). This book, published in Italian in 1896, was quickly to enjoy pan-European influence, being translated into a number of languages by the end of the century, including a French edition introduced by Georges Sorel and read early by Lenin, who encouraged a Russian translation, which duly appeared in 1898. Trotsky too read the book in the 1890s. Labriola attempted to distinguish what might be considered "direct" ideological projections of economic facts (like politics and law) from "indirect" correspondences (like art and religion), claiming "that in artistic or religious production the mediation from the conditions to the products is very complicated";[28] warned against the reduction of the former to the latter; and drew attention to the fact that, despite all social organisation, humans remained fundamentally rooted in a physical nature

[27] Morton, p. 110.
[28] Antonio Labriola, *Essays in the Materialistic Conception of History*, trans. Charles H. Kerr (Chicago: Charles H. Kerr, 1908), p. 217.

which changed slowly enough to be considered a permanent fact: in this fact, by implication, might be the solution to Marx's conundrum as to the long-lasting appeal even of "outdated" art forms. Labriola moreover called for a social psychology which might explicate what he was confident enough to depict as a full-blown dialectical scenario: "forms of consciousness, even as they are determined by the conditions of life, constitute themselves also a part of history [...] there is no fact in history which is not preceded, accompanied and followed by determined forms of consciousness, whether it be superstitious or experimental, ingenious or reflective, impulsive or self-controlled, fantastic or reasoning". [29] Althusser, then, was hardly the first to point out that Engels' famous "last instance", in which "the economic movement finally asserts itself" as the prime mover "amid all the endless host of accidents" of history, never came.[30]

Labriola did not engage directly with works of art or literature, but Georgi Plekhanov, who introduced him to a Russian audience by means of a critical essay published in September 1897,[31] certainly did. At this time Plekhanov, founder of the Russian Social-Democratic Party, was the theoretical leader of Russian communism, having not yet been eclipsed by Lenin, with whom he was to break in 1905 over their differences on armed insurrection. His major work, *Art and Social Life* (1912), attempted to apply Marx's general theory, as adapted by Engels and Labriola, to specific works, and remained enormously influential, despite Plekhanov's dwindling political fortunes, well into the Stalinist era. Two of the main reasons for his sustained popularity, even after his death in 1918, were no doubt his fairly mechanical "reflection theory" (which seemed to return art to a subsidiary rôle as a passive "reflector" of primary economic developments) and his hostility to literary and artistic experimentalism (Cubism in particular attracted his ire), both of which meant that he offered no threat to the Stalinist promotion of Socialist Realism and its counterpart, namely implacable opposition to Modernism. But *Art and Social Life* remains one of most learned and wide-ranging examples of proto-Marxist literary criticism and theory, as

[29] Labriola, *Essays*, p. 113.
[30] Tucker, p. 760.
[31] Solomon, p. 92.

do Plekhanov's other major essays, such as that on Ibsen and on French drama and painting of the eighteenth century. [32] Solomon offers a generous but well balanced account of Plekhanov's historical importance, in particular his importation into Marxism of Karl Bücher's theory of the relation between primitive art and the labour process. [33] Plekhanov's influence shows, however, that the centre of gravity of Marxist intellectual work had shifted from Germany even before the accommodation of German social democrats to the Great War definitively robbed them of any claim they may have had to be the inheritors of Marxist theory. [34]

Marx's nineteenth century heirs undoubtedly fleshed out his suggestive remarks on general aesthetic questions and attempted to show how they might accord with (or need to be adjusted to fit) his political and economic theories. In this respect they have been unduly neglected. They made a significantly lesser contribution to the analysis of specific literary texts, but the explanation for their omission from many narratives of Marxist aesthetics lies not in their empirical shortcomings but in a later historical development which engulfed them. By the end of the century the epicentre of all Marxist debate, including that around aesthetics, was moving decisively to Russia. The key turning point was undoubtedly Lenin's essay, "Party Organisation and Party Literature" (1905), which stated that "everyone is free to write and say whatever he likes, without any restrictions", [35] but reserved the right to expel from the Bolshevik Party those whose exercise of this freedom brought them into

[32] Plekhanov has been much better served in English translation than the arguably more deserving Mehring: see Georgi Plekhanov, *Art and Social Life*, ed. Andrew Rothstein (London: Lawrence and Wishart, 1953). For the essays on Ibsen and on the eighteenth century in France, see Georgi Plekhanov, *Art and Society and Other Papers in Historical Materialism* (New York: Oriole Editions, 1974).

[33] Solomon, pp. 119-24,

[34] It is worth noting that 1914 is also the point at which Karl Kautsky's participation in Marxism, which had cast a very long shadow for several decades, effectively ended. Kautsky is not discussed in any detail in this essay, because his discussions of literary topics were few and perfunctory. His real aesthetic interest was in the visual arts, on which he wrote a great deal for the Viennese journal *Zeitschrift für plastik* in the 1880s.

[35] Solomon, p. 181.

conflict with the Party line. Lenin made it explicit that his strictures applied to literary artists as well as writers on politics. He justified such a policy because the Party was a "voluntary association" whose ideological integrity was in need of protection if it was to fulfil its aims. Once it had done so and actually became the governing party in 1917, a little later making itself coterminous with the state, such a policy applied to art was obviously full of repressive potential. The evaluation of art according to its political tendency was never originally intended by aesthetically inclined Bolsheviks to preclude other kinds of evaluation or to legitimise what eventually took place under Stalin. But when, in 1931, Stalin attacked Rosa Luxemburg and her associates for being precursors of Trotskyism in his article, "Some Questions Regarding the History of Bolshevism", the rewriting of the history of the nineteenth-century beginnings of Marxist literary criticism was one of the inevitable, if more minor, consequences. Those who had endeavoured in that period to enlarge the range and scope of Marxist aesthetics would soon be past their sell-by date as a result, unless they were so intellectually compromised (or capable of being so) as to be worthy of honour in Stalin's philistine polity. Mehring in particular, having been lauded by Luxemburg, was viciously attacked by many who now occupied places in the aesthetic division of the bureaucracy – none less ardent to damn him than Lukács, the man who, Jameson reminds us, was foremost among those responsible for reorientating critics towards "a relatively Hegelian kind of Marxism".[36]

2006

[36] The details of this sorry revisionist episode are recounted by Solomon, pp. 101-2.

Marxism is, in at least one respect, very unlike a number of other critical theories. A critic does not "work with" it the way a structuralist "works with" structuralism or a deconstructionist with Deconstruction, nor does a creative writer employ it the way a surrealist may turn to automatic writing or a sonneteer choose between Petrarchan, Shakespearean or Spenserian models. Unlike certain other -isms, Marxism is not merely an intellectual method and even less an artistic technique. To "use" it or "work with" it is inevitably to subordinate one's work to, or at least to integrate it with, the political commitments which Marxism implies in a particular instance or the system of ideological beliefs it propounds in general, or both, with the intention that these shall be furthered in the world outside the text. This truth remains undeniable despite the prescriptivist atrocities (the obvious example being the Stalinist doctrine of Socialist Realism) which are the outcome of ultra-dogmatic interpretations of it.

Marxist writers or critics are not Marxists unless they are in one way or another demonstrably partisan in favour of a particular kind of socialism. In this respect alone they have more in common with, for example, avowedly Christian writers and critics than they do with *avant-garde* concrete poets or semioticians decoding the commodity-branding strategies within advertisements. The poet and the semiotician may well be Marxists, but not by virtue of their technique or their object of analysis. Nor does partisanship on its own – in the form, say, of a generalised sympathy with the downtrodden, poor and oppressed, or in the expression of a wish that the social world ought to be more equitable, just and fair – mark the Marxist. A grasp of the more systematic and philosophical dimensions of the Marxist critique of capitalism, and an understanding of what this critique requires by way of *praxis* in any "real world" conjuncture, would both need to be seen before one may consider the textual producer Marxist. Many *soi-disant* Marxist English poets of the 1930s, for example, lacked the former; a number of "armchair

Marxist" critics are likewise rather deficient when it comes to the latter. (These observations imply nothing, one should insist, about the aesthetic value of their poetry or the intellectual worth of their criticism respectively.) In short, there are arguably no "Marxist" texts at all, in the sense that Marxism always implies an additional interventionist orientation, along certain ideological lines but varying in respect of the specific nature of any historical moment, to the "real" world of contingent social relations, conflicting economic interests, and uneven distribution of power which lies outside any text. But such texts may well be part of a wider social project which is identifiably Marxist.

Terry Eagleton has proposed a useful charting of four broad "regions" in the history of Marxist cultural criticism. The terms he uses to designate these currents of enquiry are "anthropological", "political", "ideological" and "economic".[1] With the exception of the last (which describes fields such as "the sociology of literature", containing relatively circumscribed studies of the economic and legal context in which literature is socially distributed and consumed), Eagleton's categories are largely chronological phases.[2] The "anthropological" perspective within Marxist criticism is that to which Marx's own occasional reflections frequently belong, in that they often try to define art in relation to the functions it fulfils within what Marx termed the "species being" of humanity, or what more traditional thinkers may envisage to be "human nature". The questions addressed within this tradition seldom attract the contentious and tendentious political discourse which constitutes the common badge of Marxist debate, concerned as they are with fundamental issues: "What is the function of art within social evolution? What are the material and biological bases of 'aesthetic' capacities? What are the relations between art and human labour? How does art relate to myth, ritual, religion and language, and what are its social functions?"[3] Such enquiries are common from the middle of the nineteenth to the end of the first third of the twentieth century, in works by writers such as Morris, Labriola,

[1] Terry Eagleton and Drew Milne (eds.), *Marxist Literary Theory: a Reader* (Oxford: Blackwell, 1996), pp. 7-14.
[2] For a comparable three-phase categorisation, see Francis Mulhern, "Introduction", *Contemporary Marxist Literary Criticism*, ed. Francis Mulhern (Harlow: Longman, 1992), pp. 3-17.
[3] Eagleton and Milne, p. 7.

Mehring, Kautsky and Plekhanov, the five immediate post-Marx/Engels figures anthologised in Solomon's voluminous anthology.⁴ This strand within aesthetic Marxism virtually dries up with Christopher Caudwell's *Illusion and Reality* (1937), enjoying its last post-war gasps of vitality in George Thomson's two studies in ancient Greek society, *The Prehistoric Aegean* (1954) and *The First Philosophers* (1955), and in Ernst Fischer's *The Necessity of Art* (1959).

As Eagleton points out, the transhistorical nature of the "anthropological" perspective contrasts markedly with subsequent developments in Marxist criticism, which has tended to place artistic works within more precise, and indeed ever increasingly specific and localised, historical moments (usually the moments of their production or, less frequently, their consumption), implicitly laying much greater stress on historical contingency and change than on persistence and continuity. No doubt the positivist scholarly bent of the "anthropological" approach made it difficult to sustain in the twentieth century, when there were titanic issues of contemporary global politics which could clearly not, furthermore, be met by its agenda. The new phase of what Eagleton terms "political" criticism was perhaps inaugurated by Lenin's articles on Tolstoy (1908-11), in which, in a manner reminiscent of Marx and Engels on Balzac and Goethe, Lenin argues that Tolstoy transcended the limitations of his own class ideology by transferring his loyalty to the Russian peasantry in the revolution of 1905. The sharp contemporaneousness of Lenin's focus is an obvious point of contrast with "anthropological" criticism, as is the alignment of aesthetic judgments with fairly immediate political purposes. But as this immediacy suggests, and as the subsequent history of vulgar "political" criticism (especially in the Soviet Union) was to show, little of lasting intellectual value has survived from within this tendency.

In the last half century, or the decades of Eagleton's "ideological" phase, the term "cultural materialism" has often been used, somewhat euphemistically, to denote a modern form of Marxist aesthetic criticism. In some ways the term is a late twentieth-century acknowledgment of Marxist theory's penchant for the adjective: its adumbration by Raymond

⁴ Maynard Solomon (ed.), *Marxism and Art: Essays Classic and* Contemporary (Detroit: Wayne State University Press, 1979).

Williams occurred over a century after the articulation of Marx's own "historical" and later "dialectical" materialism. Williams' claim in *Marxism and Literature*,[5] where he explored the concept in most detail and at most length, was not only that it was a Marxist concept, but that it rendered Marxism more fully "materialist" than it had hitherto been. For reasons I offer in the discussion which follows, this seems a highly dubious claim.

Materialism is the doctrine at the root of all modern science. It defines the universe as consisting wholly of matter. The opposite of matter is simply its absence, as in a vacuum. On no account does the doctrine provide for positive "non-material" entities such as deities or spirits or (in the human realm) mind or soul. It would have little truck with Hegelian idealism, for instance. But in its scientific form such a doctrine has little to offer to social, political or cultural theory. To speak of human agency or of humans' abilities to conceptualise or of their aesthetic appreciation (none of which appears to be a "material" thing or event) in terms of firing neurons and synapses, for example, tells us nothing very much at all that we really want to know about those processes. Indeed, not only are such descriptions often viewed as "reductionist" (reducing the "mental" or "spiritual" to the "material") but, especially in behaviourist accounts of human conduct, they seem almost to deny the reality of those processes. If we are really simply an assembly of behaviours controlled by biochemical and other bodily events, in what sense do we have agency, for instance, and how can our conceptual abilities or aesthetic preferences be evaluated as attaching to us rather than being the mere consequences of involuntary physiological activity?

Marx was sometimes prey to this kind of reductionism, but even where he does refer to "conceiving, thinking, the mental intercourse of men" as "the direct efflux of their material behaviour" (in *The German Ideology* [1846]) he recognises that "men are the producers of their conceptions, ideas, etc." It is, after all, rather difficult to dismiss elaborately wrought philosophical systems or complex works of art or delicate collective ethical deliberations as mere "ideological reflexes". Indeed, Marx's materialism quite quickly came to accommodate what the

5 Raymond Williams, *Marxism and Literature* (Oxford: Oxford University Press, 1977).

strict materialism of a scientist ignores, namely the "non-material" categories which are inescapable in any discussion of social life, and which cannot merely be viewed as what the same 1846 text called "phantoms formed in the brains of men". To some extent the later resort to the "dialectical" variant is a tortuous compromise with Hegelian idealism, the seeming arch-enemy of materialism. By the time of Engels' letters to Joseph Bloch (21-22 September 1890) and Franz Mehring (14 July 1893), very considerable play was being allowed to "non-material" factors in determining the "form", if not the "content", of historical events otherwise considered "material".

Thus, Marxist materialism gradually travelled in a direction anti-thetical to scientific materialism in acknowledging and accommodating the "non-material" in its scheme of things. It would, perhaps, be more proper to describe Marxism not as a materialist theory at all, but in many respects as an account of how the struggle over *the possession of material things* is waged throughout history, by *means* which it considers both "material" (e.g., wars conducted with weaponry) and "non-material" (e.g. wars supported by propaganda), one of which (the "material") it considers more decisive or "determining". This compromise between materialism and idealism is no doubt why, in advanced societies, what Marxists usually mean by "material activity" is economic activity, when money, as Marx shows in volume one of *Capital* (1867), is not essentially a material thing at all but just a socially accepted metaphor for material things. Thus even a trader in oil derivatives, who usually never takes possession of the physical barrels he buys – indeed, interacts with hardly anything more tangible than data on a computer screen – is engaging in a profoundly "material activity". But the case becomes nicer when we ask if a creative writer, in modern times likewise largely placing and moving words on a similar screen, and perhaps receiving remuneration for doing so, is similarly involved in "material activity"?

Cultural materialism, as set forth by Williams, attempts to show that classic Marxism's negative answer to questions of this nature about cultural production was misguided. In other words, Williams makes the case that Marx's fundamental distinction between the "base" of material production and the "superstructure" of religious, aesthetic or philosophical ideation (or what, for the sake of a unitary term, I shall henceforth call "culture") is a false separation of domains. This position did not emerge fully formed in one text. One can see Williams struggling throughout his various studies of culture to synthesise his emphases into such a concept over almost two decades prior to *Marxism and Literature*. But his procedure in that text is explicitly to review many of the standard philosophical and methodological debates within Marxism. For instance, in a chapter entitled "From Reflection to Mediation" he argues that the key difference between "reflection" and "mediation" theories is that the former sees history as an *object* while the latter sees it as a *process*. (Williams does not point it out, but "reflection" can largely be associated with Marx and "mediation" with Engels.) Because history is obviously a process and not an object, the preference for mediation as a concept – which, to summarise Engels, posits that all (material) action is mediated by (non-material) thought – seems impossible to resist. Nonetheless, Williams does not consider mediation a concept sufficiently rigorous to attract the sustained attention of Marxists, and he locates this and many other deficiencies in the shortcomings of Marx's own original theory. Concisely put, his problem with classic Marxism is not that it is too materialist, but that it is not materialist enough. For Williams, material activity is not limited to what Marx might have termed "the production and reproduction of real life". He is concerned explicitly to extend the term to any practical activity in which humans engage which establishes, maintains or changes specifically human relationships (physically, to nature, and socially, to one another). He often refers to such activities as "constitutive" (i.e. they are an indissoluble part of historical processes and not external or incidental to them), a term he opposes to "instrumental" (in much the same way as Marx opposed "material" to "ideological"), and is concerned to demonstrate that many activities which Marx might have considered "instrumental" are in fact "constitutive".

A good example is how Williams deals with language. He cites the well-known aside on language in *The German Ideology:* "From the start the 'spirit' is afflicted with the curse of being 'burdened' with matter, which here makes its appearances in the form of agitated layers of air, sounds, in short, of language. Language is as old as consciousness, language *is* practical consciousness that exists also for other men, and for that reason alone it really exists for me personally as well; language, like consciousness, only arises from the need, the necessity, of intercourse

36

with other men." Williams praises this passage for being "compatible with the emphasis on language as practical, constitutive activity". In his view, language can never be seen as external or merely instrumental to any social process. In relating to one another, humans communicate by means of language, and their humanity cannot be conceived of without it. Indeed, in the continuation of the quoted passage, Marx goes on to distinguish the "social" nature of human relations from those of non-linguistic animals. Yet at the end of this quotation he posits a pre-linguistic order which gave rise to language. As Williams puts it (he is describing a tradition of thinkers on language as well as Marx), "'the world' or 'reality' or 'social reality' is categorically projected as the pre-existent formation to which language is simply a response". For Williams, this is only a short step from reducing the material or constitutive status of language to that of ideology or instrumentality: "the idea of language as constitutive is always in danger of this kind of reduction".

This is typical of Williams' analyses of a variety of classic Marxist categories and arguments. By close reading of works in classic and later Marxism he endeavours to demonstrate that Marx's materialist positions were often compromised, sometimes by Marx himself, and often by later Marxists, by a variety of problematic doctrines (e.g. idealism, positivism, scientism). Thus, in the passage above, language as a "material" phenomenon is reduced to the notion of language as physically produced by the body rather than as a material *activity* (i.e. one which is integral to the ways in which humans make, maintain and change the world and their place in it). The consequence, Williams goes on, is that the importance of "the practical language activities which were grouped under the categories of 'ideology' and 'the superstructure'" was similarly diminished. A sense of the constitutive nature in social practice of these activities (for which Williams uses the umbrella term "culture") must, for Williams, be restored: hence the apparent oxymoron, "cultural materialism: a theory of the specificities of material cultural and literary production within historical materialism".

The range of Williams' analyses, and his argumentative strategy, are impressive. In the first four chapters of the book he dismantles a number of "Basic Concepts", namely "culture", "language", "literature" and "ideology". In each case, he takes a concept which classic Marxism assigns to the superstructure, reveals current problems in the definition of the concept, and demonstrates that the concept can be found once to have referred to a "practical" (or "basic") activity, but that this meaning has been historically erased, by Marxism and other schools of thought. He then proposes a contemporary redefinition of the term which returns it to the "material" realm. In short, it is not Williams' intention to enhance the base/superstructure model by rendering it dialectical, like Engels, but to dissolve it altogether. This is what has led its detractors, as we shall see, to argue that cultural materialism is not (pace Williams) a Marxist theory at all, but a critique of Marxism in the spirit of post-structuralism and Deconstruction. More properly, given that its impetus and ideological affinities originate within Marxism, such observers might consider it at best a "post-Marxism".

In much of the rest of *Marxism and Literature* Williams is concerned to elaborate the implications of a position which views "consciousness" as a material rather than an ideal category. But his avowedly Marxist attempts to "make material" the categories which earlier Marxism had classified as elements of the superstructure are problematic. Firstly, he arguably confuses the "material" form an activity may take in the world with the issue of whether or not that activity itself is a "material" one (in Marxist terms) – almost the same problem as he accuses Marx of creating in his dealings with language. Writing, for example, is a material act (whether it be the physical rendering of ink on paper or the typing which places letters on a screen) and the products of writing take the form of socially circulated material commodities (such as books). But that materiality seems incidental to the social functions of writing, which are generally intellectual, informational, or aesthetic. Writing that has consensually agreed social value and importance is not primarily produced in order to manufacture physical books but so that certain non-physical concepts can be understood, knowledge acquired, or pleasures experienced. The "materiality" of writing seems almost accidental when looked at from this point of view. Similarly, when Williams points to the unquestionably material resources committed to the pursuit of apparently "non-material" activities – for example, the very considerable quantities of bricks and mortar that constitute schools and universities – he seems to be confusing the phenomenal form which such institutions have in the world with the non-phenomenal activity (in this case, "education") which takes place within them. They are (in a quite strict sense) merely material "premises" which do not lead to material "conclusions".[6]

Secondly, to return to writing as an example, the social value of its production is not "material" in the way that the social value of the production of food is "material". The "nourishment" afforded by the former is not physical or indeed even necessary to organic life – and there are many parts of the world in which such a distinction is self-evident because poverty would dictate an obvious choice between the purchase of a book or the purchase of food. Williams walks a tightrope here, because one line of defence of his general position may be that cultural materialism is actually a description intended only for "advanced" capitalist societies (and this is indeed where his emphasis lies). But if the more traditional "historical materialism" thereby remains a fit description of less developed capitalist societies, the tenets of classic Marxism return with a vengeance because it would seem that the conceptual description of the system is by and large dictated by the economic structure. In other words, it is not easy to render redundant the force of classic Marxism's stress on the differential historical importance of distinguishable activities and things. In decidedly reclaiming a "practical" rôle for "consciousness" in advanced societies, Williams seems implicitly to abjure any sense that certain practical activities may be more historically important than others. In short, his theory is close to denying all sense of priority in determination, which is what makes it difficult to accept as a Marxist theory at all, despite Williams' asseveration that it is. The base/superstructure model of historical materialism, despite its many problems, is posited on a hierarchy of determinations; the refined versions of "dialectical materialism" also accept, but modify, this hierarchy, by permitting elements of the superstructure a reciprocal (though often weak) effect on elements of the base; cultural materialism, in contrast to both of these relatively compatible positions, seems to collapse the hierarchy entirely.

Williams is very alert to this danger. A few years earlier, in his 1973 essay, "Base and Superstructure in Marxist Cultural Theory", he had argued: "It is very easy for the notion of totality to empty of its essential content the original Marxist proposition [of base and superstructure]. For

---

[6] Williams does not, however, resort to a concept like "cultural capital" as promulgated by Pierre Bourdieu, which is a similar attempt to deconstruct the traditionally opposed "cultural" and "material" and integrate "education" as a strictly materially-functioning activity with the capitalist economy.

if we come to say that society is composed of a large number of social practices which form a concrete social whole, and if we give to each practice a certain specific recognition, adding only that they interact, relate and combine in very complicated ways, we are at one level much more obviously talking about reality, but we are at another level withdrawing from the claim that there is any process of determination. And this I, for one, would be very unwilling to do."[7] Even in *Marxism and Literature* he can write, "A Marxism without some concept of determination is in effect worthless", yet go on to conclude that "determination of this whole kind – a complex and interrelated process of limits and pressures – is in the whole social process itself and nowhere else: not in an abstracted 'mode of production' nor in an abstracted 'psychology'." But if "determination" is spread throughout "the whole social process", if there is no understood prioritisation of determinants, what content does the concept have? In short, *what* is determining *what*?

Eagleton voices such reservations. Essentially, he argues that Williams has misunderstood that historical materialism is not essentially concerned with what is and is not "material" (essentially an old philosophical debate which pre-dates Marxism) but that it is "a conceptual instrument for the analysis of forms of material determination in particular historical societies, for the ends of political practice". This leads him to conclude that cultural materialism is not in competition with historical materialism at all (and certainly that it is not "within" that tradition of analysis, as Williams claims); which is another way of saying that it is not a Marxist theory. Milner is not the only critic who agrees with Eagleton on the divergence from Marxism, although he sees Eagleton's criticism as resting on an untenable faith in the classic base/superstructure distinction.[8]

Those who would call themselves cultural materialists implicitly claim to be heirs to one of Western Marxism's attempts to rethink the economistic excesses of the classic doctrine. Thus, many of Williams' emphases are reliant on the concept of "hegemony" as formulated by the

---

[7] Raymond Williams, *Culture and Materialism* (London: Verso, 1980), p. 36.

[8] Terry Eagleton (ed.), *Raymond Williams: Critical Perspectives* (Cambridge: Polity Press, 1989); Andrew Milner, *Cultural Materialism* (Melbourne: Melbourne University Press, 1989); Much of the subsequent debate around Williams' text is summarised by John Brannigan, *New Historicism and Cultural Materialism* (New York: St Martin's Press, 1998).

Italian socialist thinker Antonio Gramsci. The term was first pertinently used by Russian Marxists, including Lenin, to designate the requirement for the proletariat to take a leading (hegemonic) rôle in a revolutionary alliance with the peasantry. Gramsci, writing in prison under the fascist regime of Mussolini, in a time of defeat for the Italian working class, extended the concept to describe the strategies of the capitalist ruling class in both attaining and maintaining power. The reason the concept is so important to the theory of cultural materialism is that, in Gramsci's hands, it emphasises the profound importance of ideological as well as material determination in social processes. According to Gramsci, in advanced capitalist economies a class does not win or hold state power by sole virtue of gaining control of the means of production. To prevent its own overthrow, a dominant class must also convince a sufficient number of the state's citizens that its power is legitimate, right or beneficial. A hegemonic class must win the "hearts and minds" of the people, and it does so by mobilising the available ideological concepts and agencies to construct a picture of the prevailing social order as being consonant with nature or common sense. It follows that any successful revolutionary force must mount a successful counter-hegemonic initiative. Needless to say, the erstwhile "superstructure" is the key site of engagement in this ideological struggle.

The Gramscian concept of hegemony also underpins the theories of the French Marxist philosopher Louis Althusser, who in the mid-nineteen-seventies was the overwhelmingly dominant intellectual figure in Western Marxism. In his best known essay,[9] Althusser sets out to show how capitalist states maintain themselves, and specifically how they manage to quell dissent and disorder among their citizens. He argues that they do so by deploying two kinds of "state apparatus", one of which is "repressive", the other "ideological". It is by a combination of these approaches that a dominant class's hegemony is built and sustained. The "repressive" state apparatuses (RSAs) comprise bodies like the army and the police, which prevent or control disorder mainly (but not entirely) by physical force or violence. The "ideological" state apparatuses (ISAs), by

---

[9] Louis Althusser, "Ideology and Ideological State Apparatuses (Notes towards an Investigation)", *Lenin and Philosophy and Other Essays* (London: New Left Books, 1971), pp. 127-86.

contrast, consist of "a certain number of realities which present themselves to the immediate observer in the form of distinct and specialized institutions", from which Althusser proposes an "empirical list" comprising churches, schools, the family, the political system, trades unions, the media, and "the cultural ISA (Literature, the Arts, sports, etc.)". What distinguishes the ISAs from the RSAs is that they are plural and encourage conformity mainly (but not entirely) by "persuasion". In other words, in the terms of classic Marxism, the RSAs belong largely to "the base" and the ISAs to "the superstructure", but Althusser's key contention is that modern capitalist states rely much more on the latter for the maintenance of social compliance than they do on the former. One can see, therefore, that Williams' advancement of the erstwhile superstructure as a newly determinate force had esteemed and influential forbears. However, although Gramsci, Althusser and Williams all stress the applicability of the notion of hegemony to "advanced" capitalist societies, Williams is the only one of them whose life's work had been specifically in the analysis of culture.

If this is the inheritance around which cultural materialism was formed, has it also left a legacy enabling new lines of enquiry in the analysis of culture? One of the problems may have been that *Marxism and Literature* offers no extended applications of the theory – it cruises at a fairly high altitude of theoretical abstraction in a sometimes stratospherically forbidding prose – even to the literature of its title, never mind to culture more generally. Nor is this deficiency really remedied by Williams' later work. While there are many working in the field of culture who express an immense debt to Williams, there are few who have explicitly wished to refer to themselves as cultural materialists in the last three decades. The stellar exceptions to this observation are Jonathan Dollimore and Alan Sinfield: stellar not necessarily because their application of the theory is exemplary in the evaluative sense, but because the book they edited, *Political Shakespeare*, which nailed its colours to the mast of "cultural materialism" in its subtitle, and was published with a lengthy afterword of approval by Williams himself, became something of a bestseller measured by the modest audience numbers an academic text in literature studies can ordinarily expect.[10] A

---

[10] Jonathan Dollimore and Alan Sinfield (eds.), *Political Shakespeare: Essays in*

second and enlarged edition was published in 1994. In their foreword to the first edition of the book, Dollimore and Sinfield explain (much more briskly and with significantly less conceptual agonising than Williams) what they understand their approach to be: "[...] a combination of historical context, theoretical method, political commitment and textual analysis [... w]e call this 'cultural materialism'." The "political commitment" referred to is specified as "socialist and feminist" (not "Marxist", and feminism has no particularly privileged position either in Williams' work or in Marxism more broadly), and the quadrant of elements in which it is placed are really not derived from Williams at all. Marx is referred to on a small number of occasions in the text proper, but there is also a clear move away here from the thin air of Marxist theory towards something much more practical, unfettered, and frankly less cognitively demanding: Dollimore and Sinfield's contributions to the book essentially offer a critique of Shakespeare studies from the highly flexible position occupied by the "rainbow politics" left opposition of the day. The contributions by others – particularly Stephen Greenblatt and Leonard Tennenhouse – would more properly be categorised as New Historicist. [11] The only contributors who could claim allegiance to Marxism proper – and that of a rather old-fashioned kind – were Graham Holderness and Margot Heinemann.

However, with their relentless questioning and undermining of traditional approaches to the Bard, not to mention their combative and occasionally racy tone and style, and their willingness to dismiss age-old shibboleths and walk around theoretical quicksands for the purposes of impactful conclusions, Dollimore and Sinfield significantly altered the teaching of Shakespeare in the academy, even if only to force the proponents of traditional approaches to be explicit in defending the bases of their teaching. Sinfield's essay on the use of Shakespeare in secondary schools (probably the best known item in the volume, though most probably inspired by the Althusserian work of Balibar and Macherey in France, rather than Williams), begins where Althusser starts his essay on the ISAs, with an acknowledgment that "any social order has to include

Cultural Materialism (Manchester: Manchester University Press, 1985).
[11] On the distinction between New Historicism and cultural materialism, see Brannigan.

the conditions for its own continuance, and capitalism and patriarchy do this partly through the education system". But a purpose is restored to a critique of this system only if, as Sinfield does and Althusser does not, we understand there to be sufficient gaps within it for its dominant practices to be undermined. With respect to the formal study of Shakespeare within state schooling, Sinfield identifies an ideology of the subject Literature (one which is democratically civilising, inclusive, and formative of individual consciousness through an invitation to pupils to give a "personal response") which is in stark contrast to the assessment procedures applied to its study (which are authoritarian, exclusive, and imply "correct" responses). For Sinfield, Shakespeare is generally appropriated by the educational state ISA as a means of constructing its subjects (school pupils) within the dominant bourgeois ideology: one can see this not only in the ideological framework implicit in the questions which they are permitted to answer, but also in the questions they are not asked and the perspectives disallowed them. There is little encouragement, for example, to view Shakespeare in relation to the economics, politics, or social history of his day; to examine the history of Shakespeare's reputation and the determinations at work in the highly variable evaluations made of him in different periods; nor is there a space created in which pupils may produce non-approbatory critical discourse about Shakespeare; and they are not encouraged to reflect on the values implicit in the literary critical discourse into which they are being inducted, which is presented as being ideology-free.

Crucially, however, because such a situation is an ongoing process, Sinfield argues that it is inherently challengeable. All the same, *Political Shakespeare* had little discernible effect on the teaching of Shakespeare in British schools, which remains to this day as ideologically muddled and compromised as it ever was: indeed, at the end of the nineteen-eighties, Shakespeare became the one named author in the National Curriculum for England and Wales, which meant that reading his texts – or at least one of them – became a bizarre legal requirement in those two countries. When all is said and done, however, it is undoubtedly in *Political Shakespeare* that cultural materialism – though not particularly derived from the theoretical abstractions of Marx or Williams (whose afterword, with all the usual qualifications and circumlocutions, coming after Dollimore and Sinfield's cut and thrust, has the gravity of Jupiter) – gets the brand recognition and marketability that all successful theories require. Sinfield followed it with another long volume,[12] which once more appropriated Williams' term in its subtitle, and again was largely Shakespearean in focus, but did include work on other English Renaissance figures such as Marlowe, Donne and Sidney (a nonetheless strikingly narrow and academically traditional range of authors for a work claiming to operate under the aegis of a radical cultural, rather than a literary, theory). It did not, however, like its predecessor, add anything of significance to the theoretician's understanding of cultural materialism and, arguably in its eclecticism, had little right to advertise itself under the banner so laboriously and stringently raised in the air by Williams. Few have followed its example by claiming expressly to do so.[13]

Cultural materialism is likely to go the way of Marxism and the variants of materialism it offers. The emphases which Williams combines in the term achieved wide circulation. But this is essentially what it is, a set of emphases rather than a methodology. It informs a great deal of practical and theoretical work, but few are prepared to call themselves its unqualified adherents, not least, perhaps, because the term is thought to originate with a theorist whose work, increasingly, does not fit the temper of the times, because it failed to address now seemingly mandatory issues of race, gender, imperialism and sexual politics. In this is a final irony because, although the term is largely associated with Williams, it was not, in fact, coined by him at all.[14]

2009

---

[12] Alan Sinfield, *Faultlines: Cultural Materialism and the Politics of Dissident Reading* (Oxford: Clarendon Press, 1992).

[13] A singular exception remains the annual Williams-inspired *Keywords: a Journal of Cultural Materialism*, whose contributors likewise show little genuine allegiance to, or sometimes even knowledge of, Marxism.

[14] The credit goes to Marvin Harris, the American Marxist anthropologist, who had been using the term for many moons by the time he published a book with that very title: see Marvin Harris, *Cultural Materialism: The Struggle for a Science of Culture* (New York: Random House, 1979).

Published in the USA in 1994 and in Britain in 1995, Harold Bloom's *The Western Canon* was widely and favourably reviewed in the daily broadsheet and literary periodical press in both countries. Those who find themselves profoundly and fundamentally in disagreement with the assumptions and conclusions of Bloom's book, like myself, may be tempted simply to ignore its popular acclaim. The plaudits it has received from the non-academic press may be all it deserves, and Bloom in any case claims not to be addressing a scholarly audience: "This book is not directed to academics because only a small remnant of them still read for the love of reading. What Johnson and Woolf after him called the Common Reader still exists and possibly goes on welcoming suggestions of what might be read."[1] What follows suggests that a scholarly refusal to engage with Bloom is an unwise and inadequate response. My reasons for so thinking I shall, briefly, enumerate.

The Western Canon offers a tempting compendium, in one volume, of critical comment on everything in Western literature that Bloom considers worth reading. He even devotes forty pages at the end of the book to providing lists, chronologically arranged, of books and texts he considers make up the Western canon. He claims not to be presenting what he calls a "lifetime reading plan" (*WC* 517), but it is hard to see how else we might view the book, which counsels the avoidance of non-canonical works on the grounds that canonical works are now super-abundant. Moreover, one kind of "common reader" who might find the "reading plan" especially tempting is the non-western reader who, interested to know what he or she should read to have a knowledge of western literary culture, might turn to *The Western Canon* and use it as an authoritative guide book to help them in their studies. What I have to say will suggest that such a reader would be *misguided* rather than guided

---

[1] Harold Bloom, *The Western Canon: the Books and School of the Ages* (London: Macmillan, 1995), p. 518. Page references to this book are henceforth incorporated parenthetically into the text using the abbreviation *WC*.

by Bloom in that he offers a very misleading, tendentious and ultimately intellectually inadequate account of western literature. The compendious nature of his one-volume survey only makes that argument a necessary one.

Another reason why it is important to come to terms with Bloom is that he has an enormous reputation as a literary critic and an appreciable reputation as a literary theorist. The book upon which most of his fame depends is a rather slim volume entitled *The Anxiety of Influence: A Theory of Poetry*, published in 1973, at a time when literary theory was relatively unfashionable. Indeed, Bloom begins the book by saying that it should be seen as corrective. One of his stated aims "is to try to provide a poetics that will foster a more adequate practical criticism".[2] In other words, he considers the "practical criticism" or "close reading" of poetry insufficiently *theorised*: the book is "theoretical" rather than "practical", but only in order for the "practical" criticism of texts to be enhanced. Thus Bloom is a defender of "practical criticism", not its opponent, and, even in 1973, was attacking the school of European literary theorists whose work has since come to epitomise the term "theory". Here is what he says in the introduction to *The Anxiety of Influence*:

I am made aware of the mind's effort to overcome the impasse of Formalist criticism, the barren moralizing that Archetypal criticism has come to be, and the anti-humanistic plain dreariness of all those developments in European criticism that have yet to demonstrate that they can aid in reading any one poem by any poet whatsoever. (*AI* 12-13).

We can see from *The Western Canon* that Bloom's position has not really changed in the following two decades. Whatever else one wants to say about Bloom, one can hardly claim that has shifted with the intellectual tides that have been circulating in that time. Consistency may or may not be a virtue, but Bloom has it plentiful supply. If there is an essential difference between the theoretical presuppositions deployed in *The Anxiety of Influence* and *The Western Canon* it is simply that in the

[2] Harold Bloom, *The Anxiety of Influence: a Theory of Poetry* (Oxford: Oxford University Press, 1973), p. 5. Page references to this book are henceforth incorporated parenthetically into the text using the abbreviation *AI*.

later book Bloom expends many more words attacking "theoretical" criticism because it is, evidently, now in the ascendant. His own self-declared position as a "theorist" thus requires strict qualification: *The Anxiety of Influence* could hardly be seen as a reputable theoretical work (in terms of European theory). In 1973, however, there was very little that was "theoretical" (in the simple sense of being a reflection on practice) in Anglo-American literary criticism, and *The Anxiety of Influence* thus seemed a radical new departure. On that basis Bloom's reputation was made, and he has since become that infrequent phenomenon, the mass market literary critic. His subsequent books, whatever their quality, have all been widely reviewed, and they sell very well. One indication of Bloom's larger-than-normal audience is the price at which publishers market his books. The British paperback edition of *The Western Canon* currently sells at £10. Academic texts of 600 pages routinely sell for multiples of that sum. The presence of the book in international airport bookshops and popular book club catalogues itself bespeaks its larger-than-usual print run. If I may be permitted a supplementary anecdote of a rather Bloomian kind, I discovered seventeen hardback copies of his most recent book, *Shakespeare: the Invention of the Human*,[3] in a major bookshop in Amsterdam. I could not find any other book in the same store in such plentiful supply. People who do not normally buy literary criticism are buying Harold Bloom.

Let me dwell briefly on *The Anxiety of Influence*. I do not wish to argue here with what Bloom has to say in that book, although I find much of it eccentric and questionable. However, because he uses its theory of poetic influence throughout *The Western Canon*, I think it may be worthwhile concisely to summarise that theory. So, briefly, Bloom tells us that "Poetic history [...] is held to be indistinguishable from poetic influence, since strong poets make that history by misreading one another, so as to clear imaginative space for themselves" (*AI* 5). Let me emphasise the word that may seem strange in that quotation: "strong poets [...] *misreading* one another". For example, Bloom argues that Milton (or, rather, Milton's texts) consciously or unconsciously, *misread* Shakespeare, and that this misreading (his favoured word is *misprision*) is constitutive of their

---

[3] Harold Bloom, *Shakespeare: The Invention of the Human* (London: Fourth Estate, 1999).

greatness. Great poets labour under the influence of other great poets before them, and in order to write for themselves, or *as* themselves, they must somehow *reject* the earlier poet, get free of the anxiety of being influenced by him, fight clear of his shadow. They do this by writing great poems that the earlier poet could not possibly have written. Bloom states that this theory is, by and large, Freud's theory of family dynamics transferred onto the literary tradition, in which great poets bear the same relation to one another as father to son, so that the younger poet (the son) asserts his individuality by rejecting, or establishing his difference from, the older (the father). I point out this acknowledgment to Freud because, in *The Western Canon*, Bloom is keen to temper his earlier enthusiasm for Freud's psychological theories. He quotes with approval the critic Peter de Bolla, as saying that "the Freudian family romance as a description of influence represents an extremely weak reading [of Bloom]" (*WC* 8), although, oddly, Bloom himself later refers to the "strangely intimate family romance of great writers" (*WC* 526).

So much for *The Anxiety of Influence*. It will become clear as I continue how much that theory is still being used in *The Western Canon*. But let me turn now to the latter book, which lays down a number of challenges to what Bloom calls "the School of Resentment", a term he uses polemically to describe academics who "resent" the aesthetic and are, increasingly successfully, involved in projects which attempt to subordinate the aesthetic to something else – history, politics, economics, race, gender – in the name of something like "Cultural Studies". Towards the end of the book Bloom even specifies the six branches of the School of Resentment: "Feminists, Marxists, Lacanians, New Historicists, Deconstructionists, Semioticians" (*WC* 527). Yet in my own experience some Feminists, Marxists, Lacanians, New Historicists, Deconstructionists and/or Semioticians might, paradoxically, be as concerned as Bloom to uphold the autonomy (or at least relative autonomy) of the aesthetic. We shall, hopefully, find out.

I have already remarked on the fact that Bloom claims not to be addressing an academic audience but "the Common Reader". Yet his "common reader" is not so very common. He tells us, "such a reader does not read for easy pleasure or to expiate social guilt, but to enlarge a solitary existence" (*WC* 518). In other words, Bloom's common reader is a fairly lonely reader, demanding something large from his/her reading.

One might object, therefore, that such a reader could expect Bloom to be a little more scholarly than he is. There are no footnotes in *The Western Canon*. Nor is there a bibliography of secondary texts that Bloom has consulted for the purposes of his study. He does quote some critics, past and present, throughout the book, but apart from giving us the title of the book or essay he is quoting and, where appropriate, the name of the translator, he provides no bibliographic detail at all: no page numbers, no place of publication, no publisher, no note of which edition he has used. The same complaint might be made of his list of canonical works at the end of the book. Many of the texts he lists are the subject of considerable editorial controversy. For example, which edition of James Joyce's *Ulysses* has he read, or does he expect his common reader to read? Which translation of Franz Kafka's *The Trial* (there are at least three translations in English)? Indeed, how Bloom deals with translation throughout the book is something of a problem. It is not clear which books he has read only in translation and which he has read in the original language. He simply makes no reference to this and treats translated works as if they were linguistically unproblematic. He does tell us, in a headnote to his canonical list, "I suggest translations wherever I have derived particular pleasure and insight from those now readily available" (*WC* 531), but it is not clear if his recommendations are based on a *comparison* of available translations or not. *The Western Canon* shows a blatant disregard for the bibliographical conventions we associate with an intellectual work.

What is perhaps more serious is Bloom's reliance on anecdote in his reasoning; that is, his use of undocumented evidence, information whose sources the reader is unable to verify. "So fantastic has the academy become, that I have heard [the common] reader denounced by an eminent critic, who told me that reading without a constructive social purpose was unethical" (*WC* 518). This observation might have some force if it referred to a publicly declared position in the same or another critic's writing; as it is, it is hard to give Bloom's paraphrase of a private conversation much credibility. Two pages later he commits a more serious unscholarly act. "Teachers now tell me," he says of Shakespeare's *Julius Caesar*, "of many schools where the play can no longer be read through, since students find it beyond their attention spans. In two places reported to me, the making of cardboard shields and swords has replaced the reading and discussion of the play" (*WC* 520). The problem with this anecdote is that it fails to consider the obvious likelihood that the play is being taught *as a dramatic performance*, and that the shields and swords are probably props for use in such a performance. Indeed, Shakespeare's texts as *performative scripts* is hardly ever the way Bloom conceives of them. When he does consider performance, however, he again relies on anecdote. Consider the anecdote he tells about Shakespeare's *The Tempest*: "A friend, who teaches at the Hebrew University in Jerusalem and who was born in Bulgaria, told me about a performance of *The Tempest*, in Petrov's Bulgarian version, which she had recently attended in Sofia. It was played as farce, successfully she thought, but left the audience discontented because, she said, the Bulgars identify Shakespeare with the classical or canonical. Students and friends have described for me Shakespeare as they have seen him in Japanese, Russian, Spanish, Indonesian, and Italian, and the general report has been that the audiences were as one in finding that Shakespeare represented *them* upon the stage" (*WC* 51). It's obvious that Bloom includes these observations to bolster his view that Shakespeare is the pinnacle of high seriousness and universal accessibility, but does he expect us to attach credibility to the suggested research method? What questions did Bloom ask his "students and friends" to elicit this report? Did these individual students undertake formal audience research? Without any information of this kind, how seriously are we meant to take Bloom's assertions?

We might also wish to consider why Bloom is so reluctant, in general, to argue or debate his positions, or why when he does he should use blatantly circular or tautologous arguments. Let us begin with the refusal to argue. Despite the fact that he thinks Alice Walker's novel *Meridian* worthless, he states that he is 'not prepared to dispute admirers" of it (*WC* 30). Again, "I see no reason for arguing with anyone about literary preferences" (*WC* 518). Why not, as his entire book is about literary preferences? Perhaps because as he says, "if you can't recognize [literature] when you read it, then no one can ever help you to know it or love it better" (*WC* 520). When Bloom appears to be arguing, the argument usually turns out to be circular or merely to dissolve into assertion. If we ask why Bloom believes that the aesthetic is autonomous from the social, all he has to say about this proposition is that "its best defence is the experience of reading *King Lear* and then seeing the play well performed" (*WC* 10). Thus an aesthetic text is held up as simple, straightforward evidence of how and why aesthetic texts are autonomous of social processes. Again, we are told that "aesthetic value can be recognized or experienced, but it cannot be conveyed to those who are incapable of grasping its sensations and perceptions. To quarrel on its behalf is always a blunder" (*WC* 17). Thus the assertion that argument is inappropriate is used to excuse Bloom's lack of argumentation about his dogmatically asserted opinion. He presumably feels that this also justifies contemptuous asides or jokes at the expense of other intellectual disciplines: Marxism is airily dismissed as "famously a cry of pain rather than a science" (*WC* 518); Freudian psychoanalysis is "another episode in the long history of shamanism" (*WC* 3); "cultural criticism is another dismal social science" (*WC* 17); Plato is reduced to moralism and Aristotle to social science (*WC* 18), as if these writers or the schools of thought they generated were so easily reduced to one concept or discipline. Consequently, why Freud, Plato and Aristotle are in Bloom's canon it is rather difficult to explain; Marx's absence is at least understandable. Bloom's egregious failure to conduct himself according to the established procedures of scholarly debate seems highly contradictory when one considers that he has already attacked one set of his opponents as an "academic-journalistic network" (*WC* 4). The refusal to follow scholarly procedures is precisely what most of us would term "journalistic".

Moving on to more substantive issues, I have to confess that I remain puzzled about Bloom's account of *how* a text becomes canonical. The book is an attempt to "isolate those qualities that made these authors canonical" (*WC* 1), which I find a very odd formulation indeed. As the book makes clear, it is *texts*, not *authors*, which are or can be canonical. If we assume this to be a slip of the pen, Bloom is presumably suggesting that canonicity is potentially immanent in a text, and so he talks of "texts struggling with one another for survival" (*WC* 20). So the canon consists of those texts whose inherent qualities (rather like the genetic qualities of certain species) assure their dominance. Perhaps Bloom's reluctance to identify the Darwinian source of the metaphor owes something to the obvious fact that the evolutionary parallel dissolves as soon as one acknowledges the social arenas *in which* texts struggle for survival. Bloom's view is that texts become canonical because "late-coming authors" (*WC* 20) confront their aesthetic strength and feel anxiety in the face of it; but the passive sentence structures in the next paragraph cannot conceal his recognition that other social agencies have a say in defining the canonical and that the category is historically variable: "in each era, some genres are regarded as more canonical than others" (*WC* 20). Regarded *by whom?*, one wishes to ask. Bloom is prepared to admit that the debating chamber involves more than just authors: "aesthetic value emanates from the struggle between texts: in the reader, in language, in the classroom, in arguments within a society" (*WC* 38). But this admission that the canonical is socially constructed (and thus that the aesthetic is necessarily susceptible to *some kind* of sociological explanation) is not one that Bloom can maintain for long. By the end of the book he has returned to his initial entrenched position: "The deepest truth about secular canon-formation is that it is performed by neither critics nor academies, let alone politicians. Writers, artists, composers themselves determine canons, by bridging between strong precursors and strong successors' (*WC* 522).

One can multiply the instances at which such contradictions come to the fore in Bloom's text: "there is no socioeconomic process that has added John Ashbery and James Merrill, or Thomas Pynchon, to the vague, nonexistent, and yet still compelling notion of an American canon that yet may be" (*WC* 520); yet, "certainly the critics, Dr Johnson and Hazlitt, contributed to the canonization" of Milton (*WC* 28). Most puzzlingly of all, the qualities, assumed to be intrinsic, which Bloom finds in canonical texts – qualities which he does little more than name as "originality" and "strangeness" – are relativistic concepts which seem peculiarly unsuited to the absolutist enterprise which his own seems to be. Bloom claims to be undertaking what he calls "the quest that is the final aim of literary study, the search for a kind of value that transcends the particular prejudices and needs of societies at fixed points in time" (*WC* 62). However, judgments about what is "original" and "strange" are self-evidently implicated in temporally definite interests and needs. The very equation of the canonical with the original is in itself a fairly recent prejudice. Milton, one of Bloom's heroes, was perfectly happy with the notion that greatness could emerge from imitation: what he condemned was imitation without improvement.

One does not wish to go on simply enumerating contradictions of this kind, but it is, I think, worth noting that there are very similar problems with Bloom's conception of the purpose of reading. Bloom is not so stubborn as to suggest that something so evidently learned and socially regulated as *reading* is a matter merely of individual experience: he confesses that "reading, writing and teaching are necessarily social arts" (*WC* 36). But it seems to be the case that to read *aesthetically* (the alternative, presumably, is to read merely *functionally*) is to do no other than "augment one's own growing inner self", which is, by definition, an action which takes place outside of society altogether despite, paradoxically, the fact that it is mediated by that most social of phenomena, language. "The mind's dialogue with itself is not primarily a social reality. All that the Western Canon can bring one is the proper use of one's own solitude, that solitude whose final form is one's confrontation with one's own mortality" (*WC* 30). Rather like Bloom's notion of reading, I find it difficult to understand what model of "the self" is being proposed here. Bloom states, "I think that the self, in its quest to be free and solitary, ultimately reads with one aim only: to confront greatness" (*WC* 524). One need not be a Deconstructionist to point out that the freedom and solitude of the self are somewhat philosophically undermined if they are dependent on a continuous relationship with the canonical textual productions of other selves. To deny that reading in itself implies a nexus of social relationships begins to look like sheer perversity.

Shakespeare is the centre of Bloom's canon, his eminence is "the rock upon which the School of Resentment must at last founder" (*WC* 25). Bloom contends that he is not a Shakespeare scholar, and I should say that I am even less of a Shakespeare scholar than him. I am not the best person to respond to his account of the School of Resentment's dealings with Shakespeare, although I think I have read enough of the work to which he refers to recognise that his account is a travesty. It would not be difficult, in my view, in summarising, say, historicist work on Shakespeare by critics like Jonathan Dollimore, Alan Sinfield, Terence Hawkes or Gary Taylor, to show that such work is hardly in denial about the aesthetic status or value of Shakespeare's work.[4] But they would, of

---

4 See Jonathan Dollimore and Alan Sinfield (eds.), *Political Shakespeare: Essays in Cultural Materialism* (1985; 2nd ed., Manchester: Manchester University

course, disagree fundamentally with Bloom that aesthetic status or value are phenomena which reside beyond history and society. Let me abandon that line of argument, however, as it would clearly only lead us to the forked path where absolutists and relativists dogmatically divide. I would prefer, I think, to focus on the rhetorical function which Shakespeare performs in Bloom's discourse. If Shakespeare is the rock upon which Bloom's enemies must founder, he is also the rock upon which Bloom's canonical church is founded. His function is clearly fundamentalist or, if you like, Shakespeare is Bloom's fundament: it is in Shakespeare, to risk a pun, that we touch bottom. This is perhaps why Shakespeare's near anonymity is so significant to Bloom (Bloom in his chapter on Shakespeare bizarrely writes of his "virtual colorlessness" and his "tactics of losing his selfhood in his work" [WC 55], as if these were actual personal attributes rather than an absence of biographical – that is to say historical – knowledge about him): it makes it all the more appropriate to his vision of him as the still centre of the canonical world, the first cause which, ultimately, ensures that there is order in an apparently chaotic universe. Shakespeare is unabashedly the God figure in Bloom's secular theology, on an alarmingly literal as well as metaphorical plane. Shakespeare is not only irreducible to anything else, but we are reducible to Shakespeare. He invented us. He also invented Freudian psychology and Marxist political economy, and presumably much else which came after him:

> Here they [i.e. members of the School of Resentment] confront insurmountable difficulty in Shakespeare's most idiosyncratic strength: he is always ahead of you, conceptually and imagistically, whoever and whenever you are. He renders you anachronistic because he *contains* you; you cannot subsume him. You cannot illuminate him with a new doctrine, be it Marxism or Freudianism or Demanian linguistic skepticism. Instead, he will illuminate the doctrine, not by prefiguration but by postfiguration as it were: all of Freud that matters most is there in Shakespeare already, with a persuasive critique of

Press, 1994); Terence Hawkes, *That Shakespeherian Rag: Essays on a Critical Process* (London: Methuen, 1986) Gary Taylor, *Reinventing Shakespeare: a Cultural History from the Restoration to the Present* (London: Hogarth Press, 1990).

Freud besides. The Freudian map of the mind is Shakespeare's; Freud seems only to have prosified it. Or, to vary my point, a Shakespearian reading of Freud illuminates and overwhelms the text of Freud; a Freudian reading of Shakespeare reduces Shakespeare, or would if we could bear a reduction that crosses the line into absurdities of loss. *Coriolanus* is a far more powerful reading of Marx's *Eighteenth Brumaire of Louis Napoleon* than any Marxist reading of *Coriolanus* could hope to be. (*WC* 25)

Bloom offers this kind of argument with absolute sincerity and literalness, arguing, for instance, that Shakespeare is the first writer to depict what he calls "self-change on the basis of self-overhearing" (he cites Falstaff and Hamlet as examples) and adding that "we all of us go around now talking to ourselves endlessly, overhearing what we say, then pondering and acting upon what we have learned". Apparently, we do so because Falstaff and Hamlet taught us how to do so, whether we know this or not and, presumably, whether we have read Shakespeare or not (*WC* 48-9). I do not personally feel competent to comment on this fascinating historical thesis.

I shall, however, in closing, draw attention to Bloom's comments about the figure named J, who is viewed (by some) as the first author of the Hebrew bible. Bloom argues that this author's texts (what we now know as the books of Genesis, Exodus and Numbers) were subject to revision and censorship by a number of later priests and scribes and that, specifically, what they erased was her (for Bloom believes the writer to be female, even perhaps to be Bathsheba, mother of Solomon) construction of God as all-too-human: mischievous, jealous, vindictive, unjust, neurotic and (as his murder of Moses before the walls of the Promised Land demonstrates) finally insane and dangerous. Bloom, in one of his frequently witty moments, points out that it is something of a shock "when we realize that the Western worship of God – by Jews, Christians, and Moslems – is the worship of a literary character, J's Yahweh, however adulterated by pious revisionists" (*WC* 6).

Now, in this connection I am interested in Bloom's rather odd lack of corresponding concern about the state of Shakespeare's texts and the confidence with which he is prepared to "read off" aspects of Shakespeare's personality from those fiercely debated texts: thus, on one page alone, we are told that the texts of Shakespeare demonstrate that the man was "disinterested", "almost as free of ideology as are his heroic wits: Hamlet, Rosalind, Falstaff. He has no theology, no metaphysics, no ethics, and rather less political theory than is brought to him by his current critics" (*WC* 56). Bloom's worship of Shakespeare – I do not think "worship" is too strong a term – may have been arrived at by a procedure somewhat akin to that he claims has operated in the Western worship of God. In other words, Bloom seems to overlook any doubts that there may be about Shakespeare's texts in his keenness to construct a sublimated deity figure who can preside over the canon and operate as the ultimate guarantor of meaning and hierarchy in a world threatened with the extinction of both. It is true that he acknowledges once (and only once) the potential difficulties that the existence of competing texts of the same play can throw up. He confesses that "Shakespeare puzzles us in his apparent indifference to the posthumous destiny of King Lear: we have two rather different texts of the play, and pushing them together into the amalgam we generally read and see acted is not very satisfactory" (*WC* 52). Not very satisfactory, that is, for Bloom's conception of Shakespeare; and no sooner has he asked the question than he quickly disposes of it with a characteristic evasion: "How can there have been a writer for whom the final shape of *King Lear* was a careless or throwaway matter? Shakespeare is like the Arabian moon in Wallace Stevens that 'throws his stars around the floor,' as though the profusion of Shakespeare's gifts was so abundant that he could afford to be careless" (*WC* 52). I think we must have the confidence to identify such speculative apologetics as the arrant nonsense that they indubitably are. There is perhaps no hope of proving it, but I would dare to suggest that the existence of two competing versions of *King Lear* has nothing to do with the lofty carelessness of the play's author, and that only a more historically inclined critical procedure than Bloom's is likely to give us the enlightenment on this matter that we seek.

These matters notwithstanding, there are a host of issues which Bloom's book raises that should give critics who are historically or sociologically or theoretically inclined considerable pause. For example, the complacency with which literary study is assimilated to politics by many critics, and the tendency to arrogate texts to positions of cultural eminence on the basis of their political amenability is, I think, a very real problem in some quarters. Bloom can be blunt to the point of vulgarity about this: "if you believe that all value ascribed to poems or plays or novels and stories is only a mystification in the service of the ruling class, then why should you read at all rather than go forth to serve the desperate needs of the exploited classes? The idea that you benefit the insulted and injured by reading someone of their own origins rather than reading Shakespeare is one of the oddest illusions ever promoted by or in our schools" (*WC* 522). One could make a sophisticated answer to this kind of objection. Bloom is relying on a demonstrably fallacious distinction between interpreting and acting, between intellectual work and practical work. It's clear that intellectual work can and has changed the world. But I can't help thinking that Bloom has a point, and one could easily enlist as uncongenial a source as Marx's "Theses on Feuerbach" in support of his cause: "hitherto the philosophers have only *interpreted* the world; the point, however, it to *change* it". I read Marx's dictum not as devaluing intellectual work but asserting that intellectual work conducted without an accompanying *praxis* does not possess the degree of radicalism that it may claim for itself. And the evidence of one's senses tells one that many literary intellectuals, producing "radical" criticism, are doing little else that might be described as radical.

As just one other example, take the accusation Bloom makes about the universal lowering of standards. His argument is that, in the name of some democratic impulse, to enlarge "access", or promote "relevance", there has been a gradual devaluation, in literary disciplines more than others, he claims, of the cognitively difficult. Bloom describes this memorably: "the morality of scholarship, as currently practiced, is to encourage everyone to replace difficult pleasures by pleasures universally accessible precisely because they are easier" (*WC* 520). He points out that this simply has not happened in mathematics or the sciences, or even in the history of art or music. And again, ironically, he is able to enlist the support of an unlikely ally: "Trotsky urged his fellow Marxists to read Dante, but he would find no welcome in our current universities" (*WC* 520). I do think that what Bloom calls the School of Resentment needs to answer charges like these (let me be clear: I'm not saying they cannot be answered, simply that they need to be) but what I fear is that the all-too-polemical manner in which he issues such challenges, and the many confusions, contradictions and eccentricities of *The Western Canon*, are more likely to lead to a disparaging neglect of Bloom's complaints rather than an articulated rebuttal of them. Such neglect would simply leave the field clear for the unhindered promotion of calculated Bloomian simplicities.

1999

ETHICS, WRITING AND SCHOLARSHIP: DOES RICHARD HOGGART MEET HIS OWN STANDARDS?

Having recently been engaged on a project to do with British public radio, I decided to read Richard Hoggart's *Mass Media in a Mass Society: Myth and Reality* (Hoggart 2005), not simply because, as a colleague told me, it has a few pages on radio, but because I thought that Hoggart's considered opinion on a whole range of issues informing contemporary society and its mediation would be useful for me to know. In this decision, the element of recognition – in short, of Hoggart's reputation – undoubtedly played a part, given that, for the purposes of my project, I have ignored (because they say nothing or very little about radio) a whole raft of books of the "mass media/mass society" type. Note that, for me at any rate, that recognition is not bound up with any sense of Hoggart as a media or sociological specialist, while the books I ignore are often written by academics who could creditably claim one or both of those labels. Indeed, I did not consciously even expect Hoggart to answer the kinds of questions those other authors might debate; what is more likely is that I expected Hoggart to ask different questions and perhaps venture interesting answers.

I certainly expected a view that I considered "of the Left". In fact, the book is either an ideological hodge-podge of Left, Centre and Right, or at best is cut adrift from any coherent position designated by such terms, as Charlie Ellis in part argues (Owen 2008: 198-212). What I did not expect was to read a book that should never have been published. I did not expect a book whose public existence can owe little to its impoverished intellectual content, but is validated by the flimsiest of supports, its author's reputation alone (a reputation not regenerated by the book itself, of course). "Reputation" in this context is what creates the market for something no matter how unnecessary it is, a feature of contemporary capitalism which Hoggart repeatedly criticises in the book itself. But it is probably the only reason why my edition of the book, first published in 2004, is the 2005 reprint: without the name of Hoggart acting as a kind of brand, I doubt that it would have sold so respectably, and so quickly, that it required reprinting within a year. I am obliged to try to justify my adverse evaluation of the book in what follows, but if I do so persuasively then the first of several ironies would have to be registered. For example, here we would have Hoggart churning out a book that is otiose, out of touch, miles wide of its mark because it seems to have paid little attention to the scholarship of the past twenty years, in either media studies or sociology; and yet is probably read and bought many times more than academic volumes to which it is, methodologically and conceptually, inferior. Hereby we would find Hoggart involved, in a small way, in precisely the market-determined routines his own book repeatedly rails against.

And that was, I have to say, my continuous response all the way through my first reading of the book. I found it, indeed, nothing short of shocking and on occasions vulgar. Charlie Ellis (Owen 2008: 198) cites a number of early reviews which point out that, at worst, it is a rant by a grumbling old man; at best it is an intellectually rickety construction in which rather subjective views of contemporary British society (or the views of a particular social group, perhaps, namely those who remember the Second World War) are offered in a discourse which attempts to deploy many of the devices of impersonality and objectivity, but which is really being pressed into self-serving ends (either of the author or of the putative social group). Most charitably, one might simply consider the author to belong to a much smaller sub-culture than he thinks he does and to have made the mistake of overrating the general social import of the views he holds. But Hoggart would not see that as a criticism, as he is militant in his absolutely correct conviction that the widespread popularity of something is no argument in favour of its quality.

However, when I re-read the book I tried to gain a perspective from which I could view it with less hostility, and I shall try to suggest how that might be possible: it devolves on the question of what kind of writing, now, in the early twenty-first century, might answer the lack which, despite his very dubious arguments about this and that, Hoggart does, I think, correctly identify. That lack is caused by the ejection of moral and aesthetic evaluation from discourses around culture which has been effected by postmodernism (a word Hoggart uses only once in the book, incidentally), in society at large but also (in his view, and my own) in academic work, a serious business where one might expect it to have remained alive. In this latter respect – the general failure of the academic disciplines we variously sub-divide the field into, namely Literary Studies, Media Studies, Cultural Studies, to maintain in their discourses any strong sense of objective ethical and artistic worth, but to have witnessed and in many ways facilitated the relativisation of both – we can see why Hoggart might not have wished to bother to meet the contemporary scholarly standards of even the best academic practitioners in these disciplines. (My point here is not that there are no individual exceptions to the relativising tide within every discipline, but that the individual exceptions within the named disciplines have the appearance of being King Canutes.) In Hoggart's book there is a heavy reckoning to be paid for that divorce between ethics and evaluation on the one hand and intellectual discourses about culture on the other, although he does not describe the likely reckoning very well, nor does he suggest more than a handful of remedies to assuage the social wounds it will cause or maybe prevent its axe from falling so heavily.

Nonetheless, I do agree with Hoggart about this damaging dissolution of evaluative responsibility, and it may therefore be that his abiding worth is that he maintains, at this unfashionably late stage, this Arnoldian/Leavisite torch alight at all in the very high winds surrounding it without subscribing to the pompous elitism of someone like Harold Bloom (1995), whose *The Western Canon* builds a pyramid of worthy books around the notionally solitary reader as a protection against the chaos and vulgarity of the social life deemed to be outside it. I tend to think I knew in advance, no doubt from Hoggart's other writings, that this was the row he would continue unfashionably to plough in this book, and, though I found the volume an extremely disagreeable folly, it does prompt the question: what would writing that could properly rejuvenate the integration of moral and aesthetic evaluation with the study of culture have to be like, now, in the world in which we find ourselves? I shall fail to answer this question (which is more of an invitation to discussion than an enquiry to which I have a ready-made answer) except in the negative: such a discourse cannot now be like Richard Hoggart's. But I do believe that Hoggart's writing, although in my mind it is now an intellectually superannuated venture, is one of the few sources which still forces us to confront the question. In that alone, we might say, inheres *its* persistent value – and just as a return to the discourse of Arnold or Leavis or even (the comparison may be better in respect of Hoggart) Raymond Williams would these days be impractical for any author, nonetheless I know I am not alone in thinking that, post-postmodernism, someone with considerable intellectual authority is likely to arise who will, after some new design, successfully sail that battered boat on the waters once more.

I mention Williams also because Hoggart's book on the mass media seems to me an attempt to replicate the kind of discourse in which Williams engaged in his essay "Britain in the 1960s" in *The Long Revolution* (Williams 1961: 319-83): both are expansive attempts to write a kind of sweeping sociological survey about the contemporary, and both mix what one might call their "high" and impersonal ambitions with some very "low" and idiosyncratic perceptions. But whereas what Williams was doing, in those pre-Cultural Studies days, when academic sociology and political science were also in what we might now consider their childhood if not their infancy, had the impact of a genuinely new approach to questions of the contemporary, Hoggart's prose, more than forty years later, reads as if it were a kind of last resort, the sort of limited thing one is able to produce out of a self-imposed refusal to engage with the developments that have occurred in the interim. The difference may simply be that the two authors wrote these books at quite different points in their careers. But it is no longer intellectually tenable to produce such wide-ranging surveys if they are invertebrate; that is, if they lack the spine of evidential data, tending towards pronouncement and judgment on their many subjects without seriously engaging with the empirical realities towards which they gesture. Moreover, Williams' essay was only one (the last) in a long and highly original book, which had a clear central thesis; Hoggart's book has no opportunity for the kind of contrapuntal effects that Williams is able to produce. Perhaps most significantly, Williams' essay could easily be recognised as an enterprise firmly rooted in left-wing politics. Hoggart's, by contrast, is ideologically kaleidoscopic: if anything, although I am not qualified to carry out the discourse analysis which would prove it, it resembles the kind of discourse which elected members of Parliament probably consider intellectual. It reaches, in other words, the level of something like a Fabian Society pamphlet.

I should say that I recognise that there are all kinds of writing outside of academic and/or scholarly modes which are intellectually valuable and socially necessary: Hoggart's (and for that matter Williams') own project is such that one could never give any of their works the dispiriting and limiting label of "monograph". From the very first, in the opening words of *The Uses of Literacy*, Hoggart has genuinely, and I think valuably "thought of myself as addressing first of all the serious 'common reader' or 'intelligent layman' from any class". But while he acknowledged there that that same book "does not purport to have the scientifically-tested character of a sociological survey", he explains: "There is an obvious danger of generalization from limited experience. I have therefore included, chiefly in the notes, some of the findings of sociologists where they seemed necessary, either as support or as qualification of the text" (Hoggart 2004: xli). In my edition of *The Uses of Literacy* there are twenty-five pages of notes and a five-page select bibliography: almost exactly a tenth of the book when taken together. *Mass Media in a Mass Society* has not a single footnote and no bibliography, and shows every sign of being written without any heed whatsoever to the "obvious danger of generalization from limited experience" – a danger that, elsewhere, we usually call prejudice and/or ignorance.

And so much of the book is simply ignorant of what it speaks. The list of idiosyncratic opinions Hoggart holds, but which he presents in the book as if they have a basis in fact (while not citing or otherwise producing any evidence informing them) is extensive: the book largely consists of these opinions being delivered up out of the most slender, and often demonstrably false, certainly unverifiable, assumptions and suppositions. For example, the following, from quite early in the book, is paradigmatic (a word his chapter on language castigates, incidentally). He condemns an entire educational (or, if you prefer, training) endeavour thus: "Do these schools of journalism in British universities and further education colleges ask their students to face the ethical questions raised by their desired profession? From the answers recently given on the radio by a professor from one such school, it seems not" (Hoggart 2005: 21). He then spends a couple of sentences summarising the ethical deficiencies of what the unnamed professor from the unnamed school of journalism on the unnamed radio programme on an unnamed station on an unspecified date is purported to have said ("purported" because Hoggart provides no data which would allow us to check) and rounds off his condemnation with an irony of some enormity: "Not to raise such questions seems a dereliction of duty in an academic at any level" (Hoggart 2005: 22). But Hoggart himself can hardly lecture an academic on a duty he himself has abandoned, namely the duty to allow readers to verify one's conclusions with reference to the sources which prompted them. That is what is ethical about scholarly discourse. One could give *dozens* of examples from the book to show that this is Hoggart's habitual tendency throughout. Indeed, I do not recall a single instance in the book in which Hoggart adequately sources claims about what x or y said or wrote.

If one trusts Hoggart's judgment unquestioningly, this will not be a problem. He truly thinks that major shareholders of and members of the boards of most companies "probably" have degrees from Oxbridge (Hoggart 2005: 25). The "probably" means that one cannot say that this is factually wrong because the degree of probability he neglects to specify: but in a context such as this one there is no ethical justification for the word at all. The scholarly thing to do would be to find out, not to rely on the "probably" of one's prejudices. I suspect (but admit I do not know) that far fewer people in this category went to Oxbridge than he thinks. In print, however, I would commit myself to a factual claim only after I had undertaken the necessary enquiries. At times the bathos of these utterly bogus claims is embarrassingly laughable: for instance, Hoggart cannot believe that "Smillie" (pronounced as "smiley") is really TV celebrity Carol Smillie's name: "surely a pseudonym, or coincidence has become almost unbelievable" he says parenthetically (Hoggart 2005: 87). Of course, this may just be a cheap joke at the perennially cheerful Ms Smillie's expense, although cheap jokes are something Hoggart usually disapproves of. But Smillie is nonetheless her real name, there is no reason to think it is not, and the fact can very easily be verified. It is not a very unusual name in Scotland, and Hoggart himself probably knows that Robert Smillie, born in Belfast, was a founder member of the Scottish Labour Party in 1888 and of the Independent Labour Party in 1893, Keir Hardie's right-hand man in many ways. President of the Miners' Federation of Great Britain from 1912 until 1922, MP for Morpeth in the 1920s, he did not die until 1940, when Hoggart turned twenty-two. The name is not strange to anyone with a passing historical interest in the British Labour movement.

I do not wish to suggest that Hoggart's text is laced with personal jibes like these (Smillie is one of the few people he sees fit to name), but it is bedevilled by regrettable and unsupported prejudices of this kind. The apotheosis of this low-level hubris is the dismal chapter "Language and Meanings" (Hoggart 2005: 140-57), which reads like the outpouring of a pedantic *Daily Telegraph* reader glorying in his own out-of-tuneness with the mass of ignorant unlettered people he criticises. So (extreme laments at the passing of "sir" and at the rise of a redefined "gay" aside) we get the most astounding linguistic prescriptivism for eighteen entire pages, the spirit of which might have moved the pen of Ernest Gowers, except that Hoggart's suggested amendments are not of the kind that would have made it into Gowers' *The Complete Plain Words*. Thus Hoggart complains about titles such as "Chief Environmental Planning Officer" and suggests, absurdly, that a more appropriate term might be "Chief Environmental-Rape Officer". It would, of course, be some salvation if Hoggart's English were impeccable. But throughout his writing career he has misused the word "since" to indicate causation when in fact, for a prescriptivist, it can indicate only duration. He similarly misuses "due to" to mark causation when in fact it "properly" marks only temporal imminence. And every five or six pages in *Mass Media in a Mass Society* there pops up a sentence without a primary verb. Again, one need not labour the point too much: if you are going to use an ethical slingshot, you'd better look to the beam in your own eye, or your aim may be misdirected.

But Hoggart is consciously writing as a David facing a Goliath, and the book is a kind of desperate last wail from someone whose resources are running out and whose material is thin and whose strength is no longer great in this fight. We must remember that he published the book when he was eighty-two years old. Thus I may seem simply uncharitable and perhaps a little cruel in the criticisms and comparisons I have made. There is quite a different way of looking at the book which ignores and perhaps explains its very shortcomings: namely the impulse, in an old man, not to go down quietly, without a fight, even if the result is that he is ranting half the time. And the fight here is precisely borne out of a worthy insistence that ethics – and the corresponding duty to make aesthetic evaluation – remain at the heart of the study of art and culture.

I believe Hoggart is the last surviving remnant of this tradition – he would probably be relatively happy with the word – which, despite all their differences, binds Arnold to Leavis to Williams to Hoggart. I have never thought that Hoggart had the intellectual stature or gravitas of the other three I have named. But, in his own way – grossly distorted in the book I have discussed – he refuses to cease whispering (as he puts it) in that wind. And it is because of this insistence – not the bizarrely confused and worryingly out-of-touch discourse it has produced in this case – that I think Hoggart's life-work remains salutary, and something to carry forward.

I think he is right (both factually and morally) that the decoupling of ethical considerations (and the concomitant evaluation of cultural products and procedures) has – and I suspect we are at the apex of this development – been a disaster which the academy, and especially Cultural Studies, has all too helpfully aided. I now work in a discipline which, at its inception (for the sake of argument, let's assume that to be the Birmingham Centre, which Hoggart founded) was reworking that ethical stress in terms of politics and ideology. Twenty-five years ago, when I was an undergraduate studying English Literature, I saw this belatedly working its way through Literary Studies, as "Theory", apparently bent on destroying the seeming ideological naïvety of liberal humanism, was still doing so within the relatively clear ethical framework of socialist politics. But not anymore: Literary Studies, but especially Cultural Studies, are both now awash, if not drowned, in a tide of relativism caused by the crisis of pluralist and identity-based politics to which, ironically, "Theory" opened the gates. One still has straightforward discussions about what is "good" and "bad" but one hesitates to commit these to the illusory objectivity which writing seems to bestow. The institutions in which we carry out our teaching and research have similarly, in my experience, migrated from the collegiate public service model which I got a last glimpse of when I joined a University's staff in 1991, to the competitive business models we are now all too familiar with from experience, and, in the process, their watchword has become not what is good and right, but what, practically, in the world of education, sells and can be marketed, or can be exploited to raise research funds.

My aim in what I have said, therefore, and despite what it may have sounded like, was not simply to launch a partial attack on Hoggart by choosing one of his obvious Achilles' heels. Actually, I think what I am trying to do with Hoggart is to praise him with faint damning. When his voice is lost, the Humanities loses the last of the uncompromising ethicists and, although his practice went sorely awry in this book, he articulates the principle bravely, unwaveringly and unfashionably, at an incredibly late and unpropitious stage. He does not practise what he preaches because the slapdashness of his scholarship and argumentative procedures is no longer acceptable, just as one would be mistaken to try to reproduce in today's conditions Williams' clotted complexity, Leavis's icy and Olympian moral superiority, or Arnold's wistful, analysis-shy classicism. There is, to my mind, no one left alive in the field of the required intellectual stature who can take the baton he wishes to pass. That is what makes it difficult to see, now, what an ethically rooted study of literature, the arts, culture more generally and the social conditions which modulate it, would look like – above all, what intellectual writing, in these new conditions but with a wish to keep that strain alive, would look like. Despite all his shortcomings, then, I believe that that is Hoggart's challenge to the future of those disciplines, and I invite us to discuss whether or not it is a challenge we wish to take up or turn our backs on.

References

Bloom, H. (1995). *The Western Canon: the Books and School of the Ages.* (London: Macmillan).

Hoggart, R. (2004). *The Uses of Literacy: Aspects of Working-Class Life.* (New Brunswick: Transaction Publishers).

Hoggart, R. (2005). *Mass Media in a Mass Society: Myth and Reality.* (London: Continuum).

Owen, S. (ed.) (2008). *Richard Hoggart and Cultural Studies.* (Basingstoke: Palgrave Macmillan).

Williams, R. (1961). *The Long Revolution.* (London: Chatto and Windus).

2009

Fredric Jameson was born in 1934 in Cleveland, Ohio. He graduated from Harvard University in 1954 and completed a doctorate at Yale University in 1960, after which he returned to Harvard to commence his teaching career. From 1967 he had various appointments at the University of California, San Diego (1967-76), Yale University (1976-83), and the University of California, Santa Cruz (1983-85). In 1985 he became Professor of Comparative Literature at Duke University.

His first published volume was *Sartre: The Origins of a Style* (1961), which was derived from his doctoral thesis and, if it did not adopt the Marxist perspective for which he has become best known, showed immediately the theoretical tendencies and stylistic flair which are the hallmark of all his later work. The text which truly made his reputation was *Marxism and Form: Twentieth Century Dialectical Theories of Literature* (1971). This was followed by a series of long and intricate books, each of which has represented a milestone in the development of late twentieth century Marxist literary, cultural and social theory: the most significant among many are *The Prison-House of Language: A Critical Account of Structuralism and Russian Formalism* (1972), *The Political Unconscious: Narrative as a Socially Symbolic Act* (1981), *The Ideologies of Theory, Essays 1971-1986* (1988), and *Postmodernism, or, The Cultural Logic of Late Capitalism* (1991). In the present essay there is scope to refer in detail to only two of these key texts of Jameson's "Hegelian Marxism", the term which he embraces to denominate his critical position. This is not necessarily in his case a severe limitation, as Jameson's basic theoretical stance has remained remarkably constant throughout his career, although there has been one noticeable shift in that the objects of his critical attention have latterly derived from the realm of popular as well as high culture. The two texts selected for extensive comment have been chosen as those best illustrating this development. They are nonetheless reliably representative of his thinking as a whole.

"Hegelian Marxism"

A word needs to be said in advance about "Hegelian Marxism".

For Marx and his nineteenth-century and Soviet followers, Marxism was undoubtedly "Hegelian" in some of its analytical methods, but Marx's relation to Hegel was primarily a "negation", or "overcoming", of Hegel's philosophical limitations. Thus, for example, in a classic text like the *Economic and Philosophical Manuscripts of 1844*, we find Marx engaging in a "critical discussion of *Hegelian dialectic* and Hegelian philosophy as a whole".[1] The "Hegelian dialectic" was Hegel's novel application of an ancient Greek philosophical method to the field of social relationships to explain how history moved from lower to higher stages. For Hegel, the engine of historical change was "spirit" or "mind", or the human ability to reflect, contemplate, and theorise about the objective world as a prelude to changing it. This happened "dialectically", as pre-existent reality met its "negation" in new ways of thinking about reality, which, subsequently applied to that reality, altered or "overcame" it. The process was not, for Hegel, infinite. Indeed, he argued that history as such came to an end at the point at which this "absolute truth" was grasped. Marx profoundly disagreed with Hegel, not about the application of the dialectical method to history (which he considered the supreme achievement of Hegel's philosophy), but about the driving forces at work within history. For Marx, it was not ideation that changed social reality, but the struggle for the production and reproduction of real life, the pursuit of material interests, that was ultimately the root of all historical development.

Frederick Engels, Marx's collaborator, once famously remarked (in *Ludwig Feuerbach and the End of Classical German Philosophy* [1886]) that in the work conducted by Marx "the Hegelian dialectic was placed upon its head; or rather, turned off its head, on which it was standing, and placed upon its feet" so that "the revolutionary side of Hegelian philosophy was again taken up and at the same time freed from the idealist trimmings which with Hegel had prevented its consistent execution".[2] Engels argued that Marx had modified Hegel's dialectic in

[1] Karl Marx and Frederick Engels, *Complete Works*, vol. III (London: Lawrence and Wishart, 1975), p. 232.
[2] Karl Marx and Frederick Engels, *Complete Works*, vol. XXVI (London: Lawrence and Wishart, 1990), pp. 383, 384.

three ways: Marx was more explicit about the radical nature of historical change; he agreed that social development moved "upward" from lower to higher stages, but did not agree that this process had a terminal point; and he inverted Hegel's priorities of determination (so that matter, not mind, was the ultimately determining factor in history). Thus, for many Marxists, Marxism should *not* be thought of as "Hegelian": Marxist materialism is seen, in fact, as the "negation" or "overcoming" of Hegel's idealism; Marxist social radicalism is the opposite of Hegelian political conservatism.

Hegel could give an important place in his system to the ideational realm of aesthetics, on which subject, indeed, he lectured extensively at the University of Berlin. By contrast, Marx often explicitly endows intellectual endeavour – including matters to do with art and culture – with a quite secondary, if not altogether negligible, status within his order of determinations (and thus it comes as no surprise to find that his comments on aesthetic issues are scattered randomly throughout his work without ever coming to a focus). This poses severe theoretical problems for those (like Jameson) who find themselves committed to the social, political and intellectual premises and/or conclusions of Marxism but find themselves working, as artists or critics, in the cultural domain. "Hegelian Marxism" is one answer to the problem. In effect, it offers itself as a "negation" of Marxism, or "overcoming" of Marx's marginalisation of the importance of art and culture: just as Marx threw out the Hegelian bathwater of "idealism' without discarding the baby of the dialectical method, so "Hegelian Marxism" attempts to turn Marxist theory "off its head" by re-balancing it with an Hegelian sense of the value of ideation *without* resorting to outright Hegelian idealism (that is, without losing Marx's stress on the importance of the struggle over material interests). Predictably, much of the theoretical work in this field therefore concerns the relations (or the "dialectic") *between* material interests and the realms of art and culture. Jameson, regarded by many as the most accomplished twentieth century anglophone exponent of such an approach, thus offers a unique opportunity to judge the success of the enterprise.

Marxism and Form

Marxism and Form declares itself to be a "general introduction" to "a relatively Hegelian kind of Marxism" within a tradition which is described as "a mixture of political liberalism, empiricism and logical positivism which we know as Anglo-American philosophy and which is hostile at all points to the type of thinking outlined here".[3] We need not concern ourselves with adjudging whether or not *Marxism and Form* really *is* the kind of book which would persuade liberal bourgeois intellectuals as to the necessity of applying Marxist categories to the study of texts. The fact is that it self-consciously proclaims itself to be so, and that we are to believe that its methods may be deployed with such an audience – rather than a readership of convinced Marxists – in mind. Even so, the project immediately appears to be less compromised than it may think itself. It is not true, for example, that "Anglo-American philosophy is hostile at all points" to the notion that literature has an important social and perhaps political value; this is, in fact, a hostility more entertained by certain old-fashioned schools of Marxism. What is missing in both the former and the latter is any tradition of *dialectical* thought which accords an appreciable rôle to cultural production. The point that Jameson seems to be conceding is that there is little need to be troubled by various "vulgar" Marxist positions, as these have had no real influence within the American academy of his day. It is not the case, however, that Jameson wishes to discount them absolutely or deny them relative validity. Indeed, he ends his Introduction to the book with a curious confession as to the geopolitical limitations of his own ensuing survey of twentieth-century dialectical theories of literature:

> It is perfectly consistent with the spirit of Marxism [...] that there should exist several different Marxisms in the world of today, each answering the specific needs and problems of its own socio-economic system: thus, one corresponds to the postrevolutionary industrial countries of the socialist bloc, another – a kind of peasant Marxism – to China and Cuba and the countries of the Third World, while yet another tries to deal theoretically with the unique questions raised by monopoly capitalism in the West. It is in the context of this last, I am

---

[3] Fredric Jameson, *Marxism and Form: Twentieth Century Dialectical Theories of Literature* (Princeton: Princeton University Press, 1971), pp. ix, x.

tempted to call it postindustrial, Marxism that the great themes of Hegel's philosophy [...] are once again the order of the day.[4]

Jameson rightly indicates that these differentiations are justifiable in terms of Marxist theory. Yet the relativisation of Hegel (and of his own work) has a curious effect. It is tantamount to claiming that the other Marxisms cited (which operate within conditions of what used to be called "actually existing socialism") have no need of Hegel; or, conversely, that Western Marxism (because of the "unique questions raised by monopoly capitalism") need not see "actually existing socialism" as providing any answers. What is avoided is precisely the enquiry any Marxist – or any Hegelian – would wish to commit themselves to, namely, "which of these socio-economic systems is at a higher, and which at a lower, stage of development"? Perhaps we are to take it that the answer is implicit in the adjectives "peasant", "industrial" and "postindustrial" as applied to each of the distinctive socio-economic systems. Does it thus follow that the Soviet or Chinese socio-economic systems simply are not yet at a stage of development where they require Hegel's dialectic to inform their supposedly Marxist practice? If so, how is it that the Western socio-economic system had no need of the Marxist phase through which the other systems reached their particular level of development? Jameson's ambiguous fixation solely on issues within Western Marxism has, as we shall later see, been a principal cause of concern for commentators on his work.

Justice is not quite done to *Marxism and Form* proper by terming it a survey or an introduction. It is, in fact, a lengthy, detailed, and eloquent exploration of the Marxist-orientated work of T. W. Adorno, Walter Benjamin, Herbert Marcuse, Ernst Bloch, György Lukács and Jean-Paul Sartre, and concludes with a 110-page coda, "Towards Dialectical Criticism". Even thirty years on, the book does not seem dated, although it does appear decidedly unfashionable, not because it is Marxist, but because of the subsequent fate within Marxism of some of the figures with which it deals. Thus the most memorable sections of the book which deal with other thinkers are not those on Adorno or Benjamin (whose reputations it helped vastly to promote) but the sub-chapter on Marcuse

---

4 Jameson, *Marxism and Form*, pp. xviii-xix.

and the 100-page analysis of Sartre's *Critique of Dialectical Reason*. One would struggle to find either Marcuse or Sartre at the top of any Marxism reading lists these days (the former because he engages with the no-longer-*chic* "counter culture" of the sixties, the latter because existentialism, his lifelong concern, is nowadays hardly *à la mode*), but it is in his dealings with them that what are to become distinctive Jamesonian themes emerge with most clarity and in most depth.

The discussion of Marcuse, for example, demonstrates in extremely compact form how the dialectical procedure is for Jameson not simply something inherent in (or deducible from) the texts and authors he discusses, but is the method he too applies to those texts and authors.[5] He interprets and critiques those texts in the manner of much traditional critical discourse, but also puts them into the service of an ongoing dialectic in which he himself attempts to "negate" their limitations, not by a dismissive act of intellectual rejection or correction (Jameson, in fact, is the most generous of commentators, even to those in hostile camps), but by an ameliorating or supplementary act of construction in which he "goes through" a particular conceptualisation or argument to the "other side" of it, yielding from it what remains useful (as Marx did with Hegel) and deploying that residue in an often startlingly new configuration or application.

In the case of Marcuse, he first summarises the dialogue (or dialectic) between the twentieth century thinker and various nineteenth century theorists (Hegel, Marx, Freud and the German historian and playwright Friedrich Schiller). The theme is that of Utopian thinking, a matter of constant concern within Marxism, and particularly Marcuse's "ironic reversal" of Freud's pessimistic and paradoxical thesis "in *Civilization and Its Discontents*, which posited an irreversible and unavoidable interdependency between progress in the evolution of society and unhappiness in the repressed psyche of individual man, between individual self-denial and the diversion of psychic energy for collective purposes".[6] To use the classic vocabulary of the dialectical method, this is a *thesis* which is met by a Marcusian *antithesis* (its "ironic reversal"):

---

[5] Jameson, *Marxism and Form*, pp. 83-116; for the main discussion of Marcuse, see pp. 106-16.
[6] Jameson, *Marxism and Form*, p. 107.

"For Marcuse, on the other side of the great watershed of postindustrial capitalism, things no longer look quite the same, and it turns out that it is precisely increased sexual freedom, greater material abundance and consumption, freer access to culture, better housing, more widely available educational benefits and increased social, not to speak of automotive mobility, which are the accompaniment to increasing manipulation and the most sophisticated forms of thought-control, increasing abasement of spiritual and intellectual life, a degradation and dehumanization of existence. Thus it is that the happier we are, the more surely we are given over, without even being aware of it, into the power of the socio-economic system itself."[7]

While one of these formulations is undoubtedly a reversal of the other, it is perhaps "ironic" because it does not, in itself, offer to solve the paradox, but simply inverts its terms. Neither offers a way out of an apparent stalemate in which the hope of Utopia approaches on one axis (in Marcuse's case, happiness) while simultaneously receding on the other (individual freedom). At this point Jameson intervenes with a dialectical reversal of Marcuse which is all his own (his *antithesis* to Marcuse, or perhaps what it would be more appropriate to call the production of a new *synthesis* of Freud and Marcuse). He presents a restatement of Marcuse's insights which, in fact, yields up something which Marcuse himself does not emphasise: "the persuasiveness [...] of Marcuse's work can best be felt if we reverse these conceptual priorities and take as his basic theme not happiness, but rather the nature of the *negative* itself [, ...] the notion that the consumer's society, the society of abundance, has lost the experience of the negative in all its forms, that it is the negative alone which is ultimately fructifying from a cultural as well as an individual point of view, that a genuinely human existence can only be achieved through the process of negation."[8] By "genuinely human existence" Jameson does not mean Utopia itself but the pursuit of the Utopian idea, which "keeps alive the possibility of a world qualitatively distinct from this one and takes the form of a stubborn negation of all that is".[9] To negate the world that is is a pre-requisite to "overcoming" it

---

[7] Jameson, *Marxism and Form*, pp. 107-8.

[8] Jameson, *Marxism and Form*, p. 108.

[9] Jameson, *Marxism and Form*, p. 111.

in the search for a world to be, and this – not happiness or individual freedom in either world – is what "a genuinely human existence" consists in.

While one must admire the thoroughness of Jameson's own dialectical procedure here, it perhaps comes at a heavy price: the fetishization of a particular intellectual method seems to have reduced "human existence" to a certain method of contemplating and mentally engaging or struggling with the world, in a supremely idealist (or Hegelian) moment which neglects serious material (or Marxist) questions about the worlds of both the present and the future, and is worryingly silent about what concrete actions – if any – should be taken in respect of securing and/or balancing happiness and freedom. It is hardly surprising that many critics of Jameson have divined in his prescriptions yet another ironic reversal, this time of Lenin's famous dictum: the appropriate Jamesonian slogan would seem to be "optimism of the intellect, pessimism of the will".

Indeed, the paragraph which concludes the sub-chapter on Marcuse, which at first reading has the air of being a mere rhetorical rounding-off, does, if taken seriously, offer a disconcerting sense that what is being offered is advice to "fiddle while Rome burns", at best to compose, or at worst take solace in composing, conceptual (but properly dialectical) blueprints for an alternative future. Meanwhile, the otherwise seemingly unassailable machine of the material present grinds nearby, offering little hope that such castles in the air shall ever concretely be built. "The total system," Jameson remarks, "may yet ultimately succeed in effacing the very memory of the negative, and with it of freedom, from the face of the earth."[10] What he has to counterpose to this bleakest of possibilities is no more than the following:

Yet, whatever the outcome, it pleases me for another moment still to contemplate the stubborn rebirth of the idea of freedom [...] by the philosopher [i.e. Marcuse], in the exile of that immense housing development which is the state of California, remembering, re-awakening, reinventing – from the rows of products in the supermarkets, from the roar of the freeways and the ominous shape

[10] Jameson, *Marxism and Form*, p. 111.

76

of the helmets of traffic policemen, from the incessant overhead traffic of the fleets of military transport planes, and as it were from beyond them, in the future – the almost extinct form of the Utopian idea.[11]

"*Whatever* the outcome"? This is a notable "wobble" from any identifiably Marxist point of view. The Utopian idea does not emerge from this impressionistically evoked socio-economic system as a powerful form of immanent critique, which would require it to be tied to (or demonstrably involved in forging) a concrete political practice. Its "almost extinct form" does not appear very likely to survive the oppressive realities surrounding it, but seems more like the frailest of refuges in the face of their imminent onslaught. The frailty seems to derive from the fact that no kind of opposition to the system other than that posed by the philosopher is envisaged. As Jameson "contemplates" Marcuse's "remembering, re-awakening, reinventing", we must register the obvious conclusion that he sees no "negating" activity other than these minority ideational practices to be present on the scene. One may be tempted to cite a few empirical features of American political life in the nineteen-sixties which nominally contradict this claim. But the crucial fact is that Jameson does not do so, and for the very good reason that, throughout the Cold War period, Marxism in the most economically powerful state in the world was the pursuit of no more than a small handful of socially marginalised academic intellectuals. One may add that this is probably as true of *all* the economically ascendant nation states in the world of today (what Jameson intriguingly calls the "overdeveloped countries")[12] as it was of the United States then. Hence "Marxism and Form", perhaps, because Western Marxism has only form and no content; and the subsequent practical failure of applied Marxism in the USSR and (more debatably) China is presumably to be attributed in part to the reverse dilemma, namely that these post-revolutionary states had Marxism's content but none of its form.

---

[11] Jameson, *Marxism and Form*, p. 112.
[12] Jameson, *Marxism and Form*, p. xviii.

Theoretical Limitations

The idealist "wobbles" in Jameson's Marxism may thus be more than a matter of his conscious intellectual debt to Hegel. To be sure there are many that do derive from this source, and some of them are egregious. In the course of his extraordinarily generous appraisal of Lukács, for example, he is again tempted to "reverse the causal relationship as it is generally conceived" concerning Lukác's conversion to Marxism, and goes on "to claim that if Lukács became a Communist, it was precisely because the problems of narration raised in the *Theory of the Novel* required a Marxist framework to be thought through to their logical conclusion".[13] The answer to this gratuitous idealism may simply be the blank observation that, as Jameson's own activity demonstrates, there is no necessity to "become a Communist" to adopt a Marxist framework.

The more general concern may be whether such idealism actually compromises Jameson's Marxism as a whole, how much it suggests a purely formal commitment on his part to an intellectual system rich in resources and analytic methods which stops short of (or is of practical necessity prevented from) taking the usually concomitant leap into the much boggier world of social *praxis*. For Terry Eagleton, whose tremendous admiration for Jameson is tempered by a stringent awareness of the compromises imposed by the older critic's self-placement within an Hegelian tradition and the less negotiable fact that he works in the American academy, part of the problem lies within a "'Western Marxism' which, confronted with severe difficulties of class struggle, has abandoned a *political* starting point, has little but reworked remnants of idealist philosophy left to it".[14] He is unconvinced by Jameson's contestation in the Introduction to *Marxism and Form* that such is the nature of late capitalism that "there is no tactical or political question which is not first and foremost theoretical",[15] a line which seems to provide Jameson with a rationale for endless intellectualisation and the potentially infinite deferral of practical action. Eagleton puts his reservations like this:

[13] Jameson, *Marxism and Form*, p. 182.
[14] Terry Eagleton, "Fredric Jameson: the Politics of Style", *Against the Grain: Selected Essays* (London: Verso, 1986), p. 75.
[15] Jameson, *Marxism and Form*, p. xviii.

For my part, it is not clear that there is anything inherent in late capitalism which spontaneously selects such philosophical issues as the relation between subject and object as the order of the day, as opposed, say, to questions of the character of the state and its repressive apparatuses, problems of proletarian organization and insurrection, or the rôle of the vanguard party. There seems to me nothing in monopoly capitalism which automatically selects the names of Hegel, Lukács and Adorno as relevant touchstones, rather than – those symptomatic silences in Jameson's work – Lenin, Trotsky and Gramsci. Jameson would no doubt reply that there was indeed something immanent in contemporary capitalism which enforced these options, namely the fetishism of commodities, which while not peculiar to this epoch of class-society is mightily dominant in it. [...] But as I have argued elsewhere, too great an attention to "commodification" links the economic to the experiential only at the cost of displacing the political; and in this sense it must be grasped as itself a political option, a partial displacement occasioned by the intractable problems of class struggle in the contemporary United States.[16]

The comments here concerning commodification may actually apply most pertinently to Jameson's *Postmodernism, or, The Cultural Logic of Late Capitalism*, which was published some years after Eagleton's essay, and we shall take them up in discussion of that later work below. The significant criticism here, however, is that Jameson's self-containment within a particular form of Marxism (one supposedly "answering the specific needs and problems of its own socio-economic system") leads to correspondingly harsh restrictions on the importance of (or even discussion of) the kinds of political action which are certainly a necessary if not sufficient condition of those "needs and problems" being truly transformed. Again, the search for formal solutions seems to be pursued in isolation from matters of content, which points to a damaging dialectical inadequacy of the kind that the eleventh of Marx's *Theses on Feuerbach* indicts with powerful concision: "The philosophers have only *interpreted* the world in various ways; the point, however, is to *change* it."[17]

---

[16] Eagleton, p. 75.
[17] Karl Marx and Frederick Engels, *Complete Works*, vol. V (London: Lawrence

Postmodernism, or, The Cultural Logic of Late Capitalism

The world was certainly changed in the course of Jameson's career: it became "postmodern". His diagnosis of the cause of the change seems, at first sight, to be more classically Marxist than Hegelian. It is certainly not the philosophers of postmodernism (Jean-François Lyotard, Jean Baudrillard) or of poststructuralism (Michel Foucault, Jacques Derrida) who are to be held responsible. Hegel did once remark that philosophy always comes too late, and the grand theorisations of these thinkers as to the nature of postmodernism arrive, for Jameson, very much in the wake of its real impingement upon society. But Jameson's conviction is indubitably à la Marx: what has changed is the nature of capitalism itself, which has been transformed, particularly in the post-Second World War period, from being the sum total of a number of similar systems of state and/or monopoly capitalism operating within distinct national boundaries and under markedly differing degrees and kinds of legal and governmental regulation, to a more unified system organised on a global scale by and around multinational corporations whose activities transcend and shatter the older national divisions. Philosophical postmodernism, for Jameson, ultimately does little more than oil the wheels of this system in the cultural realm. It attempts to normalise the new world order with its relativising discourses, which propose to abolish the "master narratives" such as Freudian psychoanalysis, Marxism, scientific rationalism, and so on, which had been held up to explain the old order. All the while it ignores the "master code" which continues to determine everything, including those relativising discourses themselves, namely the newly configured ("late" or "advanced") capitalism. "Such theories," he writes, "have the obvious ideological mission of demonstrating, to their own relief, that the new social formation in question no longer obeys the laws of classical capitalism, namely, the primacy of industrial production and the omnipresence of class struggle."[18]

Of course, the cultural realm *did* change, and many shibboleths *have been* abolished, as any Marxist would expect (and not for the first or last

and Wishart, 1976), p. 8.

[18] Jameson, *Postmodernism, or, The Cultural Logic of Late Capitalism* (Durham, NC: Duke University Press, 1991), p. 3.

time: the most crackling prose of *The Communist Manifesto* describes precisely the cultural transformations wrought by industrial capitalism). *Postmodernism* is Jameson's attempt to unlock the "logic" of this transition. Among the things abolished are the old divisions between "high" and "popular" culture which had been assuredly sustained throughout the nineteenth and twentieth-century phases of realism and modernism respectively. This leads to a more general (and often absolute) blurring of the distinction between the world of commodities and the world of culture, because culture itself has, by and large, become a commodity. This is true of art (when classical works of art can be purchased by large corporations as "investments" they can no longer be thought of as standing, critically or otherwise, "outside" the market or in a position of "relative autonomy" *vis à vis* material production) as it is of similar domains which may previously have been seen as "servicing" the market without being fully integral to it (such as "information", which is now freely bought and sold like any other product, or "education", which is now a category in the balance-of-trade figures of most major economies). For Jameson, the new order at once seems perfectly explicable in classic Marxist terms (changes in the "base" of the economy or material production cause corresponding changes in the "superstructure" of the realm of thought or cultural production) but threatens to unhinge far more radically than the Hegelian dialectic (which is seen as strongly qualifying but not destroying) the binary opposition between material and cultural production. While wishing to insist on something like the position adumbrated by Raymond Williams, that all culture is material, he runs the same risk of collapsing any traditional Marxist sense of certain kinds of practice being ultimately more historically determinate than others, which is precisely one of the postmodernist positions he wishes to challenge.

Echoing Eagleton's reservations about Jameson's earlier work, we may ask if there is not a peculiarly theoretical "fetishism of commodities" being indulged here. There is more to Marxist theory than reification, and the concept itself was propounded by Marx in order that the revelation of a false condition (that we perceive our primary relations to be with a world of objects or commodities) should lead to the instatement of a true one (the knowledge that objects or commodities in fact merely mediate our human relation to others). It would not be true to say that Jameson eschews entirely such traditional binary oppositions. *Postmodernism* is commendably catholic in the scope of the cultural practices it allows to fall under its purview: Jameson takes in cinema, architecture, video, novels, photography, rock music, and more. His aim is to show, not only the commodification of these forms of production and their integration into the marketplace, but the uniquely new and often bewildering aesthetic effects they produce, which bend and break conventional concepts of space, visuality, time, ethnicity and identity (those conventional concepts all being understood as more appropriate to a previous phase of capitalist development). But he evaluates as well as describes. He finds pop art *shallow*, a matter of endless surfaces, while realist or modernist representation has *depth*. Revulsion at the bland, superficial and kitsch is not a peculiarly Marxist reaction, however, nor is a summoning-up as witness to the aridity of the present the rich aesthetic achievements of the past. The overwhelming anxiety seems to be that the cultural productions of the past (and by extension memory and history and, with them, any notion of truth as well as value) is uniquely threatened by a postmodernism which endlessly recycles and pastiches the artefacts of yesteryear, integrating all their solid and seemingly reliable "depth" into its ever-mutating and shallow "surfaces".

A concise summary like this cannot hope fully to convey the immeasurable richness of Jameson's description of the cultural consequences of late capitalist development, his exposition of the complex problems to which it gives rise, his elaboration of the widespread cognitive disorientation it has engendered, or his unflinching insistence on the need to find a path through and beyond it. His prose demonstrates that, whatever else has gone, a very welcome undercurrent of Marxist moral rhetoric has not entirely evaporated: "I must remind the reader of the obvious; namely, that this whole global, yet American, postmodern culture is the internal and superstructural expression of a whole new-wave of American military and economic domination throughout the world: in this sense, as throughout class history, the underside of culture is blood, torture, death, and terror."[19] It is curious that Jameson can here so "obviously" identify the "real" social consequences of capitalism but elsewhere in his text warn against the assumption that it is possible

[19] Jameson, *Postmodernism*, p. 5.

simply to inoculate with an injection of truth against the "pseudo-events" promoted by postmodernist practice, just as he wishes equally to deny that the moral disapprobation he himself expresses has any political valency anymore. Nor, for all the talk of class struggle which litters his text, does he pitch his tent on the ground of concrete political organisation and action. To the ongoing Marxist challenge, "What is to be done?", he proposes an intellectual and/or artistic approach ("cognitive mapping") which seems more than ever provisional and which, moreover,

> will have to hold to the truth of postmodernism, that is to say, to its fundamental object – the world space of multinational capital – at the same time at which it achieves a breakthrough to some as yet unimaginable new mode of representing this last, in which we may again begin to grasp our positioning as individual and collective subjects and regain a capacity to act and struggle which is at present neutralised by our spatial as well as our social confusion. The political form of postmodernism, if there ever is any, will have as its vocation the invention and projection of a global cognitive mapping, on a social as well as a spatial scale.[20]

"As yet unimaginable" is one way of admitting that the question will not be answered soon (at least not by Jameson); "if there ever is any" raises doubts that we should hope that it will be, by anyone else.

Conclusion

Jameson is sixty-six years old at the time of writing, and while his strictly academic career may be at its close, his immense productivity shows no signs of abatement. His voluminous publications in the last three decades, as well as whatever comes from his pen in the future, will have added immensely to the store of what is sometimes ironically referred to in left circles as "theoretical capital". The task for successors working in Jameson's tradition will be to deploy this capital in new ways – perhaps Jamesonian ways. The most obvious need is for someone to re-read Jameson himself, in particular, perhaps, with a view to doing what

[20] Jameson, *Postmodernism*, p. 54.

Jameson has hitherto refrained from doing – namely, articulating the dialectic between the Western Marxism which he has generously enriched and the intellectual legacy of the other Marxisms which he has not seen it as his business to extend. There is an especial need to put into dialogue the complementary elements of the social process which Jameson somewhat artificially separates for the purposes of analysis and which consequently appear to be out of balance in his work. Quite what will emerge on the "other side" of such a Jamesonian re-reading of Jameson remains to be seen.

2000

I

In *Mary Barton* [...] Mrs Gaskell negotiates her own problem – of how to intervene in liberal sympathy with the industrial classes – *by* writing a novel, the reading of which then leaves the *reader* with Mrs Gaskell's original problem: what to *do* in terms of concretely intervening in the kind of industrial conflict to which the novel has alerted us. Unless the reader is to take Mrs Gaskell's own solution and simply write yet another novel, the reader has been manipulated into trying to solve Mrs Gaskell's original problem *in her place*. Mrs Gaskell's strategy, in other words, is to "convert" her readers into making an active contribution she herself can avoid having to make, precisely by opting to convert others.

This is Bernard Sharratt's brief exposition of what we might call Gaskell's global narrative strategy in *Mary Barton*. It comes in the course of a mock-review of a non-existent critical work whose "overall aim is to examine ways in which certain literary texts are so structured as to entice or trap their readers into a change of mind, a reformation of view, a 'conversion'".[1] Self-consciously playful, Sharratt is nonetheless insightful. The question of literature's relationship to concrete social change *is* cunningly raised and yet avoided by fictional texts which take such change as their central theme, leaving their more exasperated readers paraphrasing Marx's aphorism on philosophers before him: novelists only *interpret* the world; the point, however, is to *change* it.[2] Today, the usual response to this frustration is to deconstruct what some see as a false opposition between "interpretation" and "change". This defence holds that an interpretation, if it gains general consent, *is* a change, because the

---

[1] Bernard Sharratt, *The Literary Labyrinth: Contemporary Critical Discourses* (Brighton: Harvester Press, 1984), pp. 51-2, 34.
[2] Cf. the eleventh, last, and most famous of Marx's "Theses on Feuerbach": Robert C. Tucker, *The Marx-Engels Reader* (New York: Norton, 1978), p. 145.

intellectual work of analysing society is integral to the process of transforming it (and it evades Marx's basic point, which is that interpretation *on its own* is not enough).

However, this is not the place to air definite views on this theoretical debate. Let me instead try to enlarge on the notion of *Mary Barton* as a "conversion" text. I choose this word rather than Sharratt's proffered synonyms ("change", "reformation") on account of the religious ideology which suffuses Gaskell's novel. It is a decidedly Christian conversion which is on offer to readers of *Mary Barton*. Gaskell's biographer, Jenny Uglow, explains clearly Gaskell's developing sense of literature as mission: "By using her art as the vehicle for her belief, writing became a religious exercise and therefore 'permissible', reflecting a feeling which had lingered on from the eighteenth century that novels were somehow frivolous and corrupting unless they had a clear moral or spiritual message."[3] *Mary Barton* is ostensibly about the relations between labour and capital, but it puts these relations into the service of a Christian myth, so that ultimately it is possible to see the novel as a fabular narrative, or parable. What this parable illustrates is the transition from the Old Testament doctrine of retributive justice (in which "life shall go for life, eye for eye, tooth for tooth, hand for hand, foot for foot")[4] to the New Testament code of fraternal pardon ("For if ye forgive men their trespasses, your heavenly Father will also forgive you").[5] As such, the ideological *locus classicus* of *Mary Barton* is the Sermon on the Mount: "Ye have heard that it hath been said, An eye for an eye, and a tooth for a tooth: But I say unto you, That ye resist not evil: but whosoever shall smite thee on thy right cheek, turn to him the other also."[6]

Gaskell was completing her novel as the opening words of a text much more influential than it were being written. It shares *The Communist Manifesto*'s sense of having reached an epochal crux ("The history of all hitherto existing society is the history of class struggles"), but the means it proposes for expunging class conflict and setting history on a new,

[3] Jenny Uglow, *Elizabeth Gaskell: A Habit of Stories* (London: Faber, 1993), p. 134.
[4] Deuteronomy 19: 21. See also Exodus 21: 23-5. All quotations from the Bible are from the Authorised Version.
[5] Matthew 6: 14. Gaskell alludes to this verse both in the title of chapter 35 and in a crucial passage of that chapter.
[6] Matthew 5: 38-9.

harmonious course is patently antagonistic to a political programme which "abolishes all religion".[7] The strife-ridden society of *Mary Barton* is governed by the law of Moses, not the law of capital. The first step towards the murder which is the most dramatic emblem of its social discord is taken by John Barton when, in the midst of a strike, he voices his opposition to the employers in terms which demand "serving out", or revenge: "It's the masters as has wrought this woe; it's the masters as should pay for it. Him as called me coward just now, may try if I am one or not. Set me to serve out the masters, and see if there's aught I'll stick at".[8] Barton says this directly after an emotive speech in which he expresses the shame of another striker who has permanently maimed a blackleg by throwing vitriol in his face. His argument is that this action is counter-productive and morally wrong: it is the employers, not "them as has none to help, but mun choose between vitriol and starvation" (p. 219), who are the enemy.

Taken out of context, Barton's speech is one of the finest pieces of revolutionary rhetoric to be found in the English novel of the nineteenth century. What we witness here is the happening which E. P. Thompson defined as *class*: "class happens when some men, as a result of common experiences (inherited or shared), feel and articulate the identity of their interests as between themselves, and as against other men whose interests are different from (and usually opposed to) theirs".[9] The narrator's antipathetic ideology, however, which casts a long shadow throughout the novel, is never more present than here. Gaskell takes pains – one of the textual signs of which is the importunate flurry of adjectives in the passage about to be quoted – which ensure that the reader does not come away from this episode with the impression that the men have achieved a state of solidarity:

> And so with words, or looks that told more than words, they built
> up a deadly plan. Deeper and darker grew the import of their speeches,
> as they stood hoarsely muttering their meaning out, and glaring, with

---

[7] Tucker, pp. 473, 489.

[8] Elizabeth Gaskell, *Mary Barton: a Tale of Manchester Life*, ed. Macdonald Daly (London: Penguin, 1996), p. 219. Parenthetical page references in what follows are to this edition.

[9] E. P. Thompson, *The Making of the English Working Class* (Harmondsworth: Penguin, 1968), pp. 9-10.

eyes that told the terror their own thoughts were to them, upon their neighbours. Their clenched fists, their set teeth, their livid looks, all told the suffering which their minds were voluntarily undergoing in the contemplation of crime, and in familiarising themselves with its details.

Then came one of those fierce terrible oaths which bind members of Trades' Unions to any given purpose. Then under the flaring gaslight, they met together to consult further. With the distrust of guilt, each was suspicious of his neighbour; each dreaded the treachery of another. (p. 220)

If the men unite in a common purpose, the price paid is an intensified disunity of mutual misgiving and fear. The enactment of the planned murder demonstrates John Barton's rejection of Christian doctrine, just as his earlier spurning of "the Prodigal" Esther fails to replicate the outcome of Christ's story of the Prodigal Son.[10]

We shall later examine more fully how "murder" is understood, and the rôle it plays, in Gaskell's novel. My claim here is that the narrator regularly acts to ensure the return of a Christian ethic which, by their actions and utterances, characters on both sides of the equation (labour and capital) work to repress. Barton is threatening a break with Christianity from his first scathing references to the gospels of Matthew and Luke. Long before the murder the narrator adjudges him to have "hoards of vengeance in his heart against the employers", to be in the throes of "monomania", as entertaining "diseased thoughts" which "excluded the light of heaven" (pp. 25, 194-5). As Job Legh sums up, "he were sadly put about to make great riches and great poverty square with Christ's Gospel" (p. 446). In this he is simply echoing Barton's own dying speeches, which are, however, confessional, repentant and guilt-ridden to the extreme that Christian morality has reimposed itself upon him. Since the day of the murder, he tells his listeners, "I've kept thinking and thinking if I were but in that world where they say God is, He would, maybe, teach me right from wrong, even if it were with many stripes. I've been sore puzzled here. I would go through hell-fire if I could but get free from sin at last, it's such an awful thing" (p. 423).

Barton's desperate request for forgiveness initially goes ungranted. Carson, the capitalist father of the murdered man, tells him, "Let my

---

[10] Luke 15: 11-32. See Gaskell, chapter 10, "The Return of the Prodigal".

trespasses be unforgiven, so that I may have vengeance for my son's murder", a statement hedged around by the narrator's own expression of appalled shock and indignation: "I would rather see death than the ghastly gloom which darkened that countenance. [...] There are blasphemous actions as well as blasphemous words: all unloving, cruel deeds are acted blasphemy" (p. 426). She takes us back to Carson's home, where, by means of a sudden regression to his childhood self, his piety is re-established:

> When he entered his house he went straight and silently upstairs to his library, and took down the great, large handsome Bible, all grand and golden, with its leaves adhering together from the bookbinder's press, so little had it been used. [...]
>
> He roused himself from his reverie, and turned to the object of his search – the Gospel, where he half expected to find the tender pleading: "They know not what they do." [...]
>
> Years ago the Gospel had been his task-book in learning to read. So many years ago, that he had become familiar with the events before he could comprehend the Spirit that made the Life.
>
> He fell to the narrative now afresh, with all the interest of a little child. He began at the beginning, and read on almost greedily, understanding for the first time the full meaning of the story. He came to the end; the awful End. And there were the haunting words of pleading.
>
> He shut the book, and thought deeply.
>
> All night long, the Archangel combated with the Demon. (pp. 429-30)

Carson's forgiveness of Barton duly follows in the morning. Indeed, Barton dies in Carson's arms at the moment the latter expressly recants his blasphemy of the evening before with the prayer, "'God be merciful to us sinners. – Forgive us our trespasses as we forgive them that trespass against us'" (p. 432). From this moment on, Carson's principled dealings with his fellow humans are offered as exemplary, their enumeration bearing the full weight of the narrator's approval:

> The wish that lay nearest to his heart was that none might suffer from the cause from which he had suffered; that a perfect understanding, and

complete confidence and love, might exist between masters and men; that the truth might be recognised that the interests of one were the interests of all, and, as such, required the consideration and deliberation of all; that hence it was most desirable to have educated workers, capable of judging, not mere machines of ignorant men; and to have them bound to their employers by the ties of respect and affection, not by mere money bargains alone; in short, to acknowledge the Spirit of Christ as the regulating law between both parties. (p. 451)

In response, then, to the contemporary crisis which Marx and Engels were busily sketching – "The bourgeoisie [...] has drowned the most heavenly ecstasies of religious fervour, of chivalrous enthusiasm, of philistine sentimentalism, in the icy water of egotistical calculation"[11] – Gaskell proposes a return to religion, chivalry, sentiment. Sharratt's question of "what to *do* in terms of concretely intervening in the kind of industrial conflict to which the novel has alerted us" is not so much begged as negated. With the exception of the elusively worded comment on the necessity of education, no "concrete" social action is implied in the passage just quoted. There can be little doubt, in any case, that these educative impulses are those so derided by Engels: "If here the workers are not educated (i.e., to obedience to the bourgeoisie), they may view matters one-sidedly, from the standpoint of sinister selfishness, and may readily permit themselves to be hoodwinked by sly demagogues; nay, they might even be capable of viewing their greatest benefactors, the frugal and enterprising capitalists, with a jealous and hostile eye. Here proper training alone can avail, or national bankruptcy and other horrors must follow, since a revolution of the workers could hardly fail to occur."[12] These "horrors" are what Gaskell anticipates and wishes to pre-empt. For her, no dissolution of the class structure is imaginable, no abolition of the bourgeoisie, as prophesied by *The Communist Manifesto*: she does not envisage a society

---

[11] Tucker, p. 475.

[12] Friedrich Engels, *The Condition of the Working Class in England* (London: Panther, 1969), pp. 151-2. I use Engels' contemporary (1845) *The Condition of the Working Class in England* as a counterpoint to Gaskell throughout this essay, not just because it is largely Mancunian in emphasis, but also because it reads like a deconstruction, in advance, of her discursive strategies in *Mary Barton*, and yet has never really been brought to bear on that novel in ways that it may.

without "masters and men". The "regulating law" of their relations is not even to be a Parliamentary one, but a spiritual bond. There is nothing, for Gaskell, to be *done* so far as prevailing economic relations are concerned. These are not perceived to be the problem. Indeed, Barton's politics are posthumously revised by Job Legh so that they appear *not* to be have been driven by essentially material interests: "what hurt him sore, and rankled in him as long as I knew him [...] was that those who wore finer clothes, and eat better food, and had more money in their pockets, kept him at arm's length, and cared not whether his heart was sorry or glad" (pp. 446-7). The revolution urged by *Mary Barton* is a revolution in the emotional and mental dispositions of individuals towards each other. As such, the novel is a thoroughly idealist enterprise.

II

Indeed, how could it have been anything else? The slightest acquaintance with Gaskell's biography shows that the two prime determinants of her ideological formation were the bourgeois class to which she belonged and the Unitarian faith to which she subscribed. Unitarianism, of course, constituted a famously "progressive" Dissenting culture, but, as Uglow remarks, "the 'progressive' Unitarian faith could dovetail very neatly with the aims of the man on the make".[13] As the wife of the assistant minister of Cross Street Unitarian Chapel, Gaskell was exposed to the particularly reactionary influences of such men. Valentine Cunningham records that "the chapel and its sanctions were dominant in Mrs Gaskell's life":

> Moral pressures [...] might have come from any chapel. But Cross Street offered peculiar resistances to what Mrs Gaskell was doing in her fiction. For Cross Street was where the bourgeoisie of Manchester worshipped God. Fifteen MPs and seven mayors had connections with the chapel, "besides many borough and county magistrates". The German merchants and businessmen of the city, the Meyers, Schunks,

---

[13] Uglow, p. 18. For an excellent and concise sketch of Unitarian thinking, see R. K. Webb, *Harriet Martineau: A Radical Victorian* (London: Heinemann, 1960), pp. 65-90.

and Schwabes, belonged to it. The Trustees and members were the millocracy, the benefactors, the leaders, of Manchester society: corn millers, silk manufacturers, calico printers, patent-reed makers, engineers; bankers and barristers; founders of hospitals, libraries, educational institutes, charitable funds, missions to the poor. The cousinhood extending outwards from the chapel was powerful indeed.[14]

There was, as we shall see, hostility to Gaskell's work from this quarter. But the suggestion that the "resistances" were only *external* to "what Mrs Gaskell was doing in her fiction" seems to me questionable. All the evidence is that such reactionary pressures are part of the *internal* workings of *Mary Barton*. What often mediates them is a judgmental narrative voice which uses this or that event in the novel as a launching pad for a brief, usually trite, typically pious, moral discourse. Examples, such as Carson's unforgiving outburst, the reader's reaction to which is overdetermined by a narrator intoning "blasphemy", have already been noted. Another key technique is Gaskell's emphasis on characters' obsessive application to themselves of an oppressive moral code which their actions objectively contest. Barton is the obvious case, but his sister-in-law Esther is another. No reader of Esther's account of the circumstances which have led her into a life on the streets (pp. 185-6) can deny that it reveals a degree of sympathy and understanding that was absent in conventional moral thinking of the period. Gaskell is here offering a socio-economic explanation for prostitution, one that runs against the grain of Biblical attainders for whoredom, resting as they did on notions of irredeemable spiritual corruption. She is not as thoroughgoing as Engels, in that she does not consider that Esther's clients are probably "the virtuous bourgeoisie".[15] Nonetheless, Esther's "Do you think God will punish me for that?" (p. 186) is a truly radical question, until it is drowned in the noise of her repeated self-condemnations, articulated and thought, which seem to answer it in the affirmative: "With her violent and unregulated nature, rendered morbid by the course of life she led, and her consciousness of her

---

[14] Valentine Cunningham, *Everywhere Spoken Against: Dissent in the Victorian Novel* (Oxford: Clarendon Press, 1975), pp. 131-2, quoting from Richard Wade, *The Rise of Non-conformity in Manchester, With a Brief Sketch of the History of Cross Street Chapel* (Manchester: 1880), p. 65.

[15] Engels, p. 158.

degradation, she cursed herself [...] How could she, the abandoned and polluted outcast, ever have dared to hope for a blessing, even on her efforts to do good? The black curse of Heaven rested on all her doings, were they for good or for evil" (p. 272). The mode of self-loathing is so pervasive in *Mary Barton* that one is tempted to declare that the novel is itself trapped in it. The narrative voice is often to be heard straining to communicate its abhorrence of the morally transgressive material which it is continually bringing to the reader's attention.

Consciously or unconsciously, Gaskell must have hoped that the self-judgmental nature of her tale would forestall the harshest criticisms of Manchester's bourgeois Unitarians. It was not to be. "My poor Mary Barton is stirring up all sorts of angry feelings against me in Manchester," she told Edward Holland on 13 January 1849, "but those best acquainted with the way of thinking & feeling among the poor acknowledge its *truth*; which is the acknowledgment I most of all desire, because evils once recognized are half way on towards their remedy." [16] The closeness of the novel to contemporary events was enough to create ill-feeling in Cross Street. The murder of Harry Carson has its origin, like that in Elizabeth Stone's *William Langshawe, the Cotton Lord* (1842), in the real-life murder of Thomas Ashton by striking workers on 3 January 1831.[17] Gaskell wrote to her publisher, Edward Chapman, on 13 November 1848, "I find every one here has most convincing proofs that the authorship of Mary Barton should be attributed to a Mrs Wheeler, née Miss Stone, and authoress of some book called the "Cotton Lord'. I am only afraid lest you should be convinced and transact that part of the business which yet remains unaccomplished with her. I do assure you that I am the author." Two days earlier, writing to Catherine Winkworth, she had in fact endorsed the rumour to maintain her anonymity, the only real protection she had from the potential wrath of the Manchester business class with which she was so strongly connected.[18] A letter of 16 August 1852 reveals the kind of difficulty she faced when that anonymity evaporated. Cunningham summarises:

---

[16] *The Letters of Mrs Gaskell*, ed. J. A. V. Chapple and Arthur Pollard (Manchester: Manchester University Press, 1966), p. 827. Not all of Gaskell's letters can be accurately dated, but dates are given in references where these have been ascertained.

[17] For other precursors of *Mary Barton*, see Uglow, pp. 191-2.

[18] *The Letters of Mrs Gaskell*, pp. 63, 62.

When Mrs Gaskell wanted to present a copy of *Mary Barton* to the Manchester Free Library in 1852, she had to seek permission from Sir John Potter, its promoter. She feared Sir John's distaste: the distaste of the mill-owning class ("Of course I cannot be unaware of the opinions which you and your brother have so frequently & openly expressed with regard to *Mary Barton* ..."). Neither did she want Sir John to think she had callously exploited the murder of Thomas Ashton by unionists in 1831 as "a mere subject for s story". As it happened, the last person to speak to Thomas Ashton had been his sister Mary who, in 1847, married Thomas Bayley Potter. When she came to the murder in *Mary Barton* Mrs Potter fainted away. The assistant minister's wife, the Potters suspected, had deliberately revived painful memories.[19]

But Potter, "a Cross Street stalwart" and, among other things, an MP who "spoke vehemently in the Commons against government legislation on factory hours and conditions",[20] would also have found *Mary Barton* difficult to swallow for quite different reasons. He would have been indignant at the apparently modest disclaimer of her Preface: "I know nothing of Political Economy, or the theories of trade. I have tried to write truthfully; and if my accounts agree or clash with any system, the agreement or disagreement is unintentional" (p. lxxiv). To the Manchester manufacturers of the late 1840s, the phrase "Political Economy" referred only to one system, that of *laissez-faire* capitalism.[21] Gaskell's disavowal of Political Economy in favour of writing "truthfully" thus carries a subversive potential.

Purporting to ignorance was almost certainly a ploy. Her own father, William Stevenson, had serialised three extended essays entitled "The Political Economist" in *Blackwood's Edinburgh Magazine* in the 1820s.

---

[19] Cunningham, p. 132, citing *The Letters of Mrs Gaskell*, pp. 195-6. It is inaccurate to state that Gaskell "had to" seek Potter's permission. Her letter makes clear that, in typically cautious fashion, she *chose* to find out in advance how much offence her donation might arouse. The Thomas Bayley Potter mentioned by Cunningham was John Potter's brother.

[20] Uglow, pp. 304, 87.

[21] Donald Read, "Chartism in Manchester", in Asa Briggs (ed.), *Chartist Studies* (London: Macmillan, 1959), pp. 32-33, quotes fascinating statements on Political Economy from the Manchester press in the period between the completion of *Mary Barton* and the writing of Gaskell's Preface. The matter was very much in the air.

These tried to lay down a theoretical basis for Political Economy as a science, partly by demonstrating how contradictory the various systems were. But Stevenson also explicitly undermined the claim of dogmatic, self-interested, practising capitalists that Political Economy was their territory and theirs alone:

> It may be urged, that those who are practically engaged in commerce, are more worthy of our confidence as instructors and guides in Political Economy; and that the facts which they have accumulated during a life of personal observation and experience, must be not only well-founded, but also directly and profitably applicable to the most difficult and complicated cases of this science.
>
> This, however, we suspect will be found far from the truth. [...] The object of Political Economy, as a science, is the increase of wealth and prosperity of communities at large, not of any class or portion of them, at the expense of another. The object of the commercial man is to benefit himself: he looks no farther; he decides on the propriety, the prudence, or the wisdom of every plan and measure, according as it is advantageous to the line of business he pursues, and, more especially, according as it is advantageous to himself individually. [...]
>
> Here, then, is one fertile source of fallacy in the facts of practical men; they state the fact and consequence of any measure, but not the whole fact and consequence; the fact and consequence as they affect their own interest, or the interest of that particular branch of trade in which they are engaged, but not as they affect the national interest. They know and feel that they are benefited by the measure, but they are ignorant, and they do not inquire, whether, while they are benefited, by their very benefit, others, and the nation at large, are injured.[22]

The burden of this passage rings out clearly in *Mary Barton*. The novel frequently seems to dramatise it. Carson's religious epiphany, for instance, reveals how self-interest has blinkered him. When Barton hectors Wilson

---

[22] William Stevenson, "The Political Economist: Essay III, Part I", *Blackwood's Edinburgh Magazine* XCI (August 1824), pp. 204-5. The three essays were published anonymously in five parts in *Blackwood's* as follows: LXXXVII (May 1824), pp. 522-31; LXXXIX (June 1824), pp. 643-655; XC (July 1824), pp. 34-45; XCI (August 1824), pp. 202-214; XCVII (February 1825), pp. 207-220.

about the effects of capital accumulation ("They'n screwed us down to th'lowest peg, in order to make their great big fortunes, and build their great big houses, and we, why we're just clemming, many and many of us") he memorably illustrates its injuriousness (pp. 72-3). The wilful ignorance of the propertied and their lack of enquiry into the conditions of the poor is starkly symbolised by Mrs Hunter, the manufacturer's wife, who passes Barton "loaded with purchases for a party" on the day that his son dies of starvation (p. 25).

Gaskell's renunciation of Political Economy was, then, one of the novel's most taboo elements, a startling break with the nostrums of her peers. But as we have seen, the narrative is one which routinely attempts to neutralise its own transgressions. The Preface itself prepares the reader for the neglect of Political Economy by a short discourse on the consciousness of the poor and, no less important, how it can be managed:

> The more I reflected on this unhappy state of things between those so bound to each other by common interests, as the employers and the employed must ever be, the more anxious I became to give some utterance to the agony which, from time to time, convulses this dumb people; the agony of suffering without the sympathy of the happy, or of erroneously believing that such is the case. If it be an error that the woes, which come with ever returning tide-like flood to overwhelm the workmen in our manufacturing towns, pass unregarded by all but the sufferers, it is at any rate an error so bitter in its consequences to all parties, that whatever public effort can do in the way of merciful deeds, or helpless love in the way of "widow's mites" could do, should be done, and that speedily, to disabuse the work-people of so miserable a misapprehension. At present they seem to me to be left in a state, wherein lamentations and tears are thrown aside as useless, but in which the lips are compressed for curses, and the hands clenched and ready to smite. (p. lxxiv)

Here, the differing and defining interests of bourgeoisie and proletariat are dissolved in a commitment to perpetual, unchanging "common interests". The "agony" of the poor, like the frustration later ascribed to John Barton, is not the agony of privation, but of *privation without sympathy* – without the sympathy, that is, of those more fortunately placed. It is not the suffering attendant upon economic disadvantage, then, which must be addressed. This is simply taken as given. The absence which must be met is that of fellow-feeling, or the demonstration of fellow-feeling, on the part of the propertied. The metaphor looming over this passage – it reveals itself in the image of the "ever-returning tide-like flood" – depicts poverty as a natural disaster, and its plea is for the middle classes to make the customary response to such a disaster: one which expresses condolence without admitting responsibility. Gaskell, in "giving some utterance" to their pain, which by definition these "dumb people" cannot do, constructs *Mary Barton* itself as a prime example of the communication of consolation. By reading her novel, it follows, working people will be "disabused" of the "miserable misapprehension" that the middle classes do not feel for them. They will thus be restored to a condition in which "lamentations and tears", the emotional displays of passive desperation, have a meaning; and in which the active, insurgent power of "hands clenched and ready to smite" is disabled. Gaskell concludes her Preface by insisting that "the state of feeling among too many of the factory-people in Manchester", if allowed to go unchecked, is one that will lead to the kind of "events which have so recently occurred among a similar class on the Continent", a blatant reference to the European revolutions of 1848. *Mary Barton* is thus to be seen as a calculatedly *political* novel, an historical intervention in the cause of counter-revolution. Gaskell said as much in a letter of 21 March 1848 to her publisher, Edward Chapman, who was dithering over the date of publication: "I can not help fancying that the tenor of my tale is such as to excite attention at the present time of struggle on the part of work people to obtain what they esteem to be their rights."[23]

Engels held that the purveyors of Gaskell's kind of sophistry – "the very people who, from the 'impartiality' of their superior standpoint, preach to the workers a Socialism soaring high above their class interests and class struggles, and tending to reconcile in a higher humanity the interests of both the contending classes" – were either neophytes or wolves in sheep's clothing.[24] We forget, perhaps, that Gaskell was herself an employer, if only on a small scale. In 1844 there were three domestic staff in the Gaskell household.[25] In March 1847 she was considering sacking her nurse,

[23] *The Letters of Mrs Gaskell*, p. 54.
[24] Engels, p. 26.
[25] Winifred Gérin, *Elizabeth Gaskell: A Biography* (Oxford: Clarendon Press, 1976), p. 70.

Fergusson, in whose arms her son had died in 1845, but whom she considered no longer able to manage her children. "I can not keep down the feeling which I yet know to be morbid," she told Fanny Holland, "that it is ungrateful to even part with one who was so *tender* to my poor darling boy, and that makes me most miserable." But dismiss her she did.[26] We cannot, of course, judge this action in virtual ignorance of its circumstances. On the other hand, the episode speaks volumes about which side, experientially, Gaskell was on.

But we should not, perhaps, set too much store by the Preface, or the long, didactic and reactionary conversation between Job Legh and Carson in chapter 37 (pp. 446-50). Gaskell was made to write both, under protest, after the novel was finished.[27] Nonetheless, in the many other passages

---

[26] Uglow, p. 157.

[27] The novel was first published, anonymously, in two volumes, in October 1848. Gaskell made a last minute proposal that the pseudonym "Stephen Berwick" be used, but the novel had already gone to press (*The Letters of Mrs Gaskell*, p. 59 [19 October 1848]). In its published form it was somewhat different from the novel which Edward Chapman had accepted for publication the previous year. Chapman asked for the title to be changed from *John Barton* to *Mary Barton*. Gaskell reluctantly agreed, adding the subtitle "A Manchester Love Story", but this was also altered prior to publication. At the same time she provided requested glosses, written by William Gaskell, to some of the dialect expressions (*The Letters of Mrs Gaskell*, p. 56 [17 April 1848]). Gaskell's polite irritation is evident in several of her letters to Chapman around this time. In the summer Chapman asked for another addition. "I hardly know what you mean by an 'explanatory preface'," she replied:

> The only thing I should like to make clear is that it is no catch-penny run up since the events on the Continent have directed public attention to the consideration of the state of affairs between the Employers, & their work-people. If you think the book requires such a preface I will try to concoct it; but at present, I have no idea what to say. (*The Letters of Mrs Gaskell*, p. 58 [10 July 1848])

In early 1849, in order to explain the perceived weakness of a particular section of the novel, Gaskell told Mary Greg of a more substantial addition she had also been forced to make:

> I can trace and remember how unwillingly and from what force of outside pressure (which is, I am convinced, a wrong motive for writing and sure only to produce a failure) it was written. The tale was originally complete without the

which dwell on economic questions, her essential complicity with *laissez-faire* is demonstrable. Note, in the following description of the outrage felt by the unemployed towards conspicuous bourgeois consumption during trade depressions, how the narrator interrupts to assert that she has access to "the truth" of the matter:

> Large houses are still occupied, while spinners' and weavers' cottages stand empty, because the families that once filled them are obliged to live in rooms or cellars. Carriages still roll along the streets, concerts are still crowded by subscribers, the shops for expensive luxuries still find daily customers, while the workman loiters away his unemployed time in watching these things, and thinking of the pale, uncomplaining wife at home, and the waiting children asking in vain for enough of food, – of the sinking health, of the dying life, of those near and dear to him. The contrast is too great. Why should he alone suffer from bad times?
>
> I know that this is not really the case; and I know what is the truth in such matters: but what I wish to impress is what the workman feels and thinks. True, that with child-like improvidence good times will often dissipate his grumbling, and make him forget all prudence and foresight.
>
> But there are earnest men among these people, men who have

part which intervenes between John Barton's death and Esther's; about 3 pages, I fancy, including that conversation between Job Legh, and Mr Carson, and Jem Wilson. The MS. had been in the hands of the publisher above 14 months, and was nearly all printed when the publisher sent me word that it would fall short of the requisite number of pages, and that I must send up some more as soon as possible. I remonstrated over and over again – I even said I would rather relinquish some of the payment than interpolate anything. (*The Letters of Mrs Gaskell*, p. 75)

John Barton's death occurs at the end of chapter 35; Esther's is reported mid-way through chapter 38. However, Gaskell cannot mean that chapters 36 *and* 37 were added later: the former relates Jem and Mary's decision to emigrate to Canada, without which their removal there in chapter 38 would appear to be extremely gratuitous. It is probable, therefore, that the insertion forced upon her was chapter 37. Gaskell's own dissatisfaction with the text of 1848 is evident: "In looking over the book I see numerous errors regarding the part written in the Lancashire dialect; 'gotten' should always be 'getten'; &c." (*The Letters of Mrs Gaskell*, p. 64 [5 December 1848]).

endured wrongs without complaining, but without ever forgetting or forgiving those whom (they believe) have caused all this woe. (pp. 23-4)

There is an extraordinary inscrutability about "I know that this is not really the case; and I know what the truth is in such matters". The import, clearly enough, is that the proletarian perspective is a deluded one: the affluent also suffer during slumps. Gaskell neglects to enlarge because this passage is self-evidently addressed to her middle-class readers, who, reassured by her assertion that economic adversity touches all, are left to supply examples from their own experience. The radical potential of Gaskell's animadversions on capitalist economics is habitually defused by the resort to cautious disclaimers and qualifications which we witness in this passage.

Donald Read reminds us that "a widening of the class gulf was not, of course, an intended effect of the new *laissez-faire* economics. On the contrary an integral part of the new political economy was its theory of social union. The work of masters and men, the argument ran, was entirely complementary. They depended on each other and had everything in common: they ought always therefore to live together in amity."[28] Gaskell was saying nothing new when she told her own class the same, or drew attention to the fact that the theory of social union was not accepted by the workers. "From the early decades of the century on," writes Michael E. Rose, "there was a growing concern about the separation of rich from poor, and a realisation of the need to neutralise conflict which might arise as a result of this separation."[29] Such neutralisation, aimed at reproducing the prevailing capitalist relations of production, is the unceasing, constantly self-renewing historical programme of the bourgeois intelligentsia. *Mary Barton* was not, ideologically, an original contribution to that project. But, cast in the populist form of romantic fiction, it is one of the most accessible and readily consumed. This may have been why Edmund Potter, a Derbyshire calico printer and, later, MP for Carlisle, bought copies of the book for his workers, much to Gaskell's delight.[30] It may also explain why

[28] Read, p. 33.
[29] Michael E. Rose, "Culture, Philanthropy and the Manchester Middle Classes" (Kidd and Roberts, pp. 104-5).
[30] *The Letters of Mrs Gaskell*, p. 66 (23 December 1848). A week later Gaskell told Chapman, "Half the masters here are bitterly angry with me – half (and the best half) are buying it to give to their work-people's libraries" (*The Letters of Mrs*

it remains a staple element of English Literature syllabuses a century and
a half later.

III

The reader unfamiliar with *Mary Barton* may be wondering why the
eponymous heroine has not yet entered the discussion. The fact is that she
was never meant to be the protagonist. One of the cruellest revisions
Edward Chapman forced on his newly discovered talent, in her view, was a
change of title. Gaskell voiced her sustained dismay to Julia Lamont on 5
January 1849:

> "John Barton" was the original name, as being the central figure to my
> mind; indeed I had so long felt that the bewildered life of an ignorant
> thoughtful man of strong power of sympathy, dwelling in a town so full
> of striking contrasts as this is, was a tragic poem, that in writing he was
> my "hero"; and it was a London thought coming through the publisher
> that it must be called *Mary* B. So many people overlook John B or see
> him merely to misunderstand him, that if you were a stranger and had
> only said that one thing (that the book shd [*sic*] have been called *John*
> B) I should have had pleasure in feeling that my own idea was
> recognized.[31]

Uglow speculates that Chapman "may have been reluctant to shock the
public by having the name of a murderer, John Barton, as the title", and
further suggests that his demand for the change reflects the perception that
"as the novel progresses Mary does move to centre stage and so does
Gaskell's enduring subject – a different kind of psychological drama, the
violent jolting into maturity and sexual awareness of a young, idealistic and
innocent girl". [32] Readers have tended to find the melodramatic
manipulation of this character too overwhelming for her also to carry this
degree of thematic weight.

Gaskell, p. 68 [1 January 1849]).
[31] *The Letters of Mrs Gaskell*, p. 70.
[32] Uglow, p. 186.

Raymond Williams felt the second half of *Mary Barton* to be "the familiar and orthodox plot of the Victorian novel of sentiment, but of little lasting interest", marked as it is by "the change of emphasis which the change of title records, diverted to the less compromising figure" of Mary: "It is not only that [Gaskell] recoils from the violence of the murder, to the extent of being unable even to enter it as the experience of the man conceived as her hero. It is also that, as compared with the carefully representative character of the early chapters, the murder itself is exceptional."[33] Lynette Felber writes of the novel's formal incongruence, "the simultaneous presence of realistic and romance elements", which she shows to be related to the text's ideological tendencies. [34] Catherine Gallagher sees the second half of the novel as an abandonment of its essentially tragic promise. [35] Only Patsy Stoneman seems to wish to redeem it in any respect, in her reading of the novel as "a critique of fatherhood": for her, "the 'murder plot' demonstrates how the dominant ideology sanctions vengeance, not succour, as the expression of paternal 'care', and the 'romance plot' offers Jem as the worker/father of the future, when workers will be 'educated [...] not mere machines of ignorant men'".[36]

I share most critics' sense of the inadequacy and tiresomeness of the murder plot and the subsequent legal melodrama. This was Gaskell's first novel and she is clearly somewhat stretched by the form. However, I want to offer the thought that the function of the murder and the consequent judicial proceedings, however prolix and incompetent their telling may be, is the creation of a community in which the social alienation of individuals is minimised (such alienation previously having been maximised). Gaskell is looking for a narrative means of dissipating the conflictual nature of the society described in the first half of the novel, but her own ideological commitments preclude plot lines which posit structural social changes. The conflict thus has to be displaced – it is made judicial rather than social – to

---

[33] Raymond Williams, *Culture and Society 1780-1950* (Harmondsworth: Penguin, 1961), p. 101.

[34] Lynette Felber, "Gaskell's Industrial Idylls: Ideology and Formal Incongruence in *Mary Barton* and *North and South*", *Clio* 18, 1 (1988), p. 56.

[35] Catherine Gallagher, *The Industrial Reformation of English Fiction: Social Discourse and Narrative Form 1832-1867* (Chicago: University of Chicago Press, 1985), pp. 62-87.

[36] Patsy Stoneman, *Elizabeth Gaskell* (Brighton: Harvester Press, 1987), p. 84.

a realm in which it can permissibly be resolved. The cooperative activity of those interested in proving Jem Wilson's innocence (positive) stands in opposition to the cooperative activity of those interested in overturning the class structure (negative). The result of the legal melodrama is a community of depoliticised individuals (Mary, Margaret, Jem, Will, Job Legh, Jane Wilson) who do not feel alienated from the society to which they belong. The minor problem cf Jem's ex-workmates refusing to rub shoulders with a suspected murderer is solved by sending him to Canada. The result is that social alienation is seen not to have its origin in class, but in radical politics: John Barton's re-entry into the narrative, after a long absence, is a mere reminder that such alienation is expiring. He is now "a wan, feeble figure" with a "clockwork tread", a "haunting ghost" paying his last respects before his own final, voluntary exorcism (p. 401).

And yet, it is Barton and Barton alone, in this novel, who voices a more radical sense of "murder" than that conceived by the judicial process. He does so when he calls Esther the "murderer" of his wife: "it was thee who killed her, as sure as ever Cain killed Abel. She'd loved thee as her own, and she trusted thee as her own, and when thou wert gone she never held head up again, but died in less than a three week; and at her judgment day she'll rise, and point to thee as her murderer; or if she don't, I will" (p. 142). The novel, of course, dedicates itself to defining murder in narrowly judicial terms which apply only to Barton. His bitter indictment of Esther is presumably to be taken as an example of his unforgiving extremism. But we are under no obligation to read it thus if we remember that Barton later turns his energies to the arraignment of the employers rather than his own class. When he does so, the notion of "social murder" clearly stays with him. It was Engels, of course, who famously accused English capitalists of being just such murderers:

> When one individual inflicts bodily injury upon another, such injury that death results, we call the deed manslaughter; when the assailant knew in advance that the injury would be fatal, we call his deed murder. But when society places hundreds of proletarians in such a position that they inevitably meet a too early and an unnatural death, one which is quite as much a death by violence as that by the sword or bullet; when it deprives thousands of the necessaries of life, places them under conditions in which they *cannot* live – forces them, through the

strong arm of the law, to remain in such conditions until that death ensues which is the inevitable consequence – knows that these thousands of victims must perish, and yet permits these conditions to remain, its deed is murder just as surely as the deed of the single individual; disguised, malicious murder, murder against which none can defend himself, which does not seem what it is, because no man sees the murderer, because the death of the victim seems a natural one, since the offence is more one of omission than of commission. But murder it remains.

"Society" here means "the ruling power of society, the class which at present holds social and political control, and bears, therefore, the responsibility for the condition of those to whom it grants no share in such control." [37] We have seen that Gaskell rejects the proposal that the bourgeoisie bears such responsibility. The murder plot of *Mary Barton* understandably, therefore, works to occlude the emergence of "social murder" as a valid concept. If it did not, the novel would be in danger of subverting the social, economic and political order it was intended to consolidate.

IV

Mary Barton, then, is the story of John Barton. He is clearly a representative figure, but not an Everyman: he does not signify the working class as a whole, but its politicised element. Essentially, the narrative is a drama of working-class radicalisation and its consequences, both personal and social. The characterisation of Barton is consistently moving in two directions. The more politicised he becomes, the more he undergoes a degeneration of the person. The embrace of active politics is equated with the erosion of humanity. On his wife's death, "one of the ties which bound him down to the gentle humanities of earth was loosened, and henceforward the neighbours all remarked he was a changed man. His gloom and his sternness became habitual instead of occasional" (p. 22). He becomes "an active member of the Trades' Union", indeed "was chairman

[37] Engels, pp. 126-7.

at many a Trades' Union meeting; a friend of delegates, and ambitious of being a delegate himself; a Chartist, and ready to do anything for his order"; but in good times his political feelings "were theoretical, not practical" (pp. 23, 25). One contrast is George Wilson, who "had no great sympathy on the questions that agitated Barton's mind" and replies to one of Barton's frequent polemics, "th'masters suffer too" (pp. 29, 73). Others are the young Jem Wilson, whose interests lie with the Barton daughter and her affections, not the father and his politics, and the elderly Job Legh, whose relation to the production process is tangential.

But the development of Barton's character as a function of his increasing difference from those around him is only one of Gaskell's strategies. Others are direct authorial judgment of the political movements in which Barton is involved, and the carefully contrived association of his public actions with his private depravity. The inflationary spiral of the trade crisis of 1839-41 leads its victims to weep, and then to curse, until "their vindictive feelings exhibited themselves in rabid politics" (p. 95). These are expressed in "desperate plans", by which is meant the intent to withdraw labour. Barton's part in these plans is related so that it seems of a piece with his addiction to opium (p. 140), just as his beating of his daughter is collocated with occasions when "strange faces of pale men, with dark glaring eyes, peered into the inner darkness, and seemed desirous to ascertain if her father was at home. [...] They were all desperate members of Trades' Unions, ready for anything" (pp. 133-4).

The portrayal of Barton indicates some uncertainty on Gaskell's part about the relations between the various elements of radical politics in this period. We learn (p. 196) that "Barton became a Chartist, a Communist, all that is commonly called wild and visionary." But Chartism and Communism were hardly synonymous. Their equation could only be made by one hostile to both or practically ignorant of either. It is conceivable that an individual Chartist might also be a Communist, or that an individual Communist might support the aims of the Charter. Communism as such, however, had no organisational existence in England until the Communist League established its Central Committee in London at its congress of June 1847. The same Congress mandated Marx and Engels to write *The Communist Manifesto*, published in February 1848. Until that date "Communism" in Britain usually denoted the doctrines of Robert Owen. As *The Communist Manifesto* indicates, English Owenites tended to oppose the Chartists,[38] which may be why the Chartist Barton is later (p. 446), and confusingly, said not to be of their number.

But Gaskell is not here aiming to enlighten her readers about the complexities of British working-class politics. Instead, she is enrolling her characterisation of Barton in the cause of a propaganda campaign against atheism. Susan Budd records that "moral-force chartism and Owenism" were "the two most important sources" of organised secularism in mid-nineteenth century Britain. [39] *Mary Barton* attacks both because, whatever differences they had with one another, Chartism shared with Owenism a nerve centre in Manchester. Owen had not only worked in the city between 1788 and 1799, becoming its most famous non-Unitarian manufacturer and being elected to the prestigious Manchester Literary and Philosophical Society.[40] He routinely came back to haunt the place, and was still active in Gaskell's day. On 1 May 1835 (conceivably the date on which the action of *Mary Barton* begins),[41] he announced in his journal *The New Moral World* the formation of the Association of All Classes of All Nations, which held its annual congresses of 1837 and 1838 in Salford. In 1837 the editorial offices of *The New Moral World* were moved to Manchester, after Owen had packed out a hall in Peter Street with an audience of two thousand (*Six Lectures Delivered at Manchester* was subsequently published in 1839):

> Manchester lay at the heart of Owenite activity, and the Salford socialists had made rapid progress in the late 1830s. Late in 1838 they had extended their activities still further when they had opened the Carpenters' Hall in Manchester for lectures, and such was their success

[38] Tucker, p. 499.

[39] Susan Budd, *Varieties of Unbelief: Atheists and Agnostics in English Society 1850-1960* (London: Heinemann, 1977), p. 10.

[40] On Owen's early Manchester period see W. H. Chaloner, "Robert Owen, Peter Drinkwater and the Early Factory System in Manchester, 1788-1800", *Bulletin of the John Rylands Library* 37 (1954), pp. 79-102.

[41] If we take the narrator to be writing in 1845 (the year in which Gaskell says she began *Mary Barton*), the date is thus the May of 1833, 1834 or 1835; if in 1848 (the year of publication), it is May 1836, 1837 or 1838. But the last three dates are inconsistent with chapter 8, which is set in the spring of 1839, four to five years after the opening episode. The evidence thus favours May 1834 or 1835 for the novel's opening, but its chronology will not bear too precise scrutiny.

that they began to make plans for a new hall in Campfield, off Deansgate. Owen laid the foundation stone for this in August 1839, the old Salford Social Institution was closed at the end of the year and the socialists looked forward to the opening of their new premises, the largest of their kind in Manchester. The Reverend J. W. Kidd, incumbent of nearby St Matthias's Church, Campfield, was not pleased: eager socialists who gathered at the building site on Sunday mornings disturbed his services, and feeling ran high on both sides. With the help of Hugh Stowell, Kidd formed a committee "for the counter-action and suppression of that hideous form of infidelity which assumes the name of Socialism", and the attempt this committee made to suppress socialism in Manchester illustrates the difficult legal position which people of unorthodox beliefs had to face in early Victorian England.[42]

We cannot know where Gaskell stood in relation to such a counter-socialist organisation. The one mention of Stowell (the vicar of Christ Church, Salford) in her extant correspondence seems uncomplimentary,[43] Kidd is not mentioned at all, and neither is alluded to by her biographer. But her opposition to Owenism was undoubtedly in the same spirit.

Let us conclude by examining what is certainly the best known passage in the novel, its climactic intertwining of Barton's character with his politics:

> John Barton's overpowering thought, which was to work out his fate on earth, was rich and poor; why are they so separate, so distinct, when God has made them all? It is not His will that their interests are so far apart. Whose doing is it?
>
> And so on into the problems of the mysteries of life, until, bewildered and lost, unhappy and suffering, the only feeling that remained clear and undisturbed in the tumult of his heart, was hatred to the one class, and keen sympathy with the other.
>
> But what availed his sympathy? No education had given him

---

[42] Edward Royle, *Victorian Infidels: The Origins of the British Secularist Movement 1791-1866* (Manchester: Manchester University Press, 1974), p. 66. I am indebted to Royle for several of the details about Owen in the preceding paragraph.

[43] "Mr Stowell was there and all the cursing Evangelicals" (*The Letters of Mrs Gaskell*, 112; 26 April 1850). Owen, incidentally, does not appear in *The Letters of Mrs Gaskell* either.

wisdom; and without wisdom, even love, with all its effects, too often works but harm. He acted to the best of his judgment, but it was a widely-erring judgment.

The actions of the uneducated seem to be typified in those of Frankenstein, that monster of many human qualities, ungifted with a soul, a knowledge of the difference between good and evil.

The people rise up to life; they irritate us, they terrify us, and we become their enemies. Then, in the sorrowful moment of our triumphant power, their eyes gaze on us with mute reproach. Why have we made them what they are; a powerful monster, yet without the inner means for peace and happiness? (pp. 195-6)

Chris Baldick identifies this discussion as the point at which Gaskell "comes to wash her hands of her proletarian hero and to recoil from him as a monster when he appears to be asserting his independence from his employers and from his literary creator". But the passage does its work not just by being "a creative misreading which wrenches the [Frankenstein] myth into new patterns". [44] The rebellious working class is equally constructed as monstrous, as "other", by Gaskell's sudden slide into the first person plural, a discursive manoeuvre which implicates the reader in a collective opposition and hostility to that class: "The people rise up to life; they irritate *us*, they terrify *us*, and *we* become their enemies. Then, in the sorrowful moment of *our* triumphant power, their eyes gaze on *us* with mute reproach." In the passage as a whole, Gaskell erects a series of binary oppositions (Barton/us, labour/capital etc.), some explicit, others implicit. The following are certainly suggested:

Barton	*us*
labour	capital
poor	rich
created	creators

[44] Chris Baldick, *In Frankenstein's Shadow: Myth, Monstrosity, and Nineteenth-Century Writing* (Oxford: Clarendon Press, 1987), pp. 87, 86. An equally fascinating reading of Frankenstein's monster as a metaphor for the insurgent working class will be found in David E. Musselwhite, *Partings Welded Together: Politics and Desire in the Nineteenth-Century English Novel* (London: Methuen, 1987), pp. 43-74.

bewildered	wise
suffering	happy
ignorant	knowledgeable
mute	articulate
defeated	triumphant

It is not just her own hands Gaskell is washing. She is inviting her readers to testify that ours are clean too, and offering us various inducements to ensure that they are, such as self-identification with the creative, wise and articulate. If these are not enough, we are encouraged in the fantasy of sharing the "triumphant power" which is seen as the ultimate reward of throwing in one's lot with the forces of capital. This is not a novel which interpellates its readers dispassionately. On the contrary, by means of its characterisation of John Barton, it tempts us into identification with a set of positive and powerful social values whose negation he signifies.

It was not only conservative discourse which in this period generated images of the proletariat as demonic and bestial. Socialist writers did the same, but with quite different ends in mind. One of the most startling passages in Engels is that in which he explains that there "is no cause for surprise if the workers, treated as brutes, actually become such; or if they can maintain their consciousness of manhood only by cherishing the most glowing hatred, the most unbroken inward rebellion against the bourgeoisie in power. They are men so long as they burn with wrath against the reigning class. They become brutes the moment they bend in patience under the yoke, and merely strive to make life endurable while abandoning the effort to break the yoke."[45] This stands Gaskell's system of values on its head, permitting Barton's humanity to be identified with his hatred, his worth with his disobedience, his effectiveness with his rebelliousness.

From the "Frankenstein" passage on, it seems to me, the reader's response to John Barton is a touchstone of his or her own ideological affinities. Only the liberals in Gaskell's audience, I would argue, can now read smoothly with the grain of her characterisation. Conservatives will find her attempts to maintain sympathy for Barton absurd, and socialists will find them bogus. But it would clearly be a mistake to think of *Mary Barton* as a mere melodrama, a simple novel of sentiment and feeling, or

---

[45] Engels, pp. 144-5.

of its author simply as the politically naïve wife of a minister, consuming her leisure hours by spinning an innocent tale of ordinary working people. In fact, *Mary Barton* is one of the most *militant* pieces of fiction to come out of the nineteenth century. In it, Gaskell embarks on a mission to persuade her readers to steer clear of the siren voices of socialism and atheism; to resign themselves to the capitalist order which the former threatens, and to embrace the consolatory Christianity which the latter rejects. These were ambitious ideological aims. They still are. Present day liberalism seeks to persuade us that capitalism is the ultimate stage of economic development; much contemporary conservatism relies on Christianity as an ideological buttress. The durability of Gaskell's novel may be a sign that it is still considered a potential means of fostering liberal/conservative consciousness.

1997

He has come, the being who was an object of fear to primitive races, whom anxious priests tried to exorcize, whom sorcerers called up at midnight without ever yet seeing him in visible form, to whom the temporary lords of creation attributed in imagination the shape, monstrous or attractive, of gnomes, spirits, fairies or goblins. After the vulgar ideas inspired by prehistoric fears, scientific research has clarified the outlines of man's presentiment. Mesmer guessed it and in the last ten years doctors have discovered the exact nature of this being's power before its manifestation. They have experimented with this weapon of the new lord of the world, the imposition of a dominant will on the human soul, which thus becomes its slave. To this power they have given the name of magnetism, hypnotism, suggestion, and what not. I have seen them playing with it like silly children playing with fire. Woe to us! Woe to mankind. He has come [...][1]

In a certain respect, there is nothing very odd, novel, or absurd about an invisible man – that is, in the house of fiction. All fictional characters are, strictly, invisible. If, from the flow of words that makes up a narrative, there emerges a figure, human features, a face, its presence can be explained only as the product of a reader's imagination, actively at work, "translating" the body of textual signs into this mental-visual form. Maupassant's narrator surmises (when he is not convinced that it has the objective reality he claims for it in the passage quoted above) that the invisible being haunting him is the hallucinatory effect of "a deep fissure in my mind and in the logical processes of my thought. Phenomena of this kind occur in dreams, in which we are not surprised at the most wildly fantastic happenings, because our critical faculty and power of objective examination are dormant, while the imaginative mechanism is awake and active."[2] What is true of dreams is true of fiction. Readers, like dreamers, do not require an elaborate

---

[1] Guy de Maupassant, "Le Horla" (1887), tr. H. N. P. Sloman, *The Mountain Inn and Other Stories* (Harmondsworth: Penguin, 1955), pp. 49-50.
[2] Maupassant, p. 45.

mechanical or technological edifice to buttress fantasy. Fantasy is precisely that which floats free of such "real" determination.

Or is it? Even to claim that *The Invisible Man* is a "fantasy" – and the term is routinely applied to Wells's scientific romances – is in the first place to risk dropping into a paradoxical abyss. The term itself, etymologically, denotes "a making visible" (*OED*). Wells must have smiled when Joseph Conrad wrote to him, placing the book in the category of "the Fantastic". The story, after all, enacts "a making *in*visible" of its protagonist, Griffin, in which respect it could only be termed an anti-fantasy. But Conrad's remark was not without an inbuilt paradox of its own: "Impressed is *the* word, O Realist of the Fantastic! whether you like it or not," was his declared response to *The Invisible Man*. "And if you want to know what impresses me it is to see how you contrive to give over humanity into the clutches of the Impossible and yet manage to keep it down (or up) to its humanity, to its flesh, blood, sorrow, folly. *That* is the achievement! In this little book you do it with an appalling completeness."[3] Conrad's praise is drawn forth not simply by the "fantastic" elements of the text, but by the "realist" grounding they are given. He is presumably lauding Wells's strenuous efforts to render his unlikely tale "plausible", both by locating its action in an "ordinary" social and geographical setting, and by offering an apparently rational, "scientific" explanation for Griffin's discovery of invisibility. The point implicit in Conrad's response, I think, is that the yoking of the "fantastic" to the "realistic" produces a narrative dynamism between two modes of representation which is, by definition, absent in unbridled fantasy. In other words, the fantastic is heightened, its qualities more keenly evidenced, by its sharp juxtaposition with the realistic. This is what Wells, at any rate, was to claim for his scientific romances almost four decades later.[4]

Whether or not this proposal is valid can be confirmed only by individual readings of *The Invisible Man*. Radical fantasists and super-realists might argue that the co-presence of realism and fantasy within the boundaries of a single text leads to a mutual neutralisation, rather than intensification, of each. Both are also likely to be perplexed as to why a novel, whose verbal form determines that the invisibility of characters is pre-given, should

[3] Quoted in Patrick Parrinder (ed.), *H. G. Wells: The Critical Heritage* (London: Routledge and Kegan Paul), p. 60.
[4] See Wells's preface to *The Scientific Romances of H. G. Wells* (London: Gollancz, 1933), pp. vii-x.

expend so much effort attempting to convince readers that invisibility is technically possible. There can be no doubt, however, that it was a prime intention of Wells to effect such readerly conviction. Indeed, in retrospect, he thought he might have failed to do so, as he told Arnold Bennett in the month after the book first appeared:

> There is another difficulty [...] which really makes the whole story impossible. I believe it to be insurmountable. Any alteration in the refractive index of the eye lens would make vision impossible. Without such alteration the eyes would be visible as glassy globules. And for vision it is also necessary that there should be visual purple behind the retina and an opaque cornea and iris. On these lines you would get a very effective short story but nothing more.[5]

But the letter also indicates that Wells was prepared to sacrifice the demands of technical "plausibility" when they fundamentally impeded his yarn-spinning impulses. Only *Griffin*'s "story", the narrative Griffin tells Kemp, can be "impossible" for the reasons offered. *Wells*'s story nonetheless manages to get written by recourse to the time-honoured device of simply omitting to mention these difficulties.

Where Wells differs from the out-and-out fantasist is in refusing the obvious fall-back position of simple reliance on the reader's suspension of disbelief. Instead, he throws up a haze of technological and pseudo-scientific detail, replete with jargon and up-to-the minute buzz words, conveniently attenuating his technical descriptions when they come close to what would be an embarrassing complexity. Here, for instance, is a typical Griffin speech, delivered mid-way through the expositional discourse which is at the heart of the book:

> "I will tell you, Kemp, sooner or later, all the complicated processes. We need not go into that now. For the most part, saving certain gaps I chose to remember, they are written in cypher in those books that tramp has hidden. We must hunt him down. We must get those books again. But the essential phase was to place the transparent object whose

5 Harris Wilson (ed.), *Arnold Bennett and H. G. Wells* (London: Hart-Davis, 1960), pp. 34-5.

refractive index was to be lowered between two radiating centres of a sort of ethereal vibration, of which I will tell you more fully later. No, not these Röntgen vibrations – I don't know that these others of mine have been described. Yet they are obvious enough. I needed two little dynamos, and these I worked with a cheap gas engine. My first experiment was with a bit of white wool fabric. It was the strangest thing in the world to see it in the flicker of the flashes soft and white, and then to watch it fade like a wreath of smoke and vanish." (pp. 57-8)[6]

This speech is only apparently expository. Its rhetorical strategies all point to the actual ineffability of what Wells purports to describe. Thus Griffin is made to delay ("I will tell you, Kemp, sooner or later, all the complicated processes. We need not go into that now [...] I will tell you more fully later"), to claim forgetfulness ("for the most part, saving certain gaps I chose to remember, they are written in cypher in those books"), to retreat into imprecise generalities ("two radiating centres of a sort of ethereal vibration"), to decline the opportunity to furnish particulars ("they are obvious enough"), and to indulge in casual name-dropping which only serves to distract from the paucity of information he has vouchsafed ("these Röntgen vibrations").[7] Naturally, these informational deficiencies are not restored later in the novel. The postponed explanation never happens, the books are not recovered, and so on. Rather, the narrative proceeds swiftly *as if* a sufficient theoretical exposition of invisibility has been given here. By the end of the paragraph, indeed, Griffin has breezily moved the discussion

---

6 H. G. Wells, *The Invisible Man: a Grotesque Romance*, ed. Macdonald Daly (London: Dent Everyman, 1995). Parenthetical page references are to this edition. Wells's subtitle has frequently been dropped from editions of the novel, but is clearly a vital pointer to the spirit in which he wished it to be understood.

7 In alluding to Röntgen, Wells is being deliberately up-to-date. Wilhelm Konrad von Röntgen (1845-1923) had in 1895 achieved fame as the discoverer of X-rays, for which work he was jointly awarded the Rumford medal in 1896. There was much discussion of X-rays in Britain at the time: in 1896 John Macintyre achieved the first X-ray cinematograph at Glasgow's Royal Infirmary. In the same year, William J. Morton and Edwin W. Hammer published *The X Ray, or Photography of the Invisible and Its Value in Surgery* (London: Simpkin, Marshall, Hamilton, Kent and Co., 1896), which reprinted Röntgen's "Preliminary communication to the Würzburg Physico-Medical Society" of December 1895, and a large number of ghostly radiographic plates, mostly of the human frame.

on to practicalities. The exposition that has been staged is a mere simulacrum. It represents a genuine theory only as much as Griffin's pantomime mask represents a real face.

Wells thus creates a twofold problem for himself. Firstly, a theory of invisibility is not required to validate Griffin's "authenticity". For the reader, and for Kemp, he is already invisible beyond doubt. From this point of view the exposition of the theory is a potentially prolix excrescence or indulgence. This "fantasist" objection might seem to be answered by the "realist" counter-argument that what Griffin's invisibility generates is not *doubt* but *mystery*, and that what is desired is not evidence to prove that Griffin is genuinely invisible (the reader and Kemp both know that he is) but disclosure of the "plausible" methods whereby he has achieved this state: "'But how was it all done?' said Kemp, 'and how did you get like this?'" (p. 80); "'Before we can do anything else,' said Kemp, 'I must understand a little more about this invisibility of yours'" (p. 86). This is where Wells meets his second difficulty, for Griffin's account does not, in fact, reveal his secrets, or does so in such an obscure and partial manner that the enigma is only redoubled thereby. In short, Wells's "realist fantasy" runs the risk of falling foul of both fantasist and realist readers alike.

What might be the benefits of taking such chances? We can examine this dilemma in the light of a comparison with a narrative which was, without doubt, a major source of inspiration for *The Invisible Man*. This is the tale of Gyges the Lydian, as told by Socrates in Book II of Plato's *The Republic*:

They relate that he was a shepherd in the service of the ruler at that time of Lydia, and that after a great deluge of rain and an earthquake the ground opened and a chasm appeared in the place where he was pasturing; and they say that he saw and wondered and went down into the chasm; and the story goes that he beheld other marvels there and a hollow bronze horse with little doors, and that he peeped in and saw a corpse within, as it seemed, of more than mortal stature, and that there was nothing else but a gold ring on its hand, which he took off and went forth. And when the shepherds held their customary assembly to make their monthly report to the king about the flocks, he also attended wearing the ring. So as he sat there it chanced that he turned the collet of the ring towards himself, towards the inner part of his hand, and when this took place they say that he became invisible to those who sat by him and they spoke of him as absent; and that he was amazed, and again fumbling with the ring turned the collet outwards and so became visible. On noting this he experimented with the ring to see if it possessed this virtue, and he found the result to be that when he turned the collet inwards he became invisible, and when outwards visible; and becoming aware of this, he immediately managed things so that he became one of the messengers who went up to the king, and on coming there he seduced the king's wife and with her aid set upon the king and slew him and possessed his kingdom. If now there should be two such rings, and the just man should put on one and the unjust the other, no one could be found, it would seem, of such adamantine temper as to persevere in justice and endure to refrain his hands from the possessions of others and not touch them, though he might with impunity take what he wished even from the market-place, and enter into houses and lie with whom he pleased, and slay and loose bonds from whomsoever he would, and in all other things conduct himself among mankind as the equal of a god.[8]

Socrates recounts the Gyges story as an example of anti-social licence and its ethical consequences. Plainly parabolic, the narrative properly ignores the mechanism of the invisibility-inducing ring. It is only interested in this supernatural marvel insofar as it disrupts the moral order of the everyday world. As such, the tale is one of absolute corruption caused by the possession and exercise of power. The thesis is not countenanced that Gyges must already have been morally corrupt so to use the power he accidentally acquired. The most just of men, Socrates claims, would do exactly the same.

The Invisible Man is obviously related to the Gyges tale, but in complex ways. It too is a parable of moral decadence, but where does Griffin's corruption begin? He tells Kemp that, once the technical possibility of personal invisibility dawned on him, "'I beheld, unclouded by doubt, a magnificent vision of all that invisibility might mean to a man – the mystery, the power, the freedom. Drawbacks I saw none'" (p. 91). One notes the telling singular here – Griffin seems never, at any stage, to have

[8] Plato, *The Republic*, tr. Paul Shorey (London: Heinemann, 1937), pp. 117, 119. Wells read *The Republic* as a youth and records, in *Experiment in Autobiography* (London: Gollancz and The Cresset Press, 1934), p. 177, "its immense significance" for him. See also Philip Holt, "H. G. Wells and the Ring of Gyges", *Science-Fiction Studies* 19 (July 1992), pp. 236-47.

contemplated the positive consequences for "man" in general, but only for "a man" (that is, himself) in particular. The reader, however, must surely wonder what benefit there could possibly be for humankind as a whole, and deliberation suggests that the obvious answer seems to be none: invisibility would appear to confer no greater advantage than the individualistic gain to be had for the person who possesses its power, and would be nothing other than a bane to everyone else.

Was Griffin's failure to see "drawbacks" the first seed of his moral decomposition, or a sign that it was already established in him? Once he has *made* himself invisible, to be sure, his sense of unreflective egoistic potency is enormously magnified: "I was invisible, and I was only just beginning to realise the extraordinary advantage my invisibility gave me. My head was already teeming with plans of all the wild and wonderful things I had now impunity to do" (p. 101). Between these two points he not only confesses to a number of outrageous (and ignominiously petty) crimes, but demonstrates a marked nihilism in accounting for them: he robs his father of money belonging to someone else, and his father commits suicide ("'I did not feel a bit sorry for my father. He seemed to me to be the victim of his own foolish sentimentality'" [p. 92]); he tortures a cat, and then lies to its owner, his neighbour ("'a drink-sodden old creature, with only a white cat to care for in all the world [...] She had to be satisfied at last and went away again'" [p. 94]; and deliberately sets fire to a lodging house full of people ("'no doubt it was insured'" [p. 101]). This moral degeneration is, like the chemical process which effects invisibility, gradual and cumulative. Griffin's becoming invisible is a literal textual event, but it is also a metaphor for the complete withdrawal from social life which his moral bankruptcy signifies. The narrative then prompts twin questions, one on the literal, one on the ethical plane: (a) is invisibility reversible?; and (b) is there a degree of moral corruption beyond which an individual is no longer redeemable?

Like the Gyges tale, then, *The Invisible Man* sets out to ignite a moral debate around the concentration of great power in individual hands. But we are perhaps now in a position to appreciate one of the narrative functions of Wells's decision to do what Socrates does not – that is, to construct a technical edifice around a fantastic notion. For one thing, Griffin's methodical pursuit of the goal of invisibility serves to establish that his turpitude is not the result of mental derangement. Indeed, his intellectual grasp of the technical issues and his relaxation of principles increase in

117

direct proportion to each other. Eventually, mere expediency becomes his only behavioural touchstone. The following is his attempt to justify to Kemp the treatment he has meted out to one of his unfortunate victims, the costumier whom he knocks unconscious and ties up in a sheet. Kemp invokes "'common conventions of humanity'" to judge this act. But those, Griffin retorts, "'are all very well for common people'":

"My dear Kemp, it's no good your sitting and glaring as though I was a murderer. It had to be done. He had his revolver. If once he saw me he would be able to describe me –"

"But still," said Kemp, "in England – today. And the man was in his own house, and you were – well, robbing."

"Robbing! Confound it! You'll call me a thief next! Surely, Kemp, you're not fool enough to dance on the old strings. Can't you see my position?"

"And his too," said Kemp.

The Invisible Man stood up sharply. "What do you mean to say?"

Kemp's face grew a trifle hard. He was about to speak and checked himself. "I suppose, after all," he said with a sudden change of manner, "the thing had to be done. You were in a fix. But still –"

"Of course I was in a fix – an infernal fix. And he made me wild too – hunting me about the house, fooling about with his revolver, locking and unlocking doors. He was simply exasperating. You don't blame me, do you? You don't blame me?"

"I never blame any one," said Kemp. "It's quite out of fashion." (pp. 118-9)

Kemp *does*, of course, blame him. His seeming dismissal of moral concerns is merely a subterfuge to maintain Griffin in dialogue until his would-be captors (whom Kemp has already summoned) arrive. What is intriguing about the passage is Griffin's reaction. He is clearly still shaken by the possibility that ethical judgments ("the old strings") might ensnare him. It is not so much that he displays a residual moral sense, but rather that he seems to perceive the potential corresponding *power* of moral evaluation – its power, that is, to mobilise society to resistance against him. It is not a lingering conscience which disturbs Griffin here, but the prospect of collective cooperation overwhelming his own individual might. It is as logical as it is reprehensible that he should proceed to propose a "Reign of

Terror" which will "terrify and dominate" the community (p. 125). The "scientific" elements of the tale help to establish that Griffin may be vicious, but that he is not mad.

Nonetheless, Wells could clearly have staged this kind of moral debate, as Plato does, without recourse to a spurious scientific explanation of invisibility. One of the funniest (or most unwittingly absurd) moments in the history of literary criticism, after all, is Mario Praz's complaint about Mary Shelley's failure to specify how Frankenstein enlivened dead tissue to make his miraculous monster.[9] Undoubtedly the technological dimension is there partly to forestall accusations of unoriginality. Wells was hardly the first to make a fiction out of bodily invisibility, but to present it as scientifically explicable was entirely new. Maupassant's story leaves the existential status of "Le Horla" in suspension: it might easily be read as the delusion of a demented narrator. In Fitzjames O'Brien's earlier "What Was It?", on the other hand, the invisible being is a decidedly objective fact and, moreover, the story contains the following speculative conversation between the narrator, Harry, and his friend, Dr Hammond:

> "Let us reason a little, Harry. Here is a solid body which we touch, but which we cannot see. The fact is so unusual that it strikes us with terror. Is there no parallel, though, for such a phenomenon? Take a piece of pure glass. It is tangible and transparent. A certain chemical coarseness is all that prevents its being so entirely transparent as to be totally invisible. It is not *theoretically impossible*, mind you, to make a glass which shall not reflect a single ray of light, – a glass so pure and homogeneous in its atoms that the rays from the sun will pass through it as they do through the air, refracted but not reflected. We do not see the air, and yet we feel it."
>
> "That's all very well, Hammond, but these are inanimate substances. Glass does not breathe, air does not breathe. *This* thing has a heart that palpitates, – a will that moves it, – lungs that play, and inspire and respire."[10]

---

[9] Mario Praz, "Introductory Essay", *Three Gothic Novels* (Harmondsworth: Penguin, 1968), pp. 25-7. To be fair to Praz, his distinction is between pseudo-scientific novelists who "try to lift the veil, be it only for a moment" and those who make no attempt whatsoever to explain scientific processes. He mentions Wells to include him in the former category.

[10] Fitzjames O'Brien, "What Was It?", *The Diamond Lens and Other Stories*

But the pair get no further than this. As the title of the story suggests, the physical reality of the invisible being remains a matter of note and query rather than explanation. Wells clearly identified the need to put more scientific flesh on these unseen bones.

Yet there is more to *The Invisible Man*'s contrived scientificity than a wish on Wells's part to differentiate his story from those who had earlier dealt with the theme. Without it, the novel would not be the comic satire that it is. For, just as Griffin's intellectual advances are made at the price of moral regression, so his lust for power, evidenced as much by his desire to transform himself as to assume control over others, is inflated by comparison with the little that his invisibility does, pathetically, achieve for him. Essentially, *The Invisible Man* is an inversion of the tale of Gyges. Griffin does not obtain real power. He is lucky enough even to receive attention:

> "The more I thought it over, Kemp, the more I realised what a helpless absurdity an Invisible Man was – in a cold and dirty climate and a crowded civilised city. Before I made this mad experiment I had dreamt of a thousand advantages. That afternoon it seemed all disappointment. I went over the heads of the things a man reckons desirable. No doubt invisibility made it possible to get them, but it made it impossible to enjoy them when they were got. Ambition – what is the good of pride of place when you cannot appear there? What is the good of the love of woman when her name must needs be Delilah? I have no taste for politics, for the blackguardisms of fame, for philanthropy, for sport. What was I to do? And for this I had become a wrapped-up mystery, a swathed and bandaged caricature of a man!" (pp. 121-2)

It is in passages like these that *The Invisible Man* reads like a "realist" critique of "fantasy", the very genre in which Wells is, putatively, working. Griffin's failure to consider the English weather and urban crowding is a trope for his active renunciation of the material basis of all collective life. His ambition is to break free of what are undoubtedly material causes of his social isolation, particularly albinism and poverty. But he has not the foresight to perceive that the visual effacement of his body will not be a

(London: Ward and Downey, 1887), p. 261.

solution to either. Instead of being recognised as "other" because of his skin's lack of pigmentation, his invisibility simply leads to his not being recognised at all. Money, moreover, has no value other than in exchange; but to exchange with others one must be capable of being acknowledged by them. In the first instance, Griffin is thus forced to *dissemble* a visual presence, in a stunning reversal of the tale of the emperor's new clothes, by becoming a man of garments. Next, he hatches a plan, "'A way of getting back! Of restoring what I have done'" (p. 122). He is learning, but learning too late, that one's social identity is fundamentally rooted in the material of the body. To forget that is to live, so to speak, in a fantasy: it is this "realist" lesson which Wells's tale, paradoxically, "makes visible".

The fact that *The Invisible Man* is in part a fictional critique of the Nietzschean "will to power" is yet another sign of Wells's extraordinary topicality. Patrick Bridgwater has pointed out that in the month the novel began to be serialised (June 1897) Thomas Common defended Nietzsche against Wells's "accusation of 'blackguardism', a charge which Wells made in *Natural Science* (April 1897): 'The tendency of a belief in natural selection as the main factor of human progress, is, in the moral field, towards the glorification of a sort of rampant egotism – of blackguardism in fact, – as the New Gospel. You get that in the Gospel of Nietzsche.'"[11] Bridgwater agrees that Wells's reading of Nietzsche was sorely misguided. But misunderstanding of the German philosopher's work was the norm rather than the exception in this period, and need not detain us. The more important fact is that Wells, according to Bridgwater, was the first English artist to pay serious attention to Nietzsche (who was not to die until 1900).

What Wells achieves in the character of Griffin, whose name itself indicates a unity of different species,[12] is an assimilation of the Nietzschean

---

[11] Patrick Bridgwater, *Nietzsche in Anglosaxony* (Leicester: Leicester University Press, 1972), p. 56. Bridgwater argues that specific Nietzschean influence is observable in Wells's *The Island of Doctor Moreau* (1896) and *When the Sleeper Wakes* (1899), and concludes that Wells read Alexander Tille's edition of *The Collected Works of Friedrich Nietzsche*, the first two volumes of which had been published the previous year: volume VII, *Thus Spake Zarathustra: A Book for All and None* (translated by Alexander Tille), and vol. XI, *The Case of Wagner; Nietzsche Contra Wagner; The Twilight of the Idols; The Antichrist* (translated by Thomas Common) (2 vols., London: H. Henry, 1896).

[12] In the context of the novel, multiple associations seem to attach to the name. The primary connection may be with the "fabulous animal usually represented as having

"beyond-man" (the word with which Tille clumsily translated the German *Übermensch*) to the Marlovian overreacher. Griffin, a "singular person", falls "out of infinity into Iping" (p. 12), just as Nietzsche's prophet Zarathustra descends from the mountains to preach his parody of the New Testament and the coming of the overman. But Griffin is at once a more minatory and more absurd figure than Zarathustra. He believes himself to be the overman as well as the prophet of his arrival. His growing megalomania culminates in the proclamation of a new dynasty, with himself as emperor (though a pathetically provincial one): "Port Burdock is no longer under the Queen, tell your Colonel of Police, and the rest of them; it is under me – the Terror! This is day one of year one of the new epoch – the Epoch of the Invisible Man. I am Invisible Man the First." Typically, however, this edict arrives at Kemp's house in "a strange missive, written in pencil on a greasy sheet of paper [...] on the addressed side of it the postmark Hintondean, and the prosaic detail '2d. to pay'" (pp. 134-5) – hardly an auspicious style in which to issue such an historic declaration. The episode is representative: Wells's satirical subversion of his overman is consistently a matter of juxtaposing Griffin's desocialised ambitions and bombastic rhetoric with the "prosaic detail" of English regional society and the necessities of material life. Like Marlowe's Doctor Faustus,[13] Griffin, in the event, barters his life and happiness for a career of farcical ignominy and a final, tragic-comic solitude.

The Invisible Man is undoubtedly the least "romantic" of Wells's scientific romances. Like every romance, it is centrally concerned with a character whose story is decidedly "out of the ordinary". But it throws into crisis this hero's experience, and the genre of romance itself, by engineering a collision between the anticipatedly "fantastic" and the recognisably

---

the head and wings of an eagle and the body and hind quarters of a lion" (*OED*): Griffin is similarly hard to categorise, and equally fearsome. But the word was also used in Anglo-Indian parlance to describe "a European newly arrived in India, and unaccustomed to Indian ways and peculiarities" (*OED*), a situation somewhat analogous to Griffin's own in West Sussex. It is difficult to know how far to extend such associations, however: more obscurely (but perhaps pertinently, given the novel's dealings with bodily colour) the word was also used in the United States (particularly Louisiana), to denote "a mulatto" (*OED*).

[13] "Sweet Mephistophilis, so charm me here,/That I may walk invisible to all,/And do whate'er I please unseen of any" – *Doctor Faustus*, III.iii.11-14.

"realistic". Wells had done this before in *The Wonderful Visit* (1895), but his more typical devices were the creation of an alternative world or radical alteration of that which was familiar. Thus the protagonists of *The Time Machine* (1895) and *The Island of Doctor Moreau* (1896) were both deliberately displaced from late Victorian England (the first temporally, the other geographically), and in *The War of the Worlds* (1898) and *In the Days of the Comet* (1906) England itself would be drastically transformed. *The Invisible Man* eschews these possibilities, however, and is therefore "a grotesque romance" in a number of senses. Firstly, it is a romance whose hero is a grotesque: one member of the novel's panoply of opinionated rustics, Silas Durgan, indeed proposes the only career for Griffin that the denizens of Iping would be likely to sponsor: "'if he choses to show enself at fairs he'd make his fortune in no time'" (p. 20). Secondly, *The Invisible Man* grotesquely distorts the romance genre by cross-fertilising it with its antithesis: Griffin falls out of the infinity of romance into the incongruously particular realism of a West Sussex village in 1896.[14] Bruce Beiderwell has, thirdly, related Wells's novel to the specific conception of the grotesque found in John Ruskin's *The Stones of Venice* (1851-3):

> He notes that the grotesque is composed of two complementary elements, "one ludicrous, the other fearful." The difficulty in distinguishing between these two elements, Ruskin maintains, arises from the fact that "the mind, under certain phases of excitement, *plays* with *terror*, and summons images which, if it were in another temper, would be awful, but of which, either in weariness or in irony, it refrains for a time to acknowledge the true terribleness." A tension between play and terror (along with a resistance to the full recognition of terror) functions as the central technique in *The Invisible Man*.[15]

---

[14] While it is not necessarily legitimate to assume chronological consistency on Wells's part, the events of the novel take place in a leap year because the twenty-ninth of February is mentioned (p. 12). Its happenings postdate the Golden Jubilee of 1887, commemorating the fiftieth anniversary of Queen Victoria's ascendancy to the throne (adverted to on p. 32), so the possibilities are narrowed to 1888, 1892 or 1896. The mention of Röntgen (p. 93) makes possible only the last of these dates.
[15] Bruce Beiderwell, "The Grotesque in Wells's *The Invisible Man*", *Extrapolation* 24, 4 (1983), p. 302.

This "attempted combination, as it were, of Thurber and Kafka"[16] makes the reading of Wells's novel a curiously contradictory and indecisive experience. In it, we witness the boundaries between certain seemingly fixed and opposed categories – romance and realism, exuberance and fear, sensationalism and seriousness, and (Wells's major preoccupations) science and art – begin to corrode and dissolve, and the possibilities of new and better syntheses emerging. In a very proper sense of the epithet, *The Invisible Man* was an experimental fiction.

1995

[16] Bernard Bergonzi, *The Early H. G. Wells: A Study of the Scientific Romances* (Manchester: Manchester University Press, 1961), pp. 118-9.

SCOTTISH POETRY AND THE GREAT WAR

> Was it for little Belgium's sake
> Sae mony thoosand Scotsmen dee'd?
> And never ane for Scotland fegs
> Wi' twenty thoosand mare need!

Hugh MacDiarmid, "Towards a New Scotland" (1934)

In a survey of English poetry of the Great War written in 1940, Edgell Rickword concluded that "the fact that the years of war failed to produce a body of poetry expressing conviction in the necessity of the struggle must have some bearing on the nature of the conflict itself."[1] However, Rickword would also probably have acknowledged that the poetry of protest which did emerge from the war, in its almost total failure to develop a social (as opposed to humanitarian) critique, demonstrated the nearly complete absence of socialist consciousness among Georgian *literati*. Indeed, he pointed out that Wilfred Owen's ignorance of Home Front rank and file movements limited severely the power of his utterance ("as it was, he took the *Daily Mail* too seriously as the expression of the people's feelings"),[2] and asserted elsewhere that Siegfried Sassoon's inability to identify capitalism as the problem in both war and peace prevented his "developing in peace-time a poetry of indignant pity and keen satire such as he wrote out of his war experience".[3]

It is, of course, revealing that the little explicitly oppositional verse that was written, such as J. M. Derwood's sonnet of December 1914, "For Whom?", is seen as so unrepresentative of English poetic temperament of the period that it is systematically excluded from war anthologies:

[1] Edgell Rickword, "War and Poetry: 1914-18", *Life and Letters Today* 25/26 (June-August 1940); reprinted in Edgell Rickword, *Literature in Society: Essays and Opinions (II) 1931-1978*, ed. Alan Young (Manchester: Carcanet, 1978), p. 156.
[2] Rickword, p. 152.
[3] Edgell Rickword, "Poetry and Two Wars", *Our Time* I, 2 (April 1941); reprinted in *Literature in Society*, p. 159.

For whom and what is this foul slaughter done?
Tell us, ye rulers mighty in your seats –
And then shall people rising 'gainst their cheats
Drive you from senate, camp, and mart, and throne:
And not in continental lands alone
But here as well in England's snug retreats,
For even here most hellish work one meets
And yet scarce dare to make one's free thought known.

My countrymen, when Europe peace declares
Midst thousands of our noble soldiers slain,
Who but the ruling class shall reap the gain
In all the lands? Toil's slaves shall be the heirs
Of yet more arduous toil, and only they
Shall have to earn the tax war's debt to pay.[4]

But, to address the critique of Owen directly, it is not obvious that a sympathetic awareness of domestic political struggles could of itself have fostered the poetic temperament which Rickword envisaged. One might justifiably hold that verse with a consciously subversive note was unlikely to emerge from an English artistic *milieu* in which the imperialist *status quo* was still either unquestioningly approved or alarmingly unacknowledged.

Dozens of kindred jingoistic metrical formulations could be cited, but John Masefield's "August 1914" is notable in that, while it peddles the familiar ideological tokens of an illusory pastoral England ("such dumb loving of the Berkshire loam/As breaks the dumb hearts of the English kind"), it also implants the misty image of desirable metropolitan capitalist

[4] Edgell Rickword and Jack Lindsay (eds.), *Spokesmen for Liberty: A Record of English Democracy Through Twelve Centuries* (London: Lawrence and Wishart, 1941), p. 387. Jonathan Mawson Denwood (1869-1933) was a Cumbrian who wrote mainly about the region, co-authoring a book of poems, *The Shepherds' Meet*, published in Cockermouth in 1913, and writing several later prose volumes. His admittedly amateur poem makes no appearance in the key anthologies edited by Parsons or Silkin (see footnotes 24 and 25 below for references), or in S. S. Hussey (ed.), *Poetry of the First World War* (London: Longman, 1967), or in Brian Gardner (ed.), *Up the Line to Death: The War Poets 1914-1918* (London: Methuen, 1976). Many other amateur poems do.

advance for which the war was truly being waged ("some idea but dimly understood/Of an English city never built by hands"). This combination of myth and dream formed an armour which could be dented, but not pierced, by the otherwise impressive Sassoonian condemnation of the army hierarchy, or the laudable solidarity in physical suffering with German soldiers evinced by the likes of Isaac Rosenberg.

But the erection of *English* cities, one would have thought, was not the vision which inspired 320,589 Scotsmen to volunteer for the wartime army (that is, almost half of the entire total of 688,416 Scots who served in the 1914-18 forces, 78,000 of whom, or 11.3%, died as a result).[5] If one were looking for a truly oppositional poetry, one might expect it to have issued, if anywhere, from an internal colony of that Empire whose economic dominions the war was an attempt to consolidate and extend. The fact that Scotland produced nothing of the kind is, in certain respects, not so very surprising. Statistically, a higher proportion of eligible Scots (26.9%) voluntarily entered the army than of any other nationality in the British Isles: England and Wales, classified together, yielded 24.2%, and Ireland 10.7%.[6] As J. M. Winter is at pains to show, although on the whole twice as many professionals and white-collar workers as manual workers enlisted,[7] the general support for the war from the industrial working class, even in occupations which had shown a propensity for industrial militancy prior to the war, cannot be denied: "the compatibility of class consciousness and patriotism could have no better illustration".[8] But the curious phenomenon of Scottish "patriotism" in an English war is not something which Winter is concerned to examine. The low Irish figure bespeaks a much more widespread lack of complicity with the English war effort than that present in Scotland, and, although Winter wilfully avoids the issue, the historical explanation for this is transparently clear. The Home Rule struggle in Ireland before the war fostered a national consciousness which, in wartime,

---

[5] J. M. Winter, *The Great War and the British People* (London: Macmillan, 1986), pp. 28, 68, 72. The figures reflect place of enlistment rather than country of origin, but in the absence of more detailed statistics we shall simply assume that the number of Scots who volunteered outside Scotland roughly equals the number of non-Scots who enlisted in Scotland.

[6] Winter, p. 28.

[7] Winter, p. 33.

[8] Winter, p. 35.

mobilised a more effective resistance to English imperialism than any available to non-nationalist Scottish socialism. The Irish Home Rule movement was always, of course, historically in advance of the Scottish: without the former there would have been little pressure for the latter. But as Michael Keating and David Bleiman have persuasively argued, the emphasis on Home Rule was crucially in decline in Scottish labour circles in the years preceding the war: "In the early years of the century, however, the overriding trend within the labour movement was towards integration with England and a downgrading of the Home Rule cause."9 Resurgence of nationalism among Scottish socialists was largely, then, an effect of the war itself. My argument here is that Scottish war verse was so dependent on a combination of English literary models and English literary temperament that a corresponding growth in conscious poetic nationalism is hardly detectable in it.

Yeats's airman, himself a volunteer, shows how verse can articulate the complexity of English imperial dominion. Recognising that the war is not one from which "my countrymen, Kiltartan's poor" are likely either to lose or gain, he rationalises his uncompelled enlistment by appealing to "a lonely impulse of delight" which immersion in war offers to satisfy. His position is thus thoroughly distinguishable from the historically delusioned anglomania of a poem such as W. N. Hodgson's "The Call" ("Ah! we have dwelt in Arcady long time"). The airman, on the contrary, has a quite unblinkered perspective on the "waste" of Irish history under English rule. His seizure of the opportunity to indulge his "impulse" is a function of, rather than an escape from, his nation's oppression. The choice of death presents itself as the logical conclusion in circumstances of social impoverishment:

> I balanced all, brought all to mind,
> The years to come seemed waste of breath,
> A waste of breath the years behind
> In balance with this life, this death.

"An Irish Airman Foresees his Death" favours active over passive suffering, and as such can be assimilated in some immediately obvious respects to the

9 Michael Keating and David Bleiman, *Labour and Scottish Nationalism* (London: Macmillan, 1979), p. 56.

ideological matrix which led Yeats to suppress the war poets when compiling *The Oxford Book of Modern Verse* (1936):

> I have rejected these poems for the same reason that made Arnold withdraw his *Empedocles on Etna* from circulation; passive suffering is not a theme for poetry. In all the great tragedies, tragedy is a joy to the man who dies [...]
>
> If war is necessary, or necessary in our time and place, it is best to forget its suffering as we do the discomfort of fever, remembering our comfort at midnight when our temperature fell, or as we forget the worse moments of more painful disease.[10]

The politics of this censorious plea for voluntary amnesia are sufficiently familiar, extending from the ideological orthodoxy of the Great War itself. "An Irish Airman Foresees His Death" is a legitimate poem, in Yeats's terms, because the airman's "impulse of delight" may be equated with the "joy" of the tragic hero; but that neat rationalisation is thrown into disarray by the weary defeatist tone in which the announcement of his tragic enterprise is delivered. The poem indicates something of the understood social complexity which informed Irish responses to the war, whether of resistance or complicity. If nothing comparable came out of Scotland, the relatively late popularity of nationalism there must offer at least a partial explanation for the failure.

Many Scots, then, were deeply committed to the Empire at the struggle's outbreak. But as the war effort progressed its aims and conduct were increasingly queried, and the modifications in Scottish assent often carried latent, in some cases unconscious, national traces. There could hardly be any greater pillar of the war establishment, for example, than John Buchan. Born in Perth in 1875, Buchan had travelled on a familiar anglifying educational path: Hutcheson's Grammar school, Glasgow University, then Brasenose College, Oxford. Like his fictional hero Richard Hannay, he had had a spell in colonial South Africa between 1901 and 1903. As an ex-soldier under forty-five when war broke out, he was eligible to serve, but was medically unfit. He thus continued as a partner in the Edinburgh publishing

---

[10] W. B. Yeats, "Introduction", *The Oxford Book of Modern Verse*, ed. W. B. Yeats (Oxford: Oxford University Press, 1936), pp. xxxiv-xxxv.

firm of Thomas Nelson, being responsible eventually for overseeing the twenty-four volumes of Nelson's *History of the War*. But his indefatigable support for the war also gained him entry into a variety of established institutional posts. He was a war correspondent for *The Times* and attached as an observer to Haig's GHQ. He worked for C. F. G. Masterman's propaganda department, known only as Wellington House (the name of the London building it occupied), one of a group of writers so involved, which included Masefield, Alfred Noyes, Anthony Hope and Hilaire Belloc.[11] In 1917 he became head of the British propaganda services, as Director of Information.

Richard Hannay's national origins are glossed in the opening paragraphs of *The Thirty-Nine Steps*, where we are told that "my father had brought me out from Scotland at the age of six, and I had never been home since; so England was a sort of Arabian Nights to me, and I counted on stopping there for the rest of my days."[12] If that slippage from Scotland to England is rather curious (it seems to differentiate yet at once identify them), the heavily romanticised depiction of both in *The Thirty-Nine Steps* is consonant with this declared ignorance. Hannay finds life in England extremely boring until his fortuitous and fantastic involvement in an international conspiracy allows him to satisfy his boyish wanderlust and mania for adventure, apparently unquestionable excitements which historical circumstances look set to perpetuate, if the final paragraph of this flashy narrative is anything to go by: "Three weeks later, as all the world knows, we went to war. I joined the New Army the first week, and owing to my Matabele experience got a captain's commission straight off. But I had done my best service, I think, before I put on khaki."[13]

Buchan's fictional *alter ego* continued to "serve", however, in *Greenmantle* (1916) – which opens as he is convalescing from an injury sustained at the Battle of Loos[14] – and *Mr Standfast* (1919). In the opening

---

[11] See Stuart Sillars, *Art and Survival in First World War Britain* (London: Macmillan, 1987), pp. 18-19. The general participation of the *literati* in Britain's propaganda effort is well documented in Peter Buitenhuis, *The Great War of Words: Literature as Propaganda 1914-18 and After* (London: Batsford, 1989).

[12] John Buchan, *The Thirty-Nine Steps* (Edinburgh: William Blackwood, 1915), p. 10.

[13] Buchan, *The Thirty-Nine Steps*, p. 252.

[14] John Buchan, *Greenmantle* (London: Hodder and Stoughton, 1916), p. 1, where

pages of the latter Hannay experiences an access of spiritual enthusiasm for the "Old Country" which he had earlier found so sickeningly dull, enjoying a sudden ethnic epiphany on the ridge of a Cotswold hill:

> In that moment I had a kind of revelation. I had a vision of what I had been fighting for. It was peace, deep and holy and ancient [...] It was more; for in that hour England first took hold of me [...] I understood what a precious thing this little England was, how old and kindly and comforting, how wholly worth striving for.[15]

The most striking feature of this passage now – an index of the flatness of the prose and the utter conventionality of the sentiments – is surely its failure to compel assent from the reader. This judgment holds for all of Buchan's novels.

By comparison, Buchan's lesser known war verse is remarkably Scots-inflected. The seven items in the "Inter Arma" section of his *Poems Scots and English* (1917) are all written in Lowlands vernacular, being typically monologues put into the mouths of representative members of the serving Scottish soldiery. Thematically, most of these poems are on the march towards various forms of reconciliation arising from the horrors of war, whether it be the individual's reconciliation with God ("On Leave"), that between Rome and Presbyterianism ("The Kirk Bell"), or between competing nationalisms ("Sweet Argos"). But they also exhibit an impressive range of tone, both across poems (compare the elegiac "Fisher Jamie" with the rumbustious "Fragment of an Ode in Praise of the Royal Scots Fusiliers") and within poems (the speaker in "Home Thoughts From Abroad" being jolted from his daydream of returning home by the realisation that he has peopled his reverie with the slain). The major

the war is characteristically portrayed as a blend of adventure and schoolboy high jinks: "there was no prouder man on earth than Richard Hannay when he took his Lennox Highlanders over the parapets on that glorious and bloody 25th day of September. Loos was no picnic, and we had some ugly bits of scrapping before that".
15 John Buchan, *Mr Standfast* (London, Nelson, 1919), pp. 23-4. Sillars, pp. 133-4, places this passage and others from Mr Standfast in the context of contemporary mythic conservative representations of England in various art forms. Foster, p. 117 (see note 17 below for reference) discusses how the presentation of Clydeside elsewhere in the novel is consonant with Government policy.

achievement of these poems, collectively, is that they hail a Scottish audience, attempt to provide an aesthetic appeal to a specifically Scottish, as distinct from British, patriotism. But in doing so they never descend into the bland jingoism of Buchan's prose hero.

Take, for instance, "On Leave", whose speaker finds himself, like Hannay in the passage from *Mr Standfast* quoted above, contemplating his "old country" from an elevation. He has returned for a week after eighteen months at the front, "fitsore, weary and wauf", during which his young child dies ("The pin had faun oot o' the warld,/And I doddered amang the bits"). Following the burial of the infant, he climbs the Lammerlaw, "The stink o' the gas in my nose,/The colour o' bluid in my ee,/And the biddin' o' Hell in my lug/To curse my Maker and dee". What he sees only reminds him of the front:

> I saw a thoosand hills,
> > Green and gowd i' the licht,
> Roond and backit like sheep,
> > Huddle into the nicht.
>
> But I kenned they werena hills,
> > But the same as the mounds ye see
> Doun by the back o' the line
> > Whaur they bury oor lads that dee.
>
> They were juist the same as at Loos
> > Whaur we happit Andra and Dave. –
> There was naething in life but death,
> > And a' the warld was a grave.
>
> A' the hills were graves,
> > The graves o' the deid langsyne,
> And somewhere oot in the Wast
> > Was the grummlin' battle-line.

There follows a lyrical section in which a distinctly Scottish landscape and memories of youthful rural pursuits ("Guddlin' troot in the burns,/Howkin' the tod frae his lair"), by gentle osmosis, lift the speaker out of his despair.

But if the poem eventually rallies its readers, by means of an appeal to the pastoral glories of Scotland and Scottishness, towards a re-engagement with hope, it has nonetheless managed to plumb the depths of a sombreness which, by comparison, Richard Hannay seems constitutionally incapable of experiencing.

It is true that Buchan's war poems, like those of Charles Murray, whom we shall examine in due course, are in thrall to a Housmaniac, nostalgic rusticity. It is hardly surprising that they want to resist, deny, refuse to contemplate Scottish modernity, or the political possibilities it offers. The difficulty for any invocation of Scottish patriotism in the context of war, it has to be remembered, is its historical antagonism to England and Englishness. To insist on Scottish traditions, the Scottish land, Scottish military prowess, is to risk the encouragement of anti-unionist sentiment. The No Man's Land between such patriotism and nationalism is very narrow. For all the ostensible lightheartedness of Buchan's "Fragment of an Ode in Praise of the Royal Scots Fusiliers" (which gives us the Kaiser speaking in Scots), it needs to be noticed how it demotes the English, among other nationalities, in making its point about Scottish bravery and belligerence:

> "I went ower far
> When I stertit this war,
> Forgettin' the Fusilier Jocks.
> I could manage the French and Italians and Poles,
> The Russians and Tartars and yellow Mongols,
> The Serbs and the Belgians, the English and Greeks,
> And even the lads that gang wantin' the breeks;
> But what o' thae Fusilier Jocks,
> That stopna for duntin' and knocks?
> They'd rin wi' a yell
> Ower the plainstanes o' Hell;
> They're no men ava – they are rocks!
> They'd gang barefit
> Through the Bottomless Pit,
> And they'll tak Berlin in their socks, –
> Will thae terrible Fusilier Jocks!"

Murray, in his *A Sough O' War* (1917), takes greater chances than this. In "Wha Bares a Blade For Scotland?", perhaps the most eloquent specimen of pro-enlistment copywriting to come out of the war, he calls up "the cairns o' the Covenanters whaur the martyrs' banes are laid" and those other separatist folk heroes, Wallace and Bruce, as examples of patriotic conduct to be followed in the current crisis.

Where it is addressing or appealing to a Scottish identity, then, war verse has inherent tensions and contradictions, intimately bound up with the peculiar placement of Scotland within the Empire. Buchan and Murray's own imperial views are well formulated by Colin Milton in one of the few critical engagements with their poetry:

> In the case of individuals like Buchan and Murray, interest in and respect for local customs, patterns of life and forms of speech was not only not inconsistent with support for the British Empire, but intimately related to that support. Both represented a particular tradition of imperialist thinking which was essentially federalist in nature and which conceived of empire as a voluntary union (in the end, if not at the beginning), linking different cultures and countries in a way that would bring the advantages of large-scale co-operation without compromising the essential integrity of the individual components.[16]

It is no surprise, then, that quasi-nationalist difficulties come to the surface most evidently in pastoral, where they can to a degree be managed on account of the genre's occlusion of modernity.

Given this fact, one might anticipate a more radical articulation when these matters are dealt with from an urban focus. In terms of general political discourse, of course, this expectation is fulfilled. It is undeniable that the west of Scotland sustained the most ambitious and prolonged mass anti-war agitation of any area on the British mainland. There is no need to engage here in a narrative of wartime "Red Clydeside", which belongs more properly to a fully historical discourse: the issue has in any case become

---

[16] Colin Milton, "Modern Poetry in Scots Before MacDiarmid", *The History of Scottish Literature, vol. 4: Twentieth Century*, ed. Cairns Craig (Aberdeen: Aberdeen University Press, 1987), p. 26. It should be said that Milton is more negligent of Buchan than I am, perhaps for good reason.

something of an historiographical labyrinth. [17] The debate about the importance of the social and industrial struggles on Clydeside of these years will no doubt continue to centre on the issues of how far they demonstrated a principled popular opposition to the war, and how far a representative pragmatic protest against the intolerable social conditions which the war engendered. In either case, the lack of a correspondingly critical artistic utterance in this quarter is what concerns us. General agreement about the poverty of Scottish literary endeavour in the period offers only a partial understanding of the failure.

Indeed, I am in a position personally to muddy the waters somewhat further. Going through my own grandfather's papers several years ago, I found an untitled poem dedicated to a friend killed in the same Battle of Loos which Buchan's jingoistic hero finds so glorious:[18]

Young, lithe, adventurous,
Quick your response to the call
To fight the foes of your country.
Ne'er a thought that you might fall.
But battles for you are now over,
Your bosom now is cold.
In the soil of a foreign battlefield
What was mortal now's left to mould.
For war pities nought an aching heart.
Nearest, dearest, all must part.
You have passed from the fray
Of the daring and brave,
From sorrowing friends
To a premature grave.
Your years, they were happy
But alas, how few.
Farewell, young martyr.
Adieu! Adieu!

---

[17] For an investigation of the various competing "versions" of this history, see John Foster, "Red Clyde, Red Scotland", *The Manufacture of Scottish History*, ed. Ian Donnachie and Christopher Whatley (Edinburgh: Polygon, 1992), pp. 106-24.
[18] The date of the poem is uncertain. The author, Hugh Daly, was born in 1896, and died in 1974.

The feature of this which I most want to note is not its evident untutoredness, but the fact that its author was a war volunteer (he was turned down on medical grounds), worked in the Clydeside yards, took part in the rent strikes and other agitations of wartime Glasgow, and later became a communist. This progress might be taken to represent a personal political radicalisation as a result of the war experience, but in fact this writer bears out Winter's thesis remarkably well: his patriotism and his socialism do not seem to have been mutually exclusive. Specifically, there is no nationalist hesitancy at all in "to fight the foes of your country". Technique aside, this could be W. N. Hodgson ("England to Her Sons"), or Herbert Asquith ("The Volunteer"). It certainly qualifies James D. MacDougall's well known socialist generalisation of 1927, "Jingoism was at a discount in Glasgow from the very beginning of the war". [19] On the contrary, this versifying is as untroubled by scepticism as the majority of English efforts.

Yet the most sceptical Scottish poet of the war is also the most ignored. Dugald Sutherland MacColl's verse is not formally consummate, but its themes are politically informed, and unique in registering variations in response between urban and rural Scotland. This has not won him a place in any notable war anthology: his mark is made only in Gardner's collection by "The Miners' Response" (a four-line squib which makes much of the contradiction between military and industrial uses of the word "strike") and he is enigmatically absent from others, especially Royle's. MacColl was born in Glasgow in 1859 to a Presbyterian minister and the daughter of a banker.

[19] Quoted by Trevor Royle, "Introduction", *In Flanders Fields: Scottish Poetry and Prose of the First World War*, ed. Trevor Royle (Edinburgh: Mainstream, 1990), p. 21. Many of the Scottish poems I discuss in this article can be found in Royle's valuable anthology, which is the first of its kind and brings together much forgotten verse by John Buchan, W. D. Cocker, John MacDougall Hay, Violet Jacob, Roderick Watson Kerr, Joseph Lee, Hugh MacDiarmid, Donald MacDonald, Pittendreigh MacGillivray, Ewart Alan MacKintosh, John Munro, Neil Munro, Charles Murray, Murdo Murray, J. B. Salmond, Charles Hamilton Sorley, and Mary Symon. One of the incidental revelations of Royle's edition is just how anglocentric anthologies of first world war verse can be, even when they are trying consciously to present an "alternative" picture of poetic production in the period: neither Violet Jacob or Mary Symon, for instance, appear in Catherine Reilly (ed.), *Stars Upon My Heart: Women's Poetry and Verse of the First World War* (London: Virago, 1981), despite being considerably more interesting poets than many who do.

His father became minister of Kensington Presbyterian church in 1873, and he was subsequently educated at University College, London and Lincoln College, Oxford. He became a well known figure in the British art world, dying in 1948. Never a combatant, his first world war poetry, collected in *Bull and Other War Verses* (1919), contains a series of vigorous satires on the sanctimoniousness which arose on all sides during and immediately after the conflict. "Another Neutral", for example, imagines a French interrogation of the Pope in which the latter's supreme contempt for any declared commitment is laid bare:

"The 'Lusitania' – there at least
Was an appalling crime?"
"Most injudicious: human lives
Are more than stone and lime.
It pained me greatly, though I did
Not say so at the time."

This is what one might expect from the son of a Presbyterian minister, of course, but it is also in an accord with MacColl's general position on the war, set out in the long "Preface" to *Bull and Other War Verses*, where he contends that he wrote under the conviction "that in a conflict of such scope and kind neutrality, when not enforced by weakness, must damn the nation that maintained it".[20] It is no surprise, then, that America rather than Germany is the most lambasted of the participants, on account of its late entry into the fray and its attempts to steal the show in constructing a post-war global order. Much of the humour is in MacColl's deployment of Old Testament parallels: "The Ark: A Fable of Henry Ford" is a long, knockabout poem which likens the famous industrialist to Noah, while "A League of Nations" compares Woodrow Wilson's brainchild to the Tower of Babel. It is perhaps not so hard to see why MacColl's lively humour should be excluded from war anthologies assembled in the spirit of Owen's dictum that the poetry is in the pity.

As for politics, MacColl is deeply ambiguous about socialism. He complains in the "Preface" of Wilson's refusal to negotiate with Germany compared to his preparedness to entertain "the wickeder tyranny of the

[20] Dugald Sutherland MacColl, "Preface", *Bull and Other War Verses* (London: Constable, 1919), pp. vii-viii.

137

Bolsheviks", [21] and "War Savings" is a clever example of flyting at the expense of the Independent Labour Party. But these animosities issue less from allegiance to a contending faction than a searing Carlylean disdain for industrialism as a whole, which is seen as the prime cause of the conflict:

> Unlimited industrial exploitation and commercial competition are not Peace but War, and if a Pax Americana is to guarantee the resumption and intensifying of these, our last state will be worse than the first. The "War" was the application of science by Germany to a violent furthering of the industrial and commercial scramble. But the peaceful war began before that. Its root was the invention by England in the late eighteenth and early nineteenth centuries of a scientific industrialism applied to limitless production, without consideration of the worth of the objects produced or the effect of their production upon the life, the numbers, and the character of her people. England was first in the field and captured the markets of the world, but brought into existence in the process a population without tradition or inheritance, went far to destroy all that makes England a country worth living in, and in particular shaped her policy for the development of industry and commerce to the hurt of agriculture and the breed of men it nurtures. In this we were imitated, and on the way to be surpassed. [22]

In spirit this comes close to that other much better known war sceptic and Carlylean, D. H. Lawrence, and MacColl's heavily qualified endorsement of socialism at the end of the "Preface" (it "may be a doubtful experiment, especially in a country that adores wastefulness") [23] recalls Lawrence's similar and persistent vacillation. But there is equally little truck with modern capitalism or imperialism. "Bull: A Transposition", a comic poem of 528 lines, is so named because it transposes the story of Job to that of modern England, "a Trader in the West/Whose name familiarly was Bull", and envisages the war as Bull's trial by his maker. Here, for instance, is Bull's dawning perception that the productivity of the German is outstripping his own:

[21] MacColl, p. xi.
[22] MacColl, pp. xiii-xiv.
[23] MacColl, p. xix.

Bull stirred uneasily to see
His careless old commercial line
Grow to a monster shape, while he
Lagged, a reluctant Frankenstein;
The tune of *Deutschland über Alles*
Was not that of the Crystal Palace.
Nevertheless, his diplomats
And leading journals never ceased
With mild propitiating pats
And offerings to approach the Beast,
Trusting the formidable alien
Was kindly hearted, if Hegelian.

Clumsy as MacColl's metre and diction can be, this poem shows him at his most sustained, witty and erudite. The tone occasionally approaches the ironic poise better known to us from George Dangerfield's later, if more consistently brilliant comic history, *The Strange Death of Liberal England* (1936).

Where Scotland features in MacColl, it is in his more clichéd verse. "France's Day" is a piece of "Auld Alliance" sentiment and "What We Are Fighting For" a curious exercise in allied propaganda, in which each nation is given one or two stanzas (though England gets three and Scotland four) to state its war aims. The "England" section presents contrary voices from "The Country" and "The Town", and "Scotland" is similarly divided:

Lowlanders
To thriftless England we have lent,
The frugal life, the fervent mind,
And where the wanderers of us went
A mighty realm of human kind
Keeps guard upon the seven seas,
And orders the Antipodes.

Us too the fog has sore beset
The din of wheels, the reek, the mud,
But not commuted in us yet
The thrillings of the battle-blood;

From close and wynd, from cot and manse,
Old wayfarers, we turn to France.

Highlanders
To fight for loyalty outworn,
For leaders fallen, for cause betrayed,
The battle lost, the hope forlorn,
This, from of old, was all our trade;
And scanty is the remnant here
Among the pastures of the deer.
Yet from the corrie and the glen
Where lingers any fighting clan
Sutherland, Gordon, Seaforth men,
Black Watch, we muster to a man.
Charge Cluny, Murray, with the steel;
On Fraser, Appin and Lochiel!

It is easy to dismiss this slice of Caledonian kitsch and fail to note its symptomatic deflatedness: "what we are fighting for" is, in this light, precious little, as the urban working class in the "England" section has already declared ("we would give nothing: we gave all"). All that prevents the giving of nothing is "a face forgot", some residual, almost dissolved, primordial national affinity, but not one based upon any recoverable material reality. While he has none of Yeats's formal grace, MacColl succeeds in expressing a related sense of futility, even in participation.

By contrast with the systematic neglect of MacColl is the routine celebration of Charles Hamilton Sorley. Another victim of Loos, Sorley is the one Scottish trench poet regularly memorialised, but his nationality is usually seen to be of questionable relevance to his contribution. Jon Silkin understandably (perhaps) does not even mention it,[24] and Ian Parsons laconically and misleadingly remarks only that Sorley "was of Scottish descent on both sides".[25] Actually, Sorley was born in 1895 to William Ritchie Sorley, then Professor of Moral Philosophy at Aberdeen University,

[24] Jon Silkin, *Out of Battle: the Poetry of the Great War* (Oxford: Oxford University Press, 1972), p. 74.
[25] I. M. Parsons, "Biographical Notes", *Men Who March Away: Poems of the First World War*, ed. I. M. Parsons (London: Chatto and Windus, 1965), p. 74.

but the family moved to Cambridge in 1900, and he had a conventional English public school education. Had the war not occurred he would have studied at University College, Oxford, at which he had won a place in 1913. When the war broke out he was attending the University of Jena before taking up his Oxford studentship, which gave him a somewhat unique perspective on the Anglo-German conflict, one which, in the sonnet "To Germany", could envisage future reconciliation even in the earliest days of the struggle.[26] The poet addresses his German counterparts thus in the sestet:

When it is peace, then we may view again
With new-won eyes each other's truer form
And wonder. Grown more loving-kind and warm
We'll grasp firm hands and laugh at the old pain,
When it is peace. But until peace, the storm,
The darkness and the thunder and the rain.

High praise has been attached to this poem. One critic feels that it

[...] demonstrates an understanding of the historical significance of the crisis which was unique among the younger war poets. Although most Britons saw the war superficially in terms of the popular catchwords and patriotic slogans, Sorley valued his experiences in Germany and tried to account for the human failures that lay behind the folly of nationalistic rivalry. [...] Thus Sorley could measure the depths of a tragedy which Brooke and Grenfell ignored and which his elders – the Kiplings, the Newbolts, and the Watsons – interpreted only in external terms of outraged national honour and retributive confrontation.[27]

[26] Even this feeling, among the rank-and-file soldiery, may have been more the rule than the exception. In the early days of the war there was a great deal of fellow feeling across enemy lines, culminating in open mass fraternisations in No Man's Land in and around Christmas Day, 1914. As the war became more bitter such demonstrations of fellowship were not to be repeated. See Modris Eksteins, *Rites of Spring: The Great War and the Birth of the Modern Age* (London: Black Swan, 1990), pp. 159-87.

[27] John H. Johnston, *English Poetry of the First World War: A Study in the Evolution of Lyric and Narrative Form* (Princeton: Princeton University Press, 1964), pp. 62-3.

Does "To Germany" deserve this singular tribute? In it, the hostilities are diagnosed as stemming from a lack of vision, a failure to see the essential human kinship of soldiers on both sides. But it is the specific status of this figurative blindness which the poem neglects to interrogate. Is it an inflicted disability, an ideological product of an implicitly criticised social and economic system, or a freak consequence of a somehow "natural" human condition? One might ask the same of the "storm" metaphor which describes the conflict itself. Is this to be accepted with the resignation we might adopt in the face of meteorological inclemency, or does it signify a deliberate and thus challengeable political policy of *Sturm und Drang* on both sides? "To Germany" cannot solve these perplexities because it finds itself trapped within the ignorance enunciated in its octave:

> But gropers both through fields of thought confined
> We stumble and we do not understand.

This is an acknowledgment of limitation, a confession within the poem that there are matters about which it must remain inarticulate, questions it can raise but cannot answer, things beyond its ken.

A better known sonnet of Sorley's, "When you see millions of the mouthless dead", suffers from similar constraints:

> When you see millions of the mouthless dead
> Across your dreams in pale battalions go,
> Say not soft things as other men have said,
> That you'll remember. For you need not so.
> Give them not praise. For, deaf, how should they know
> It is not curses heaped on each gashed head?
> Nor tears. Their blind eyes see not your tears flow.
> Nor honour. It is easy to be dead.
> Say only this, "They are dead." Then add thereto,
> "Yet many a better one has died before."
> Then, scanning all the o'ercrowded mass, should you
> Perceive one face that you loved heretofore,
> It is a spook. None wears the face you knew.
> Great death has made all his for evermore.

This has been admired for its lack of triumphalism, its refusal to aggrandise death as heroism. But the main difficulty is in the restricted range of options the poem offers to its addressee(s). Although they are not specified, it is conceivably the relatives of dead combatants and/or their surviving comrades who are being apostrophised. But the proscriptions and prescriptions uttered by the speaker are, significantly, directed only towards coping with individual grief or managing the emotional horror of genocide. They do not encourage the exertion of political pressure which might prevent either. The anacoluthic awkwardness of "It is a spook" betrays the poem's evasiveness. The conditional clause which precedes it raises expectations of an active verb at the beginning of the penultimate line. But it is never the poem's (or Sorley's) mission to incite action or resistance. Sorley was only twenty when he died, and his verse inevitably suffers from too exacting an analysis, being essentially juvenilia. Its most notable feature has always been the boundaries it observed rather than those it crossed.

Charles Murray, the one Scottish poet of 1914-18 who was able occasionally to sustain a memorable complexity of both language and thought, was by comparison an elder of the Scottish literary establishment. He turned fifty in the month after the war broke out, and had already achieved celebrity in his native north east with the publication of the collection *Hamewith* (1900). Although born in Alford, Aberdeenshire, from the ages of twenty-four to sixty he worked in South Africa as a mining engineer, serving in the South African Defence Corps throughout the war. Accusations of exilic nostalgia and sentiment would not be entirely inappropriate to much of Murray's output, and *A Sough O' War*, a short and variable collection of fifteen items, has certainly many obvious signs of war gung-ho-ism which detract from its technical accomplishment and the liveliness of its dense Scots vocabulary. In the title poem, in "Wha Bares a Blade For Scotland?", "To the Hin'most Man", and "Bundle an' Go", Scotland's modern backwater status in martial and imperial accomplishment is registered and regretted. These poems talk up the war as an opportunity for national pride, which they see as an index of a *machismo* which can now not only be declared but demonstrated ("Gie's but the weapons, we've the will,/Ayont the main, to prove again/Auld Scotland counts for something still" ["A Sough O' War"]). "The Thraws O' Fate" is spoken by a farmer appalled that the accidents of birth dates make himself too old and his son too young to prove their manhood in combat:

I gang nae mair to markets, o' kirk I've tint the gait,
    At smiddy an' at mill I hear the cry
For men, an' here I hing my heid an' ban the thraws o' fate,
    That I was born sae early an' Donal cam' sae late.

This is revealing about Scottish masculinity, but it is more concerned to naturalise than to investigate it. Yet the most intriguing feature of most of Murray's war verse – its depiction of Scotland as a depressed region, both psychically and economically – is present even where it purveys this cranky and perverse military enthusiasm. Murray is not engaged in writing Scots calques of the "Arcady long time" strains of some English war poeticising.

Indeed, the ignorance or disregard of Murray's two finest performances by anthologists of war poetry are little short of scandalous. "Dockens Afore His Peers" and "Fae France" exhibit both a searing vernacular energy and a sustained satirical vigour, by comparison with which Owen can appear stilted and Sassoon tame. Dockens is an affluent and influential farmer attending an exemption tribunal, whose verbally tremendous and wholly self-interested dramatic monologue succeeds – by contrived warmth, then insinuation, followed by minor grumbling, punctuated by appeals to reason and scornful dismissals of patriotic duty, and finally supplemented by indirect financial threats upon his listeners – in winning total exemption from combat for his son. Brief quotation does it little justice, for the poem essentially needs to be read as a whole: its power lies in its flow, the cumulative force with which Dockens "ups the ante" until the issue becomes one of naked material interests. The poem does not deviate from the popular commitment to the war which it is always Murray's mission to incite, but its political power is not dissolved on this account. Rather, the poem's extreme scepticism about the subterfuges of capital explodes the Pelion of idealist trumpetings which made up a great deal of war discourse to expose the Ossa of its material foundations. Dockens' own monologue is a progressively less diplomatic series of argumentative postures which, when they produce no result, culminate in an appropriately hostile set of ultimata to each individual member of the board:

Hoot, Mains, hae mind, I'm doon for you some sma' thing wi' the bank;
Aul' Larickleys, I saw you throu', an' this is a' my thank.
An' Gutteryloan, that time ye broke, to Dockenhill ye cam' –
"Total exemption." Thank ye, sirs. Fat say ye till a dram?

He is offering to declare war unless they "buy" his peace; and when they do, ironically, the bargain is sealed with a patriotic token.

The speaker of "Fae France" possesses comparable colloquial volubility, but comes from a rural underclass. Writing with great cheer from a hospital bed after being wounded, "wi' nocht to dae but fite the idle pin", he recalls an incident of three years before which resulted in the local sheriff imposing a fine that was "byous hard on me,/For fat wi' lawyers, drinks, an' fine, it took a sax months' fee". He kept his head financially above water, he admits, by very prodigal poaching. The sheriff's son, it transpires, is an officer in the regiment in which he has enlisted, and after being injured on an evening sortie is courageously carried back to base by the poacher. The son is not portrayed as lacking in bravery; indeed, the poacher and his comrades admire his soldierly industriousness and his ability to communicate with them in their own local tongue. But what we are asked to savour is the rich irony that the same strength, intelligence and resourcefulness which make a man a criminal can also make him another's saviour. This is not lost on the poacher when he receives a letter of gratitude from the sheriff's wife:

His mither sent a letter till's, a great lang blottit screed.
It wasna easy makin't oot, her vreetin's coorse to read;
She speir't could she dae ocht for me, sae I sent back a line –
"Jist bid yer man, fan neist I'm up, ca' canny wi' the fine."

There is a certain witty inevitability about that: it could close the poem. But in fact there is much more to "Fae France": the tale of the sheriff and the poacher is the central section of the poem, but it is framed by an introductory section in which the poacher explains his decision to enlist, and a lengthy conclusion in which he recounts how he was injured and describes recurring dreams he has of being back in Scotland. As a recognisably pastoral indulgence, this close need not concern us greatly, except insofar as it contrasts starkly with the economic hardship he has really known, and which the opening section of the poem details. He has enlisted, and intends to remain so after the war, we discover, because life in the ranks, with all its grim labour and riskiness, is materially more secure than anything home has to offer:

I ken that I cam' here awa' some aucht days aifter Yeel,
An' never toon nor fee afore has shootit me sae weel;

They gie me maet, an' beets an' claes, wi' fyles an antrin dram –
Come term-time lat them flit 'at likes, *I'm* bidin' faur I am.

This is a renunciation of Scotland, or at least of the bitter rewards offered to its populace in return for its incorporation into the Empire, that is quite unique in the otherwise romantic pro-combat verse of the first world war. No doubt the feeling issues partly from Murray's own condition of exile. It is also, it should be noted, momentary. Towards the end of "Fae France" Murray tries to recoup the sense of individual submergence in nationhood which these lines forgo, but, significantly, he is unable to tie such yearnings neatly together into one of the eloquent but anodyne patriotic formulae which litter his verse. Rather, he exploits the epistolary nature of the poem simply to allow it to break off, to silence itself ("but, wheesht!") and subdue the political discontent to which recognition of the reality of life in modern Scotland would inevitably lead. As a whole, the poem is about finding the resources to go on living in a state of casualty, physical on one level, social on another. In so doing it is as repressive as it is expressive.

What can we conclude from the general political complicity of Scottish poetry with the aims and values of the official discourses of 1914-18? We can confidently repeat Edgell Rickword's observations about English poetry of the same period, while perhaps now being able to explain our initial surprise at the fact of their applying also to Scotland. The "Scottish Renaissance" of the 1920s and 1930s offers a contrast which is only partly accounted for if we offer a merely formalistic explanation of it. It is absolutely clear that the "re-birth" was not of verse in Scots: there had been plenty of that in the years before and during the war. Buchan was as scornful of kailyardism as MacDiarmid was to be. The basic problem for Scottish poets before MacDiarmid was, to be sure, the enslavement of some to English literary models, but of more to English literary temperament, particularly their acquiescence in Empire and bourgeois consciousness. Only when the post-war welding together of socialism and nationalism occurred were there sufficiently tensile pre-conditions for the forging of a distinctly Scottish poetic identity. This is to say, poetic revolutions are seldom solely formal in origin: the pressure for aesthetic renewal is also often an ideological one.

1994

146

POLITICS AND THE SCOTTISH LANGUAGE

> The dooble tongue has spoken and been heard.
> — Hugh MacDiarmid[1]

In this essay I examine the relationship between Scottish and English cultural identity. My main area of concern is the presence of this relationship in Scottish literary writing of the twentieth century, although I begin by indicating something of the pre-history of the tensions inherent in the relationship in this period, before proceeding to investigate how the presence of a larger and more powerful neighbouring nation has influenced the work of particular Scottish writers. Readers unfamiliar with Scottish/English cultural debates may find it helpful to consider the relation between Canada and the United States as somewhat analogous. The analogy is far from perfect as far as politics goes (Scotland and England share political institutions and much else and, though separate countries, co-exist within a single state conglomerate, the United Kingdom), but useful in terms of the comparable population imbalances and corresponding differences in cultural influence and power.

I

In the Scottish popular imagination, William Laughton Lorimer's Scots translation of the New Testament has rapidly passed into mythology as the one in which the Devil speaks in English. The misconception has no doubt thrived on account of the approval such an idea excites, adding as it does a welcome biblical dimension to the demonisation of the English in which many Scots exult. Those who go so far as to flick through the

---

[1] Hugh MacDiarmid, "To Circumjack Cencrastus", *The Complete Poems of Hugh MacDiarmid*, ed. Michael Grieve and W. R. Aitken (Harmondsworth: Penguin, 1985), vol. 1, p. 182.

posthumously published translation will search in vain, however, if they seek the distinguished classicist's Sassenachal Satan. There is an appendix, ostensibly reproducing one of Lorimer's draft translations of Matthew 4.1-11, which reads as follows:

> Syne Jesus wis led awà bi the Spírit tae the muirs for tae be tempit bi the Deil.
> Whan he hed taen nae mait for fortie days an fortie nichts an wis fell hungrisome, the Temper cam til him an said, "If you are the Son of God, tell these stones to turn into loaves."
> Jesus answert, "It says i the Buik:

> > *Man sanna líve on breid alane*
> > *but on ilka wurd at comes*
> > *furth o God's mouth."*

> Neist the Deil tuik him awà til the Halie Citie an set him on a ledgit o the Temple an said til him, "If you are the Son of God, throw yourself down to the ground. For it says in the Bible:

> > *He shall give his angels charge concerning thee,*
> > *and in their hands they shall bear thee up,*
> > *lest at any time thou dash thy foot against a stone.*

> Jesus answert, "Ithergates it says i the Buik: '*Thou sanna pit the Lord thy God tae the pruif*'."
> Aince mair the Deil tuik him awà, this time til an unco heich muntain, whaur he shawed him aa the kingdoms o the warld an their glorie an said til him, "All this I will give you, if you will only go down on your knees and worship me."
> Than Jesus said til him, "Awà wi ye, Sautan! It says I the Buik:

> > *Thou sal wurship the Lord thy God*
> > *an him sal thou sair alane."*

> At that the Deil loot him abee, an immedentlie angels cam an fettelt for him.[2]

---

[2] William Laughton Lorimer, *The New Testament in Scots*, ed. R. L. C. Lorimer (Harmondsworth: Penguin, 1985), p. 455 ("Appendix II: *Interpretatio*

This is not, in fact, what Lorimer senior wrote, because Lorimer junior has editorially modified him. A footnote from the latter tells us that "my father spells the Deil's English like Scots mispronounced, and the Deil provides his own English translation of the passage he quotes from Ps. 91. My father's Scots phonetics merely labour the point. In the transcript here printed, I have accordingly substituted conventional English spelling; and by quoting from the Authorised Version the Deil reminds us how much influence it has exerted in Scotland during the last three hundred and fifty years."[3] Elsewhere Lorimer junior confides that his father claimed to have destroyed all extant copies of his apocryphal rendering of the Temptation "since it had never been intended for publication", but that one had been discovered by chance after his death. "Once having plucked this brand out of the fire, I could not finally bring myself to suppress so characteristic an example of his wit; and I have accordingly printed an edited transcript of it." [4]

This prodigal son's failure to resist temptation (a compound dereliction: he can neither suppress the draft or deny himself the pleasure of "improving" it) is a parable in itself, ripe with instructive irony. The obvious objection is that Lorimer *père* had the fidelity of his translation in mind, a priority which properly led him, in the final draft, to have the Devil and Jesus speak in the same tongue, and positively to exclude his own intermediate *jeu d'esprit*.[5] But this is a mere fundamentalist observation. Altogether more interesting is the fact that Lorimer *fils*, who knows he has apprehended his father's "wit", seems not to credit its subtlety. Is it not meet that the fallen Lucifer, speaking in "Scots mispronounced", should sound like an anglicised Scot or an Englishman dissembling Scottishness; that he who was one of us, or would pretend to be one of us, should have his whited sepulchre status betrayed either way by his faulty phonetics? [6] Instead, the man who spent a decade

apocrypha"). Lorimer's idiosyncratic use of diacritical marks to indicate pronunciation is explained by his son in "Appendix IV: Spelling and pronunciation", pp. 465-9.
[3] Lorimer, p. 455. If the Devil is quoting from the Authorised Version (Psalms 91: 11-12) he is doing so inaccurately.
[4] Lorimer, p. xxi.
[5] Cf. Lorimer, pp. 6-7.
[6] Notwithstanding that the celestial pre-history of Satan and his identification

painstakingly translating the New Testament into Scots has his own laborious Scots phonetics "substituted" by "conventional English spelling"! It would be rather hard to argue the case that the end – a satirical stab at the English and their oppressively controlling language – is justified by the "improving" means. The "correction" of Scots, after all, has forever been a mainstay of that apparently oppressive control.

When it comes to textual authority, the younger Lorimer's version is certainly bankrupt, and its claim to enhance the original's implicit intent is demonstrably ill-conceived. Nonetheless, when these issues are put aside – that is, should we choose to pretend that they do not matter – the draft as published can be seen as a spiritually resonant allegory of the dilemma posed for generations of Scots by the greater economic power of England. After the Reformation, the newly Calvinist Scotland's "auld alliance" with Catholic France deteriorated: "Scotland opted for the most drastic religious innovation possible, along with an agreement with England which would safeguard it."[7] Henceforth, Scotland was offered access to English and other foreign markets at the price of largely dancing to England's political and cultural tune. In other words, shown the kingdoms of the world, the Scottish Jesus got down on his knees and worshipped the English Devil. One of the largest concessions made was linguistic, a fact accounted for by three things: the failure of the Scottish Reformers to produce a Scots bible;[8] the resurgence of English literature in the reign of Elizabeth; and the Union of the Crowns in 1603. The last is probably the moment at which English linguistic ascendancy becomes irreversible. King James moved his court from Edinburgh to London. His *Counterblast to Tobacco* (1604) made it clear that his own preference for Scots in writing was now at an end, and the Scottish *literati* took note and

with Lucifer (i.e. Venus, the morning star: see Isaiah 14: 4-12) is, of course, apocryphal too (a tradition which begins with that other great biblical translator, St Jerome, and reaches its apogee in Book X of Milton's *Paradise Lost*).

[7] Christopher Harvie, *Scotland and Nationalism: Scottish Society and Politics, 1707-1977* (London: Allen and Unwin, 1977), p. 27.

[8] The long-standing charge that the Reformers were actively anglicising influences, particularly in the person of their leader, John Knox, has been persuasively rebutted by R. J. Lyall, "Vernacular Prose before the Reformation", *The History of Scottish Literature, Volume 1: Origins to 1660 (Medieval and Renaissance)*, ed. R. D. S. Jack (Aberdeen: Aberdeen University Press, 1988), pp. 163-81.

followed suit. Most decisively of all, in 1607 James gave instructions for the preparation of a new English bible. So many aftercomers have been eclipsed by the 1611 Authorised Version that the Scots, to this day, have managed to produce no fuller a rival than Lorimer's. The Scots-speaking Christ's nay-saying to the English Satan (of Lorimer junior's version) can thus be read as the rejection which, historically, Scotland failed to deliver to England. Lorimer senior's entire *New Testament in Scots* is, correspondingly, the monumental embodiment of a hope that it may not be too late (in matters of language at least) for the Scots to reverse that historic neglect and the consequent loss of cultural autonomy.

Living monument or sterile folly? The key parable is surely that of the seed scattered on barren or fertile ground. A New Testament in Scots produced in 1583 might have made a profound historical impact. The one which appeared in 1983, albeit to moderate celebration, has not and will not.

II

I now offer the first of several quotations of which the attempt to reproduce a Scottish vernacular version of contemporary English is the most immediately noticeable feature:

> But even that was wrong cause he couldnay sit about waiting I mean if he was fucking waiting what was he waiting for, it was here right now man know what I'm saying, if ye wait, it's got to be for something. Naybody waits to get surrounded. He wasnay gony wait for that christ almighty if ye knew ye're gony get captured then ye get to fuck, ye get fucking out man know what I mean ye get to fuck, ye dont fucking wait; that's the last thing. Ye get to fuck. Cause nothing went back to normal. There was nay fucking normal, whatever the fuck it meant, normal, stupit fucking word. Whatever the past was it was ower and done with. There wasnay gony be nay fucking big cuddles, nay kiss-and-make-up scenes; that was out the window, as far as that went, it was all washed up. So okay. So it was now. So he needed dough. He had to get squared up. And he didnay have the time to wait. That other wee bit of business, he could maybe push it through; he just needed a start, if he could punt the shirts; a knock-down price, it didnay matter,

just something, he just needed something. Once he got that. But even without it.[9]

The passage is chosen, on account of its linguistic representativeness rather than its exceptionality, from the Scottish novel of recent years which has attracted more popular attention than almost any other. The narrative situation – a blind Glasgow down-and-out is attempting to convince himself that his run of bad luck might be reversible – is not particularly important. Nor need we concern ourselves too much with the technique: no one familiar with the stream-of-consciousness mannerisms to be found in most national variants of literary modernism will be perplexed by Kelman's fusion of first and third person perspectives. But those habituated to reading prose fiction in Standard English, or unfamiliar with the *patois* of the Glasgow working-class male which he seems to be transliterating, are likely to experience a considerable sense of estrangement in the presence of Kelman's style.

These readers usually have to work hard to decode (or, if one feels the process requires a stronger verb, translate) Kelman's vernacular into the linguistic norms with which they are familiar. Understandably, they often fail to ask (because they mostly cannot hope to know the answer) if Kelman's attempt to reproduce the *patois* is accurate, contestable or misleading. Indeed, by default, they invariably assume accuracy. It is possibly his placement in such a cultural and linguistic position that leads one (German) reader to commend Kelman's "uncompromising critique of the convention in English fiction of draping the 'third-party voice' in a neutral guise, whereas in most cases it colludes through its adoption of Standard English with that sociolect's élitist value system". His unverified conclusion is that Kelman's style is systematically subversive of such "average fiction".[10]

---

[9] James Kelman, *How Late It Was, How Late* (London: Secker and Warburg, 1994), p. 273. A dialect glossary may help here: "couldnay" = "couldn't"; "ye" = "you"; "naybody" = "nobody"; "wasnay" = "wasn't"; "gony" = "going to"; "didnay" = "didn't"; "stupit" = "stupid"; "ower" = "over"; "punt" = "sell". Incidentally, this passage demonstrates what I understand to be a unique feature of Glasgow English: is there anywhere else in the anglophone world in which "fuck" is a place to which one may be commanded to go?

[10] H. Gustav Klaus, "Kelman for Beginners", *Les Cahiers de la Nouvelle* 22

Such a conclusion is certainly the one which would be drawn by any reader prepared to trust Kelman himself, speaking here in promotion of his own work:

How do you recognise a Glaswegian in English literature? He – bearing in mind that in English Literature you don't get female Glaswegians, not even the women (*sic*) – he's the cut-out figure who wields a razor blade, gets moroculous drunk and never has a single solitary (*sic*) "thought" in his entire life. He beats his wife and beats his kids and beats his next door neighbour. And another striking thing: everybody from a Glaswegian or working-class background, everybody in fact from any regional part of Britain – none of them knew (*sic*) how to talk. What larks! Every time they opened their mouth (*sic*) out came a stream of gobbledygook. Beautiful! Their language a cross between semaphore and morse code; apostrophes here and apostrophes there; a strange hotchpotch of bad phonetics and horrendous spelling – unlike the nice stalwart upperclass (*sic*) English hero (occasionally Scottish but with no linguistic variation) whose words on the page were always absolutely splendidly proper and pure and pristinely accurate, whether in dialogue or without. And what grammar! Colons and semi-colons. Straight out of their mouths. An incredible mastery of language. Most interesting of all, for myself as a writer, the narrative belonged to them and them alone. They owned it. The place where thought and spiritual life exists. Nobody outwith the parameters of their socio-cultural setting had a spiritual life. We all stumbled along in a series of behaviouristic activity (*sic*); automatons, cardboard cut-outs, folk who could be scrutinised, whose existence could be verified in a sociological or anthropological context. In other words, in the society that is (*sic*) English Literature, some 80 to 85 percent of the population simply did not (*sic*) exist as human beings.[11]

As an implied manifesto this makes an adequate show of being "uncompromising", even going so far as liberally to commit to paper a

(Summer 1994), p. 135.
[11] James Kelman, "The Importance of Glasgow in My Work", *Some Recent Attacks: Essays Cultural and Political* (Stirling: AK Press, 1992), p. 82.

fistful of elementary grammatical errors to shake defiantly at the linguistic standardisers it attacks. The paradox which has consequently to be explained is that a reader of Kelman's work who is intimately familiar with the *patois* of the Glaswegian working class – and the present writer can claim the distinction of having thrived from the ages of three to fifteen in a public housing district which a character in one Kelman novel knowledgeably calls "an awful place to live"[12] – is highly unlikely to find his rendering of it "uncompromising". Indeed, the reaction of this very particularly positioned reader to Kelman's handling of Glasgow speech is virtually the reverse of those I have been describing. For me, reading Kelman is rather akin to looking in a mirror which, although it sends back an image of oneself which is recognisable, does so with a flatteringly soft focus. I am aware that this is so remote from all standard comment on Kelman that it may appear outrageous. The obligatory analysis therefore follows.

If we were to ask how well the passage quoted from Kelman's *How Late It Was, How Late* actually captures the *patois* under discussion, in terms of the dialectal and accentual accuracy of its transliteration, it would be difficult to arrive at an answer which honours Kelman's ear. Admittedly there are felicitous congruences between demotic Glasgow speech and Kelman's version of it. *Couldnay, ye, nay,* and *stupit* are all acceptable attempts to render the appropriate Glaswegian pro-nunciation, respectively, of *couldn't, you, no* and *stupid*. Similarly, the passage incorporates a number of recognisably local dialect terms: *cause (because); gony (going to); to get squared up (to get even* or *to get tidied up); wee (little);* and *punt (sell, get rid of)*. One's reservations about Kelman's abilities in this regard, however, rest on many more examples, and can be distilled into three categories.

Firstly, there is an overall lack of consistency of treatment. Why is the contraction *dont* printed without the apostrophe to mark the point of elision it would have in Standard English *(don't)* while *it's* appears throughout in its Standard form? Why are *got to* and *get to* printed in their standard forms (Glaswegian dialect: *goty* or *go tay* and *getty* or *get tay*) while *going to* is rendered in dialect *(gony)*? Secondly, why are some accentual features, which one would expect to see indicated by non-

---

[12] James Kelman, *A Disaffection* (London: Secker and Warburg, 1989), p. 315.

standard forms, consistently standardised? The most pervasive example of this practice is in Kelman's treatment of the verb ending -ing, represented in the International Phonetic Alphabet as [ɪŋ], which one would have expected him to transliterate regularly as -in [ɪn]. One would have anticipated that the personal pronoun I [aɪ] would have been rendered as A or Ah [ə], but it appears throughout as it would in transliterated Received Pronunciation (i.e. the most prestigious non-regional accent spoken in England, often referred to as "BBC English", actually spoken by only 7% of English people). Wis [wɪz] would be a more defensible rendition than was [wɒz], oot [uːt] more likely than out [aʊt], wi [wɪ] more satisfactory than with [wɪθ], windy [wɪndɪ] more probable than window [wɪndəʊ], and noo [nuː] more appropriate than now [naʊ]. Thirdly, the orthography of a number of Kelman's forms, although deviant with respect to Standard English, arguably fails to convey the requisite pronunciation: examples are naybody (I would argue for naybiddy), wasnay (wisnay), and ower (oor). In short, the evidence from this representative passage is that, far from representing demotic Glasgow speech consistently, in mainly non-standard forms, and with due regard for the potential of deviant orthography accurately to indicate local pronunciation, Kelman is often demonstrably doing the opposite. He actually renders cognate forms so differently that his procedure at times appears random; he uses considerably more standard than non-standard forms; and many of the non-standard forms he adopts are open to question. Indeed, we might be giving Kelman's handling of the vernacular its due if we were to call it ersatz Glaswegian.

Kelman has occasionally attempted a more dedicatedly phonetic approach, in short texts such as "The Hon" and "Nice to Be Nice". But these are early experiments. The first appeared in an amateurishly produced, limited edition pamphlet, the second in a collection issued by a small Scottish publishing house.[13] In Kelman's début with an English publisher,[14] there is nothing so linguistically outré. Nor has there been in the many fictions that have since been published from London on his behalf. Kelman's later, more conservative transliteration is not to be

---

[13] To be found, respectively, in Short Tales from the Night Shift (Glasgow: Print Studio Press, 1978) and Not Not While the Giro (Edinburgh: Polygon, 1983).

[14] James Kelman, Agnes Owens and Alasdair Gray, Lean Tales (London: Jonathan Cape, 1985).

scorned on the assumption, then, that he is technically incapable. On the contrary, it is a carefully modified version of the *patois*, one that renders it acceptable to the reader attuned to the forms of Standard English without abandoning the defamiliarising effects (for such a reader) of occasional deviations from those forms.

To the reader conversant with the *patois*, on the other hand, Kelman's fictional discourse is one which conspicuously signals its repression of that marginalised vernacular in the very limited and inadequate ways in which it attempts to preserve it within a predominantly standardised range – in its relatively *easy translatability*, one might say. Repression without abandonment is, as I have said, a common syndrome of the culturally marginalised, and, once placed under scrutiny, Kelman's writing certainly appears to abrogate – more than it advocates – Scottish language. It is trapped in such a contradictory double movement by its desire to maintain the international audience (which reads texts predominantly in Standard English) it originally won – and this is the paradox – by its appeal to that audience's hegemonic patronage of the seemingly culturally aberrant. By what other means could his work have fared so well at the hands of London reviewers, or performed so creditably in the best known annual competition of the English literary establishment, the Booker Prize for Fiction?[15]

Nor is Kelman the only example. The one Scottish novel of recent years which can claim to have reached an even larger international audience than anything by Kelman – Irvine Welsh's *Trainspotting* – offers a similar patchwork, in which an apparently self-sufficient vernacular voice necessarily yields to the insistent code-switching demands made by the standard: "He wis takin nae mair notice though. Ah stoaped harassing him, knowing thit ah wis jist waistin ma energy. His silent suffering through withdrawal now seemed so intense that thir wis nae wey that ah could add, even incrementally, tae his misery."[16] Note in

---

[15] *A Disaffection* reached the final Booker shortlist; *How Late It Was, How Late* won the prize and was engulfed by media comment, most of it preoccupied with the novel's repetitive use of taboo (rather than Scottish) language.

[16] Irvine Welsh, *Trainspotting* (London: Secker and Warburg, 1993), p. 6. "Wis" = "was"; "takin" = "taking"; "nae" = "no"; "mair" = "more"; "Ah" = "I"; "stoaped" = "stopped"; "thit" = "that"; "jist" = "just"; "waistin" = "wasting"; "ma" = "my"; "thir" = "there; "wey" = "way"; "tae" = "to".

particular the concession made to the written standard here by the placement of the adverbial phrase (which would have appeared at the end of the sentence were the intention to transliterate spoken language), and how the narrator's -*in* endings are freely interchangeable with -*ing*.

I perhaps need to make it explicit that these remarks on Kelman and Welsh do not constitute, and are not intended to support, a prescriptivist critique of their failure to achieve a pure mimesis of spoken language in their writing. Not only are they under no obligation to do so, but the very notion that there are scriptural conventions which could secure such an unmediated mimesis is, I think, already widely repudiated (as is the related idea that speech is "authentic" language while writing is merely "representational"). My purpose, on the contrary, is merely to discredit, by means of relatively rudimentary descriptivist remarks, any supposition that readers of Kelman or Welsh may have (observation having led me to believe that such readers are legion) that their styles *are* straightforwardly mimetic of the demotic speech, respectively, of Glasgow and Edinburgh. One can certainly identify linguistic elements which make it clear that the contrivance of mimetic effects is being essayed; but the attempt is demonstrably less thoroughgoing than many readers are aware, and the accuracy of the mimesis considerably more debatable than they imagine.

Indeed, as I have already suggested, these writers can just as easily be said to be *repressing* demotic speech. The degree to which they do so can be suggested by citation of a contrary example, whose semantic content, conveniently, expresses an intransigent attitude to the dilemmas of translatability and cross-cultural understanding I have set out to explore. The author is a Glasgow poet, Tom Leonard. His poem (quoted in full) declares a refusal to apologise for the linguistic localism, not only of itself, but of most of the author's other phonetic texts, which are equally inaccessible to ears (and eyes) attuned to Standard English:

GOOD STYLE

helluva hard tay read theez init
stull
if ye canny unnirston thim jiss clear aff then
gawn

get tay fuck ootma road
ahmaz goodiz thi lota yiz so ah um
ah no whit ahm dayn
tellnyi
jiss try enny a yir fly patir wi me
stick thi bootnyi good style
so ah wull[17]

This text, at once demotically ordinary yet poetically extraordinary, ostensibly addresses those readers who are so linguistically positioned that they cannot understand it: in an idiom which they will not recognise, it explains its refusal to embody its content in an idiom which they might

[17] The last of Leonard's *Six Glasgow Poems* (Glasgow: Other People, 1969); reprinted in Tom Leonard, *Intimate Voices 1965-1983* (Newcastle upon Tyne: Galloping Dog Press, 1984), p. 14. To apologise for "translating" into Standard English a poem which refuses to apologise for its own untranslatability would be to expose myself to the accusation that I lack a sense of irony. I therefore offer, wholly without apology, the following (inexpressibly inadequate) standardised version of Leonard's poem, as devoid of punctuation as its original:

GOOD STYLE

extremely difficult to read these isn't it
still
if you can't understand them just go away
go on
fuck off out of my way

I am as good as all of you I am
I know what I'm doing
I'm telling you
just attempt any of your clever language with me
I'll kick you with considerable effectiveness
indeed I shall

On the other hand, readers who are able to decode the original without considerable effort may rightly demand an apology for a translation which so ineptly travesties it. If so, they prove rather than confute my argument: this poem is really intended for such linguistic *cognoscenti*, but pretends to address itself to *ignoramuses* in the thrall of Standard English.

recognise. The difficulty is compounded by the "non-official" nature of the language in which the poem is written: the beleaguered apparent addressee is unable to resort to the manuals which usually offer assistance in such rebarbative circumstances, for no such help is readily available. But, in fact, the poem is written partly for the spectatorial gratification of those whom it *does not* ostensibly address: its ideal reader is one who, already appreciative of the aurally and visually *recherché* possibilities of its *patois*, responds to the poem's invitation to redouble that appreciation by considering the hopeless plight of the *seemingly* interpellated reader. In other words (as it were), the poem seems to hail a reader who approaches it from a position "outside" the language in which it is written; yet its achievement is to affirm and approve, for a reader with the requisite "inside" knowledge, the exclusionary power of that language. The reader who has to puzzle over what this poem is saying is peremptorily told, in effect, to get out of the poet's way: "get tay fuck ootma road" – literally, "get out of the street where I live" – is an imperative which radically emphasises the text's commitment to localism. The poet meets the prospect of his text being "held up" by/to linguistic standards perceived to be more "proper" than its own ("jiss try enny a yir fly patir wi me") with the threat of a bruising collision. But "stick thi bootnyi good style" (an impeccably Glaswegian proletarian idiom, incidentally) also enacts the poem's ultimate irony: the one immediately recognisable English phrase of the poem, used also as its title, acclaims as a "good style" its wholehearted embrace of a vernacular "bad style", in a total *bouleversement* of the usual power relations between the official language and its marginalised variants. Leonard's text does not repress its linguistic localism in order to prevent speakers bound by the constraints of Standard English from feeling dis-enfranchised (neither does it self-interestedly do so to increase its potential marketability). It operates in precisely the reverse manner. One can hardly imagine a Booker Prize judge, sitting in a bay window in Hampstead one fine Sunday morning, weighing up its merits, even patronisingly. Unlike Kelman and Welsh, Leonard hardly takes care to ensure that his vernacular is so moderately signified that it offers no serious obstacle to a reader linguistically placed "outside" it. On the contrary, in the poem, it is such a reader who is envisaged as constituting the obstacle. Leonard's figurative advice to readers like this is to ignore his work rather than attempt its impossible "translation" into the terms and conditions of the standard. All the evidence suggests that readers unable to understand this advice have nonetheless taken it. Unlike Kelman and Welsh, Leonard has not enjoyed vast international recognition of his achievement. The price of the kind of success which his work seeks is, by definition, this kind of failure.

III

The literature of twentieth-century Scotland has always had to struggle to maintain an identity in the presence of its internationally dominant neighbour. Even when a temperamental resistance to the aesthetic models offered by English literary discourse has asserted itself, the brute fact of English economic ascendancy (most acutely felt, by Scottish writers, in England's virtual monopoly of the publishing industry and consequent control over access to international audiences) means that cultural and linguistic concessions to England and Englishness are perforce the norm rather than the exception. The unaccommodating recalcitrance of Tom Leonard – shared, although usually in less politically provocative fashion, by a very small number of writers (almost exclusively poets) who continue to use Gaelic or Scots or various local dialects as a medium – is an infrequent phenomenon. The position typically adopted – its most conscious and articulate exemplar, in the twentieth century, probably being the poet and translator Edwin Muir[18] – is quasi-abandonment of the very notion that a separate, indigenous literary culture can be sustained in the shadow of England. Although this does not preclude the continued use of Scottish motifs, settings or (at least in reported speech) dialect, Standard English is nonetheless the favoured medium of Scottish writers who subscribe to this view. The third way is to seek a negotiated settlement, with varying degrees of linguistic compromise between idiomatic Scots and Standard English: one sees this heteroglossic negotiation being enacted in Kelman and Welsh, but also, earlier in the century, in a writer like Lewis Grassic Gibbon. My intention

[18] The key text is Edwin Muir, *Scott and Scotland: The Predicament of the Scottish Writer* (London: Routledge, 1936).

in this paper so far has been to suggest that the formal radicalism of such compromises is often exaggerated: their repression of the vernacular is every bit as important as their measured vocalisation of it, and the linguistic freedom which they seem, *prima facie*, to signify, can be viewed, under closer scrutiny, as a quite contained liberation.

However, we can note further that these three broad positions within Scottish literary culture are almost perfectly replicated at the political level. The three alternative governmental scenarios in Scotland throughout the twentieth century have been: (a) complete political separation from England (that is, *nationalism*); (b) acceptance of English political rule (that is, *unionism*); and (c) autonomy from England in some, but by no means all or even most, aspects of political life (that is, *devolutionism*). It goes without saying, perhaps, that a Scottish writer who favours Standard English, for example, is not crudely to be designated a unionist in politics. But the clear popular consensus in Scotland, established in the last twenty-five years, confirmed by a national referendum in 1997 and the subsequent re-establishment of the Scottish Parliament in May 1999, is in favour of a limited devolutionary rather than a nationalist or unionist political future for the country. This is as pleasing to liberal sentiment in England as it is to moderate opinion in Scotland. It is impossible to disassociate this negotiated settlement in the political order from the otherwise inexplicable popularity in Scotland *and* England of writers like Kelman and Welsh who, although concerned at the level of content to depict subcultural or subversive modes of living, do so at the level of form by deploying an *ersatz* vernacular whose relationship to Standard English is calculatedly *devolutionary* in nature.

This picture would, however, be somewhat incomplete if I were to conclude without some consideration of the one twentieth-century Scottish writer – Hugh MacDiarmid – who cannot readily be positioned at any point in the tripartite linguistic spectrum I have defined. The Scottish poet Douglas Dunn, in the most judicious assessment of MacDiarmid's towering yet rickety presence in twentieth century Scottish letters, notes MacDiarmid's aim (expressed in *Lucky Poet* [1943]) to write in "quite untranslatable Scots",[19] by which he meant not a language

[19] Douglas Dunn, "Language and Liberty", *The Faber Book of Twentieth-Century Scottish Poetry*, ed. Douglas Dunn (London: Faber and Faber, 1992), p. xxiii,

which anyone spoke, but a synthesis in which the vernacular was supplemented by elements, past and present, of the various dialects of the Scottish Lowlands. Dunn indicates the profound contradictions to which such an objective gave rise, in particular the irreconcilable attempt both to resurrect a Scottish identity which was perceived as having been overwritten by English culture since the Act of Union of 1707, and simultaneously to emphasise and account for the experience of modernity:

> MacDiarmid went far beyond the customary critical task of trying to create the taste in which a new poetry could be appreciated. He leapt from his own unpredictable inspiration towards the would-be deliverance of a nation-language. His action can be seen as extraordinarily generous; or it can be seen as an attempt to externalize an interior bigotry, a great heave of will, or a charge against history's facts and fences. ... [T]he poet was obliged to remake Scottish poetry on the basis of a pre-1707 mentality. That is, *write as if history had never happened*; or write in such a way that history would be rewritten, and unknitted, in the work. Both, I think, are involved. But the first is a forlorn choice, and the second, to say the least, a challenge. In terms of modernism, though, it can be seen as MacDiarmid's Scottish equivalent of Pound's eccentric scholarship, Eliot's literary erudition, or William Carlos Williams's belief in the American Grain.
>
> The difference is that MacDiarmid was trying to make a nation as well as poetry. He did so with a language that through disuse had become the victim of an inbuilt preterite. Vernacular, Doric, Braid Scots, Scots, Synthetic Scots, Plastic Scots, Aggrandized Scots, or Lallans, were and are (but, by and large, they are all one) instruments with which to cleanse the Scottish psyche of generations of English influence. It was for decades, and remains, a language unexposed to

quoting Hugh MacDiarmid, *Lucky Poet: A Self-Study in Literature and Political Ideas* (London: Methuen, 1943). Dunn points out that *Lucky Poet* post-dates MacDiarmid's vernacular verse of the 'twenties and 'thirties. It should be added that *Lucky Poet* is itself highly emphatic about the desirability of an internationalist outlook in aesthetic matters. MacDiarmid was no narrow nationalist philistine.

actual contact with changing intellectual and domestic life. It is a language with very few, if any, new words. Indeed, it is a language in which old words are used in poetry with the force of neologisms, the shock of the unfamiliar.[20]

The essential point, for my purposes, is that MacDiarmid's vernacular verse is not only untranslatable to the English, but, because dependent on a scholarly philology, also deeply rebarbative to the modern Scots whose sense of national identity it is designed to cultivate. The self-contradiction is evident even in the shortest lyric:

THE WATERGAW

Ae weet forenicht i' the yow-trummle
I saw yon antrin thing,
A watergaw wi' its chitterin' licht
Ayont the on-ding;
An' I thocht o' the last wild look ye gied
Afore ye deed!

There was nae reek i' the laverock's hoose
That nicht – an' nane i' mine
But I hae thocht o' that foolish licht
Ever sin' syne;
An' I think that mebbe at last I ken
What your look meant then.[21]

If the test of a text's marginality is the requirement that its own margins be filled with explanatory glosses, even for the readers to whom

[20] Dunn, "Language and Liberty", pp. xx-xxi.
[21] Hugh MacDiarmid, "The Watergaw", Grieve and Aitken, vol. 1, p. 17. A prose paraphrase might run as follows: "THE INDISTINCT RAINBOW. One wet early evening, in the cold weather after sheep-shearing, I saw that rare thing, an indistinct rainbow, with its shivering light, before the onset of rain; and I thought of the last wild look you gave before you died! There was no smoke in the lark's house that night – and none in mine; but I have thought of that foolish light ever since then; and I think that maybe at last I know what your look meant then."

it could claim to address itself, then this is as marginal as we are likely to get. The comparison with Leonard's "Good Style", whose power derives from playing-off readers who are "inside" against readers who are "outside" the *patois*, is revealing, for there is no reader who is "inside" the language of "The Watergaw". The linguistic beauty of the poem, for *any* reader, derives largely from the alienating, not the familiarising, effect of its vocabulary. There is no Scot for whom "yow-trummle", "antrin", "watergaw" and "on-ding" are all recognisable elements of lexis. Mac-Diarmid's vernacular poems evidently predispose themselves to a Scottish readership; but even to such an audience they give off a tremendously scholastic, and sometimes antiquarian, whiff. MacDiarmid himself repeatedly expressed the appeal to him of "a poetry full of erudition, expertise",[22] but he never properly confronted the dilemma that such verse, in a country with a small and already highly anglicised intelligentsia, was the narrowest of foundations on which to build an indigenous culture with any pretensions to hegemonic status.

This is, in the end, to say that MacDiarmid's project was, politically, utopian. It attempted, in Scottish soil, to nurture together contraries which can be united, precisely, nowhere: modernity and antiquity, nationalism and internationalism, élite and mass and, dare one say it, margin and centre. Its refusal to accept the three-item linguistic menu from which every other Scottish writer of note in this century has chosen (attempted transliteration of a living vernacular, Standard English, or an *ersatz* compromise between the two) is as singular and unusual as the occurrence of utopian thinking within a polity bounded almost exclusively by nationalist, unionist or devolutionary possibilities. It is this which makes MacDiarmid's both an immeasurably more restricted *and* an infinitely more expansive cultural initiative than the other literary enterprises discussed herein.

2001

---

[22] Grieve and Aitken, vol. 2, p. 1019.

I

In 1968 a twenty-five page booklet, printed by Macdonald of Edinburgh for "The Fiery Star Press", priced at six shillings, made an unassuming, and largely unnoticed, appearance on the shelves of certain of the capital's bookshops. At the same time, the privately published work was posted to a number of its author's friends and acquaintances, provoking a sheaf of personally communicated responses which has, thankfully, been preserved. [1] These epistolary reactions ranged from the tersely appreciative to the amicably perplexed, from the morally horrified to the theologically corrective. One of the respondents referred accurately to the text as being full of "savage outbursts of autophobia", and felt that "such a work has a valid existence in publication only when the author has rendered himself interesting for some other reason".

John Herdman's *Descent* is indeed among the oddest of literary *débuts* and, had it not been supplemented by later, more substantial and mature work, its inglorious neglect would be entirely pardonable. [2] Part of the difficulty in understanding *Descent* is that the reading protocols one might bring to bear on it are not self-evident. The text is a monologue in ten sections, some of which take the form of short philosophical disquisitions, while others are the meditations of a distressed and tortured psyche wrestling with itself. Beyond the intimation of certain anecdotal facts in his personal history, we learn little about the outward identity of the nameless narrator. Herdman, who has categorised *Descent* as a "confessional essay", has acknowledged that its voice "is my own,

---

[1] The correspondence can be consulted in the Herdman materials in the manuscripts section of the National Library of Scotland, Edinburgh (hereafter referred to as "Herdman Papers"; see ACC. 11089/5/vii).

[2] Herdman's most accomplished works to date are the novella *Imelda*, in *Imelda and Other Stories* (Edinburgh, Polygon, 1993), and the novel *Ghostwriting* (Edinburgh, Polygon, 1996).

though obviously filtered through a lot of literary influences" and that he was, at the time, "a distinctly dysfunctional individual". [3] The indebtedness to Rimbaud's *Une Saison en Enfer* and *Les Illuminations*, to Dostoyevsky's *Notes from Underground* and Rilke's *Notebooks of Malte Laurids Brigge*, may not have been uppermost in the minds of the personal acquaintances to whom Herdman sent the text in 1968: the indeterminateness of the distance between the author and narrator, and the consequent uncertainty as to whether masks are being cast off or assumed, clearly caused difficulties for several of them.

Yet *Descent* is anything but a psychoanalytic outpouring. It structures itself by appropriating or reworking the hellish imagery and existentialist themes of the texts cited. The narrator, unable to achieve anything more than a "deadly confusion" in the relationship between his inner and outer worlds, tells us (in section II) that he holds his inner world dearer, but that at times it seems "endowed with a crablike malice". He describes it as a cancer upon the life he leads "in the world of human intercourse", but he has already described cancer, with self-conscious perversity, in terms of "the miraculous principle of its growth and the hidden beauty of its development". He waxes lyrical about intoxicating moments when he does experience ties and obligations and a sense of communal belonging, even fashioning "masks" which allow him to indulge in this sense of social authenticity. But these moments, which he calls "happiness", disappear as his "inner life" reassumes dominance. His existence oscillates between these incommensurable worlds. Before the external world can demand a share of his attention it seems hugely antagonistic, and there is a brooding passage in which, at such moments, he feels like Roderick Usher, the expiring character in Poe's tale; and then, finally, he remarks that in this confusion between "the tortuous vagaries of the mind" and the "grasping for the actual" he feels "at one with my weary time and culture". The section closes with an explanation of what it is that "nourishes" the inner self, and it turns out that these are virtually all things from the past: "old history books, quaint Victorian drawings of Elizabethan voyages, Old Testament phrases, exotic place-names like Bhutan and Tegucigalpa, mathematical symbols, old coins, obscure

---

[3] Macdonald Daly, "An Interview with John Herdman", *Southfields* 6, 1 (1999), p. 86.

species of sea-life, [...] ruined keeps". Thus is the inner life mapped on to the past, richly resonant, while the outer life belongs in a spiritually impoverished present; and this disjunction is said to be typical of contemporary experience.

The dichotomy also determines the unreaderly form of *Descent*. Appalled by the diversions of the outer world – the ways it has of seducing one from "minding the business of one's own soul; which is after all a full-time occupation, and very hard work" – the authorial personality "descends" into itself, and the text correspondingly eschews narrative, event, and dialogue ("I am quite done with speech – speech, that most dangerous form of action") in favour of melancholy broodings on will and pride and appalling dreams full of oppressive half-significance.

One could say that *Descent* presages elements on which Herdman's later work would come to focus. To speak of content, these are: questions of will and pride; of the possibilities of spirituality in a grossly corrupt material world; theological obsessions; existential anxiety; psyches on the brink of collapse; and an all-pervading fascination with physical and situational abnormality. To speak of style, there is a distinct flair for short set-piece passages which, by accretion, allow the text to develop segmentally, as a series of distinct but related meditations or mini-stories. On the other hand, one might argue that Herdman's later work has essentially been an elaboration (but, most crucially, as we shall see, a *narrativisation*) of *Descent*. Either way, this early production, written when its author was only twenty-three years old, is a key to understanding not only Herdman's potential, but also his achievement.

II

John Herdman was born, "with the umbilical cord twisted round my neck",[4] in Edinburgh on 20 July 1941. He was the elder child of parents

---

[4] Most of the biographical information and all of the unfootnoted quotations in this Introduction are taken from Herdman's unpublished and alarmingly candid "spiritual autobiography", *From Whence Comes My Aid* (completed 1985). A copy is among the Herdman Papers, but will be generally unavailable until the author's death. I thank John Herdman for his permission to consult and quote generously from the manuscript.

who enjoyed considerable affluence, his father being a grain importer in Leith; and who shared the still "almost Victorian" value system of the professional upper middle class of the city. Herdman has written that "in spite of all the resentments and hard edges in our domestic relationships we were in many ways a very, and even unhealthily, close family: 'discord,' as I put it in one of my novels, 'being an infinitely more compelling bond than harmony'."

At two-and-a-half months Herdman was baptised in the Church of Scotland. In his childhood years he "plunged indiscriminately" into the "basic resources of a traditional Victorian and Edwardian library" offered by his parents' and grandparents' homes. He claims that from this early age his favourite reading matter was the Bible, especially the Old Testament, and that this was of considerably more significance than the family's "usually fortnightly" visits to St Cuthbert's church. He started writing prose and verse pieces at the age of seven ("In content they would be a psychoanalyst's paradise, characterised as they were by a pre-occupation with cruelty and violence and a repelled fascination for dirt"), but his talents in this direction "went into a hibernation from which I sometimes think they never wholly emerged" at adolescence. He was sent to Angusfield House, an independent Edinburgh prep school, for five years, a period which he remembers mainly as one in which he came to be aware of a general alienation from his own body and his lack of sociability. At eight or nine his father began to take him regularly to Scottish National Orchestra concerts in the Usher Hall, from which developed a passion for classical music, but from his early attempts at music-making he was forced to conclude that it was not the direction in which his future pointed.

In the autumn of 1952, Herdman's parents sent him to New Park, a preparatory boarding school in St Andrews, where the family had relations (Herdman's cousin was the school doctor). It was here that the eleven-year-old came to feel not only "acutely exposed and lost" but also became convinced of the "absolute reality of evil, both in others and in myself ... For New Park in the early fifties had horrors on offer which seemed to come straight out of *Tom Brown's Schooldays*." These mainly took the form of physical and psychological bullying among the boys, to which the teachers turned a blind eye or "tacitly encouraged ... as character-forming and backbone-stiffening". It was here that Herdman first made the acquaintance of D. M. Black, later an accomplished poet,[5] the pair sharing their nascent literary efforts with each other; and developed a devouring passion for Sir Walter Scott's novels, reading "about a dozen of the monsters in a couple of years", and producing short stories in imitation of "the Wizard of the North":

> One of these stories could almost have been inspired by Samuel Beckett, had his great trilogy been available to me at that time. It concerned a "hermit-miser" called Hezekiah Finch who resided in a hovel in the Borders, living by theft and beggary and continuously drunken ("And if he was given not the spirits free, he always had a stout stick to wield over the back of the unfortunate bar-boy"). Hezekiah "was about sixty-five years of age, over six feet in height, and thin as a rake. He had a long, matted grey beard, stuck together with dried egg-yolk, soup and other food. His sparse grey hair came over his ears, and his beak nose stuck out like a vulture's. He wore foul, tattered clothes, and was covered with lice, as he had never had a bath for twenty-eight years." This unattractive personage, who of course was the black sheep of a family descended from Norman barons, had amassed by theft and mendicancy the unlikely sum of £850,000, but he kept his ailing son Leonard a prisoner in his repulsive hovel. Leonard, a talented but consumptive youth, was writing "a book telling of the wretched life of his father, which he hoped some day to give to some passer-by, accompanied by a letter to the police advising them to arrest his father as the foulest thief and vagabond for miles around." Losing patience, however, this filial young man brought the story to an abrupt and premature conclusion by cleaving Hezekiah's skull with an axe when he came home drunk one evening. It is good at any rate to relate that this cautionary tale had a happy ending, for "with the dead brute's fortune he was cured of T.B."

After two years at New Park, Herdman won an entrance sholarship to Merchiston Castle public school in Edinburgh, where his "unhappiness

---

[5] The friendship was renewed in later life and has resulted in a voluminous (and ongoing) correspondence, much of Black's contribution to which can be consulted in the Herdman Papers.

was more low-keyed and less spectacular", and the fact that he began to envisage a career as practical as law suggests the extent of the influence its over-systematised regime had on him. It was at Merchiston that Herdman's acquaintance with modern literature began. He recalls "starting not with the giants but with those who were most talked about at the time – Hemingway, Steinbeck, Graham Greene, George Orwell and Pasternak". He also read Joyce's *A Portrait of the Artist as a Young Man*, and was introduced to T. S. Eliot in the classroom, but "understood him scarcely at all". Specialising in History, Herdman took his A-levels and prepared for entrance to Cambridge. Shortly before leaving the school he was admitted to full membership of the Church of Scotland.

By the summer of 1959 Herdman had secured a place at Magdalene College, Cambridge, his official aim being to pursue a History degree followed by studies in Scots law at Edinburgh and a career at the bar, "though I had a private idea that I might write novels as a hobby". In the December he won an open scholarship to Magdalene and, in the New Year, "a temporary position was manufactured for me in the family business on my mother's side, Melroses the tea and coffee merchants, who had their head office in Leith". This was his parents' way of helping him gain some experience in the "real world". There followed an extended period of travel on the continent, and in October 1960 he went at last to Cambridge.

Herdman stayed in Magdalene for his entire three years. His account of the time is perhaps the least relentlessly melancholy of his autobiography. During his first term he spent more time on Joyce's *Ulysses* ("it took me about six weeks") than the History he should have been reading. This was a significant turning point. Not only did Herdman embrace Joyce's *non serviam* ethic, but he also nursed an ambition to emulate his artistic achievement: "from that time on I was single-mindedly determined to be, in Eugene O'Neill's phrase, 'a writer or nothing'":

> My hero-worship of James Joyce – it could not be described as anything less – had a number of far-reaching consequences for my future life and development. In the first place it encouraged a certain *folie de grandeur* in terms of my literary aspirations and my estimation of my own talent. My discovery of the possibilities of the

pseudo-priestly rôle of the artist gathered up all the dangerous potential that lay buried in my nature for a compensatory self-aggrandisement; a self-assertion, indeed an almost mystical self-certainty, which at once gave meaning to my inveterate sense of aloneness and difference, and compensated my equally deeply-rooted feelings of physical, practical and sexual inferiority. It also made for a perilous single-mindedness, a commitment to put all one's eggs in the basket of literary ambition, and to regard any such compromise with the bourgeois-philistine world as a safe or conventional career as disqualifying one from the status of artist-priest, indeed as almost a kind of mark of the Beast in such a context. It goes without saying that the nurturing of such an attitude involved the growth and conscious cultivation of a truly demonic pride.

Secondly, the Joyce-identification defined in a new way my sense of alienation from my parents' world, and turned it into a conscious rebellion against their values. This of course is a familiar enough story, but the form it took in my own case was very much determined by a Joycean sense of style. It was within this influence, too, that I came to be aware for the first time of my Scottish cultural heritage; but here the effects were more complicated, and modified by other factors. Cambridge has made me aware of being Scottish in a way I had never been before; but at first, after the example of Joyce, my reaction was to reject the local, the provincially limited, in the life I had known, in favour of a championing of European culture, in a spirit which assumed the relative unimportance of national cultural differences compared with the shared insights and perceptions of the great artists of the west. Soon, however, my reading not only of Joyce but also of Yeats and Beckett made me stress equally the divergence of the Celtic consciousness from the Anglo-Saxon stream. I felt more intimately at home with these writers – and, indeed, with many continental writers – than I did with most English poets and novelists; and with my discovery of the poetry and politics of Hugh MacDiarmid a year or two later, my conversion to a Scottish nationalist cultural position was not long delayed.

His *"folie de grandeur"* could only have been encouraged by the award of a runner-up prize of one guinea in the short story competition of the magazine *Granta*, in recognition of "a sub-Lawrentian tale written before my Joycean experience had completely taken over my approach to writing". There were two additional practical consequences of this suitably epiphanic conversion to Joyceanism. Firstly, Herdman changed course and began reading for the English Tripos, lapping up Lawrence, O'Neill, Beckett, Brecht, Yeats, Dunbar, Henryson, Marlowe, Donne, Swift, Blake and Coleridge (among others), taking Dickens as a special author and the Romantics as a special period in his final year. He also abandoned his Christianity virtually overnight, recognising his beliefs as shallow, and acting under the pressure of a sense that being a modern writer and being a Christian ("the provoking exception of T. S. Eliot could safely be dismissed as an aberration") was a contradiction in terms. He claims, however, never to have become an atheist.

Herdman was awarded a double first and received his degree in June 1963. From the age of twenty-one he had been in receipt of "a small income from a trust fund, which was enough for me to live on, though I was not to have control of the capital until I reached twenty-five". It was this which enabled him to turn his back on both legal and academic careers, much to the disappointment of his father. He sailed to New York for a three-week sojourn, during which he witnessed the "dumb trance" of its citizens at the assassination of John F. Kennedy. Back in Edinburgh, tensions increasing between himself and his father, he moved out of the parental home and tried unsuccessfully to apply himself to writing, becoming "very subject to hypochondria and morbid brooding", as well as anxiety attacks and symptoms that sound close to psychosis. He associated this condition with his lapsed Christianity, and tried in vain to revitalise a sense of religious vigour. Eventually he found a "palliative" in a book edited by Christopher Isherwood, entitled *Vedanta for the Western World*, which "sought to introduce the wisdom of the east to the children of the west ... and [whose teaching] accorded well with the religious-minded artists whom I admired, especially Blake". Further reading in the *Bhagavad Gita* and the *Upanishads* helped to keep his recurring "apocalyptic terrors" at bay.

The June of 1964 found Herdman in Cambridge once more, visiting old friends and reading Rimbaud and Rilke. In July he gained suitably Joycean work in an appropriately Joycean city (Zürich, where Joyce had, of course, written the greater part of *Ulysses*). He found both his job (as an English teacher in a private language school) and his lodgings (with an evangelical Christian landlady) oppressive, but stuck it out for two months before returning to Edinburgh in September. It was in Zürich that the "distinctly dysfunctional individual" began to write the prose poems which would later become *Descent*. The work was finished in Edinburgh during the following winter of worsening "apocalyptic anxiety neurosis".

III

The texts collected in the present volume[6] are the most substantial fruit of his writerly activity in the decade following the composition of *Descent*. They represent both the development and variety of his style and themes, while exhibiting certain constancies of influence and preoccupation.

Herdman himself has characterised the thematic development in his novellas as one which begins with a concern for questions of the will and of self-assertion, "with the individual pitting himself against society in some way, seeing himself as marked out to defy society by being an individual, perhaps not in any more social a sense than that, but simply by being an individual and asserting a sense of his own rightness over against the claims of society. But I was always aware at this time of the *hubris* involved in such an attitude, and I think what ... *A Truth Lover* and *Pagan's Pilgrimage* ... are really about is the religious dilemma, ultimately, of where this form of self-assertion (which I suppose could be called Nietzschean) leads the individual."[7] Where it often leads the protagonist is away from dominance by "will" to an acceptance of "truth", the latter involving at least a partial integration into the society which he had earlier been in revolt against. This development is explored in modes which are meditative and primarily existential (*A Truth Lover*), but also comic (*Pagan's Pilgrimage*).

The constant influence is Dostoyevsky, "the colossal presence" and "supreme novelist" whose ethic of redemption through suffering Herdman came to embrace wholeheartedly in the nineteen-seventies.

---

[6] John Herdman, *Four Tales* (London: Zoilus Press, 2001). Parenthetical page references are to this edition.

[7] Daly, "An Interview with John Herdman", p. 87.

The text which hovers over *A Truth Lover* is clearly *Notes from Underground*, although Herdman's spleenful narrator, unlike Dostoyevsky's, emerges partially reformed, Raskolnikov-like, from his misanthropy; and while the narrator of *Pagan's Pilgrimage* comes consciously to understand that he is *not* a Raskolnikov (p. 102), this very insight makes it clear that the novella takes its cue from *Crime and Punishment*.[8]

In his autobiography, Herdman explains at some length his thematic intentions in these novellas. Here he is on *A Truth Lover*:

> The misanthropic Straiton is a man whose excessive devotion to "truth" and the idea of his own integrity is revealed as a function of pride. Witnessing a gratuitous act of violence in a pub, he decides for arbitrary reasons of his own that he will refuse to give evidence if called as a witness, determining to use this occasion as a touchstone of his self-belief. Accordingly he decamps for Paris and Switzerland, where a series of picaresque encounters underlines not only his wilfulness but also a certain perverse cruelty in his nature, which sours his relations with those he meets.
>
> In his enervating idleness he makes himself believe that he is performing "invisible work, the work of the spirit", but gradually he begins to feel sick at himself and decided that the time has come for him to return home and face the consequences of his act of will. [...]
>
> Unwilling however to take the risk of disturbing the motive structure of his life, "my belief in truth and the efficacy of my own will", he retreats into a womb-like passivity, hiding himself away as a kitchen-hand in a Highland hotel. He is capable of honesty, though scarcely yet of therapeutic action; but he does form the resolve to drive out the "burrowing beast" within him, with the only weapon he possesses, "the resource of understanding, of knowledge, of intelligence".

---

[8] *Crime and Punishment* is, in every way, Herdman's master text. Its influence can be found even in the details. For example, the scene in "Clapperton" in which the eponymous anti-hero plants his wallet in an umbrella stand to incriminate his host (p. 123), owes something to Part Five, Chapter Three of Dostoyevsky's novel, in which Luzhin plants a hundred rouble note on Sonia (an ill-fated stratagem which is similarly exposed).

The final scene of the novella, in which Straiton takes an epic walk through the Lairig Ghru pass in the Cairngorms, is consequently meant to be read as a redemptive passage, in which he "sees his journey to the bleak summit of the pass as imaging his ascent into the chilly abstractions of his will and his mental life, and his return to the warmth, richness and friendliness of the lower slopes as corresponding to the possibility of re-entering life and humanity". The figure who comes down from the heights is at last aware that he is no Zarathustra descending from his isolation in the mountains to preach the will-to-power to his fellow *übermensch.*

Redemption through suffering never was fashionable stuff. Does this make it difficult for the many readers who do not share the ethic to appreciate Herdman's achievement? I think not. It is possible to read *A Truth Lover* in a much more Nietzschean mode than its author perhaps thinks – that is, to see Straiton's accommodation to conventional societal modes of living as a capitulation in which he abjures his freedom and fails to see through the consequences of acting in accordance with it. His interest as a character certainly resides in his defiance. Nowhere is this more so than in the centrepiece of the novella, the clash between Straiton and the Sheriff Substitute (pp. 21-3), a verbal *tour de force* which, although it results in his being given a prison sentence – or *because* it so results – Straiton must surely be seen as winning? Such a reading makes Straiton's dilemma more ambivalent than his author perhaps knows or cares to admit. The issue at stake may therefore be to what extent Straiton's distinction as a free individual is threatened *both* by his will (how *free* is it if it is an alien within, a "burrowing beast"?) *and* by his accommodation to the dictates of his society (which seems to produce a dampened, quiescent identity robbed of much of its autonomy). We might legitimately enquire whether the balance between these two extremes which Straiton can be read as having finally achieved is, in fact, the "truth" he really desires or not. The power of *A Truth Lover* resides in its posing, rather than solving, these questions.

It does so in a vein of fairly high seriousness. However occasionally comic Straiton's sometimes self-indulgent confession is, comedy is never the dominant mode or mood of *A Truth Lover*. Much of Herdman's later work is, however, primarily comic, although it seldom fails to be underwritten by the signature of a prevailing mordancy. Thus, "Clapperton" offers us an hilariously awful day in the truly wretched life of its eponymous anti-hero, but with the disturbing suggestion that every day is, by and large, as equally terrible for him. "Memoirs of My Aunt Minnie", although the most comic of the texts in the present collection, nonetheless lays bare in detail the hysteria and violence which sometimes attend intellectual deprivation.

In some instances the choice of comedy has clearly been dictated by the genre in which Herdman has chosen to work. Thus he realised that *Pagan's Pilgrimage*, which is a narrative of a "holy killer", could not be done "straight" in the manner of his main inspirations (*Crime and Punishment*, Hogg's *Confessions of a Justified Sinner* and Hoffmann's *The Devil's Elixirs*), partly, no doubt, because the genre itself can no longer enjoy the ideological support of widespread religious faith but also, more practically, because Herdman's killer is destined to fail by persuading himself (or finding himself persuaded) not to commit the final deed. The disproportions between his executionary fervour and the quotidian realities of his life are the rich source of the novella's humour. However, by the end of the narrative Herdman has managed again partially to redeem his anti-hero. While his impracticality as a schemer and his inadequacy as a person have set him up to be the butt of the story, Pagan appears at its conclusion to have come to an effective half-understanding of his limitations, or to be the recipient, as he contemplates the poignancy of the family relations and character of his intended victim, of what "I suppose that those with religious inclinations might term ... grace" (p. 102). The ambiguity of his new condition is, however, also emphasised by the missionless status it brings – without a fantastic personal crusade to channel his evaporated sense of rebellion, Pagan at last feels a kind of humble contentment. But the novella's final paragraph insists that there is also an emptiness at the heart of this peace, into which "the restless ghost of my dead dreams insinuates itself" and might once again take hold.

The present collection brings into print again the most valuable work of John Herdman's youth and allows readers once more to chart the development of a presence in Scottish literature which now spans almost four decades. Despite his varied and voluminous activity, Herdman's work has been consistently overlooked by critics, a neglect which would seem inexplicable only to those unaware of many parallel cases in literary history.

2001

It was the summer of 1991. I had just completed a doctorate on D. H. Lawrence and Marxist criticism and, while my travels in the byways of Soviet anti-aesthetics seemed somehow not to have blunted my enthusiasm for the revolutionary doctrine, I was in thorough emotional revolt against all narratives modernist and realist. I was thus somewhat demob-happy and uniquely susceptible to the seductions of a fiction that combined radical Marxism with postmodernist aesthetics, had such a paradoxical thing existed, which I was fairly confident it did not. That was before I encountered a thin yellow book whose spine jutted out further than the others on the fiction shelf of a Glaswegian second-hand bookshop. This jutting-out was a sure sign of a small press publication done in A5 dimensions, an ungainly size for a book of fiction, but one at least (like their cheap duotone covers) that allowed these semi-professional rarities easily to be detected.

This specimen was called *The Aleppo Button*, was published by Malice Aforethought Press, and contained thirteen stories by one Ellis Sharp, in 110 pages.[1] Despite my usual experience of disappointment with small press publications (whose professional shortcomings – almost invariably poorly edited, often amateurishly typeset, usually containing multitudes of howling linguistic and typographical errors – tend to be matched by writing to which, at best, one can be only aesthetically indifferent), this one instantly got me where it mattered: it opened with a tall tale, which I read in its entirety on the spot, standing there in the bookshop, in which Joseph Stalin did not die on 5 March 1953, but faked his decease, swam to England, and by 1957 "was a familiar figure on the promenade at Bognor". Indeed, so popular did Iosif Vissarionovich Dzhugashvili prove with the West Bognor Conservative Association, and so prized was his "personal knowledge of the horrors of Seychellism", that he became the local MP ("the previous MP having disappeared off the pier one foggy evening"), although he did feel obliged to enlarge the list of aliases drawn upon in his Russian period (Koba, Ivanovich, Gayoz Nisharadze, K. Cato,

---

[1] Ellis Sharp, *The Aleppo Button* (London: Malice Aforethought Press, 1991).

Chizhikov, Vassil, Stalin itself) by changing his name to Julian Iron.

The story (reproduced on pp. 54-61)[2] was a hoot – written with great tonal poise, linguistically complex, and confidently taking the imbecile thematic liberties of all great satire – but its idiosyncratic killer touch, for me, was that it seemed to be as well versed as I was in the recondite details of Stalin's insane life and showed a brilliant awareness of the comic potential in much Soviet history, something that any humourful student of the subject soon comes to appreciate. As I have intimated, the author could not have hoped for a more ideal reader: indeed, having bought the book and devoured it later that day at one sitting, I had a peculiar sense, which can surely only happen once or twice in a lifetime, that the book had been written especially for me.

Or perhaps I should say *half the book*. I have in this astringently sifted selection retained four of *The Aleppo Button's* thirteen stories, although I could quite easily, on grounds of quality, have included two or three more, such as "Dead Paraguayans" (a forerunner to the later story which gives the present selection its title) and the manic monologic lecture of "The Aleppo Button" itself. The stories which I disfavour – and for me this will emerge as a general rule in relation to Sharp's fiction, as well as being a principle of selection to which I have largely adhered in putting together this volume – tend to be the shorter squibs in which, although all his typical verbal pyrotechnics are there to be enjoyed, narrative is thin or non-existent, and one has the feeling that his imagination has not been allowed the full obsessive rein it seems to display when in the throes of spinning a yarn. Sharp is generally at his best, despite the seeming aesthetic monstrosity of his consistent and explicit coupling of fiction with dogmatic politics, when he allows himself to do something as traditional as to unfold a story at leisure. He would perhaps eschew my preference for his more "readerly" stories – and I hope that readers of this volume will go back to the original volumes and test that preference for themselves – but, for me, Sharp at his most memorable is not the author of two-page streams of consciousness or brief propagandistic philippics, many instances of which can be found in the five volumes of

[2] Ellis Sharp, *Dead Iraqis: Selected Short Stories of Ellis Sharp*, ed. Macdonald Daly (Seattle: New Ventures, 2009). Parenthetical page references are to this edition.

tales I have here cannibalised. *The Aleppo Button* has several examples of both "writerly" and "readerly" texts, and likewise announces most of the literary techniques and thematic preoccupations Sharp was to pursue throughout the coming decade. The typical Sharp story of the 1990s is usually some kind of blistering critique of mainstream (Conservative, Labour or Liberal) politics, or of fascist or Stalinist barbarism, or a frankly partisan promotion (laced with a seemingly alien wild humour) of either classic Marxist ideology or Leninist-Trotskyite *praxis*. But critique and promotion alike are conducted by means of grotesque Swiftian narration and the deployment of a welter of literary devices as far removed from realism (socialist or otherwise) as could be imagined, all served up in a prose style that glories in the slipperiness, precision and poeticism of the English language.

It is no coincidence to me that the longest story in *The Aleppo Button*, "Dobson's Zone" – which fantastically relates the narrator's intermittent connections with his friend Dobson, who exhibits a ragbag of incommensurable obsessions which he somehow tries to synthesise (namely the Loch Ness monster, the paramilitary career of Che Guevara, and crop circles) – is also my favourite, not least because one passage in it (pp. 16-17) explicitly foregrounds what more narrowly conceived political fiction tends to ignore, the necessary magic of words on which the entire enterprise of creative writing, even political fiction, depends:

On our last evening together, drinking whisky, and then more whisky, and then yet more, I have never forgotten how we came (whose idea was it – his or mine? I no longer remember) to open up his Thesaurus at random, selecting quite arbitrarily a single, humble word, and chuckling as our fingers promiscuously roamed back and forth across the pages, up and down, between and below, touching every inch and scrap, every glorious, throbbing vowel and consonant and crackling, pulsating fiery connotation, until at last, drenched in sweat, half-drunk, utterly fatigued by our endeavours, we tumbled into a wordless, innocent and dreamless sleep. Ah, what it is to bathe in language, to cavort there, unashamed, ecstatic, up to the very ceiling of one's mind in beauty and resonance, drifting and gliding amid the harmonic choruses, the plangent chords, hearing the sweet hum of pluralism, soaring across the dazzling ranges of multiplicity, then falling, falling, dizzy, satiated, drained and drowsy, soothed by excess of meaning! (Chess, by contrast, has always struck me as rather a bore.)

When Dobson sets out to "manufacture a mystery" and thus achieve immortality, he does so with a programmatic awareness of *form* rather akin to this love of the workings of language: "for a hoax to be successful and to endure after the perpetrator's death various essential ingredients were required". The "zone" he goes on to describe turns out to be his invention, the inexplicable crop circle. However, it might equally well be a trope for Sharp's fictional *oeuvre*: "It must, in short, provide a Z.C.F.M. — a ZONE for the CONVERGENCE of FECUND MULTIPLICITY" (p. 30).

Much of this "fecund multiplicity" is to be found in the flights of linguistic fancy into which any Sharp story is at any point liable to soar, sublimely, often without warning. "The Bloating of Nellcock", for example, is a savage satire on the career of Neil Kinnock, then leader of the British Labour Party, who is depicted as a wind-filled Gargantua, a man masquerading as an immense balloon, met in so gas-engorged a condition that the story serves as the fuse which precipitates his imminent momentous explosion. Nellcock's bloatedness is a metaphor for Kinnock's linguistic bombast, which, fittingly enough, is described with a corresponding and carefully crafted fustian:

> At the age of six his future as a deipnosophist seemed certain. Guzzling filched apples, he loved to prattle. Hogging the pie, he invariably piped up and rattled on. Devouring fried eggs and beans, he became voluble, prolix. At puberty he used to perorate under the sheets. One day he became lost in a welter of subordinate clauses and did not return until dusk, panting and red-faced. At sixteen he loved nothing better than to rise to speak, ejaculating in full view of passers-by. How he spouted, shuddering! How he loved to stand on stumps, tuning his rant, oblivious to the pain of the amputees. (p. 44)

We are informed that "'Bloater' is found between 'blitzkrieg', which has one meaning, and 'blob', which has four or five" (pp. 48-9). The narrator, who is writing a book on Nellcock which he has yet to finish, enables himself to do so by following in action the logic of these lexical collocations: he carries out a fatal blitzkrieg on this particular blob by puncturing Nellcock with a harpoon, thus going considerably further in his treatment of his subject than either of Nellcock's previous biographers, who bear in their names ("Dunlop" and "Michelin") their own complicity with his repellent inflatedness. Thus does Sharp make literary our common fantasies of political assassination, a theme to which he returns: a later story, "Nixon's Dog", has the narrator blasting the corrupt American President to smithereens in 1962, long before he can assume office – and the year of the release of *The Manchurian Candidate*, the brainwashed-zombie-assassin movie which Nixon ironically urges the protagonist to see.[3]

The present collection opens with one of the later stories in *The Aleppo Button*, "To the Wormshow". It deserves its priority on account of its first sentence alone, which paradoxically makes it sound like the opening of an epic *Bildungsroman*: "My earliest memory?" But this is just one of the ways in which it succinctly exhibits the typical constituents of a Sharp story. For example, upon paradox there is heaped impossibility: the narrator's earliest memory seems to be of the sensations experienced as an ejaculated spermatozoon – a successful one, as it necessarily turns out. Then there is the literary allusiveness which is penumbrally at work in nearly all of Sharp's writing: the inspiration for this concise five-page monologue is Laurence Sterne's bloated *The Life and Opinions of Tristram Shandy* (1759-67), a text also narrated in the first person which likewise begins (and pretty much remains) temporally concerned with events before the hero's birth, and is discoursing metaphorically about the spermatozoon (or "homunculus") by its second page. Similarly, the narrator of "To the Wormshow" refuses to emerge from the womb until a protracted four-and-three-quarter years after his conception in August 1945 or, in other words, for the entire duration of the post-war British Labour government.[4] But

---

3 Ellis Sharp, *Lenin's Trousers* (London: Malice Aforethought Press, 1992), pp. 72-87.

4 As ever, there is probably some Marxist sub-text at work, which readers are increasingly unlikely to recognise. In this case, it is Leon Trotsky's immensely funny Darwinian characterisation of the Fabians: "English pigeon-fanciers, by a method of artificial selection, have succeeded in producing a variety by a progressive shortening of the beak. They have even gone so far as to attain a form in which the beak of the new stock is so short that the poor creature is incapable of breaking through the shell of the egg in which it is born. [...] Having been induced to enter the path of analogy with the organic world, which is such a hobby with [Ramsay] MacDonald, we may say that the political skill of the English

this thematic politicisation of a literary device is itself taken over, at the end of the story, by a resumption of an intensified voice of satire, in this case the revelation of the young infant's first "actual" memory, served up in prose evoking nausea at and loathing for the world; these are the cadences and semantics of Swift once more. The style returns again and again in Sharp: reading for the first time the later "Dead Iraqis" or "The Henry James Seminar at My Lai" (pp. 109-116 and pp. 229-238 respectively), one is probably feeling something similar to the appalled amazement of the original readers of Swift's "A Modest Proposal". It is this element of balance or, conversely, dynamism – between the often mistrusted rhetoric of a morally outraged Marxist politics and the more ambivalent and playful deployment of literary language and devices – that seems to me to distinguish Sharp's finer work.

In "Shooting Americans, with Emily", a story in Sharp's second collection, the narrator records the following anachronistic conversation with Karl Marx: "I remarked that whereas a writer's best book is always the first, a singer's best album is always the second. Marx immediately disproved this with references to Malcolm Lowry and Joni Mitchell" (p. 72). And it could be disproved by *Lenin's Trousers* itself: Sharp's second is also his best collection. Only because I wished to represent a broad range of Sharp's work across the 1990s have I reluctantly excluded from the present selection "Martina" (a story based entirely on a single typographical error), "Nixon's Dog" (even with its somewhat pat ending), and "Da-Da Vogt" (a furious obsessional monologue put into the mouth of Marx). *Lenin's Trousers* presents (though not exclusively) a number of "alternative histories", or engineered collisions between different ontological worlds, to employ some of the vocabulary then current in discussions of much "postmodernist" fiction.[5] So, in the winter of 1846, Emily Brontë bribed a girl from Haworth to impersonate her while she read a gun catalogue in a nearby cave. In the summer of the following year, "having made the final revisions to her manuscript", she went to

---

bourgeoisie consists in shortening the revolutionary beak of the proletariat and thus preventing it from breaking through the shell of the capitalist state." See Leon Trotsky, "Where is Britain Going?" (1925), *Leon Trotsky on Britain* (New York: Monad Press, 1973), pp. 74-5. Sharp actually uses a quotation from this text as the epigraph to the Kinnock satire (p. 43).

[5] See, for example, Brian McHale, *Postmodernist Fiction* (London: Methuen, 1987).

Liverpool, where she "disguised herself as a cabin boy and obtained employment on one of the vessels being used to transport British troops across the Atlantic". She spent the rest of her life engaged in a guerrilla war, sniping at U.S. imperialists in Central America, eventually dying in her lover's arms after a particularly heroic shoot-out. And here is the serious while absurdly comic feature of Sharp's recycling of past cultural icons, lore and booty: unlike a great deal of postmodernist fiction, his intentions are consistently political in nature. What reader of *Wuthering Heights* has speculated, between chapters 9 and 10, that Heathcliff's mysterious disappearing act may be explained in terms of a revolutionary sojourn such as that enjoyed by his creator in "Shooting Americans, with Emily"? But with knowledge of the latter, who could revisit Brontë's novel without considering the possibility?[6]

The technique and its effects recall the superbly violent yoking-together of heterogeneous legends we find, among others, in the earlier collocation of Che Guevara and the Loch Ness monster. Appropriation of revolutionary politics for the purposes of absurd humour is ubiquitous in Sharp, but, rather than the knowing, nudging, trivialising iconoclasm which is a tic of much postmodernist narrative, the result seems to be exorcism of the earnestness, the deadly lack of play, which has ironically come to characterise much subversive politics. These stories don't seek to convert one to revolutionary causes, in the manner of propagandistic prose or Socialist Realist fiction, but rather draw attention to the failures of imagination, the excesses of solemnity, and the linguistic deadness which has hitherto accompanied almost all previous representations of such politics.[7] Thus "Lenin's Trousers" (pp. 77-108) describes at great

[6] Indeed, Heathcliff is missing for the climactic years of the American Revolutionary War and returns in September 1783, the year of its conclusion: "'Have you been for a soldier?'" is one of Nelly Dean's first questions to him. He deliberately neglects to answer it. See Emily Brontë, *Wuthering Heights* (Harmondsworth: Penguin, 1965), p. 133. It has not escaped the present writer's attention that this novel was first published under the pseudonym "Ellis Bell", indicating, perhaps, a further dimension of allusion on our author's part, just as his surname may involve a Sharp nod towards a Swift predecessor.

[7] An earlier exception would be Martin Rowson's *Scenes From the Lives of the Great Socialists* (London: Grapheme, 1983), although, as a collection of cartoon drawings, this does little other than restore comedy to Marxism. The medium is not sophisticated enough to prompt any profounder response.

length how "there is not one Lenin but three Lenins that people write about" – "Saint Lenin", "Lenin the Monster" and "Lenin the Revolutionary Socialist" – only to point out that "whichever of these three Lenins you happen to prefer, it is a fact that none of them showed any interest whatsoever in trousers". But by playing with the possibility of this interest a story (incidentally rooted in truth) gets told of the most unusual kind – and of course it also comically demonstrates, though not without a deep residue of seriousness, the important "materiality" of trousers compared to the negligible "idealism" of the prevalent characterisations of Lenin. *Cherchez l'étoffe*, one might say.

John Constable, *Landscape, Noon* (*The Hay Wain*) (1821)

In "The Hay Wain" (pp. 117-47) we encounter the most concentrated and profound of Sharp's transformative appropriations, as well as the most serious in tone. This opens at noon in Manchester on 16 August 1819 with Jack Frake, a once-renowned Shakespearean actor, "hit one day in the street by a cart, bad leg injury, career in decline". Frake gets caught up in the Peterloo Massacre, kicks a soldier, and is spotted doing so by the yeomanry, which means he must run for his life and, wanted for high treason, "set his actor's talents to work" in disguising himself and going underground. "A month later he's in Norwich, three days later at Ipswich", moving from bolthole to bolthole. Close to collapse, he finds "a white house, deep in mist", and manages to conceal himself for a night in an empty box room at the top of it. "He wakes five hours later to the sound of housemartins chattering ourside the window and a dull bronze glow over everything from the noonday sun. Goes to the window. Sees, over on the far bank, a man in his early forties, sat on a folding chair, reading a book. No, not reading a book. Holding a sketch pad and pen. Making two or three strokes, then pausing to look across the river. Looking right at Jack Frake."

It is "almost noon". The house, it turns out, is Willy Lott's Suffolk home; the artist, John Constable. One commentator complains of the famous picture, "exhibited as *Landscape Noon* [it] is now so well known that ... it is ... never looked at, and its 'novel look' is taken for granted".[8] If Sharp's dramatically contrived collocation of English labour history's most notorious slaughter with English bourgeois art's most popular idyll makes us look anew at the latter, it also makes it impossible to see in it what Cormack's ideological purblindness makes out:

Here in the centre is, again, the focal point of the design, which consists of two horizontally opposed diagonals. One leads the eye over to the right to the haymaking, where the white shirts of the haymakers provide rhythmic accents on the horizon. [...] The white smock of the drover nearer at hand is balanced by the light tone of the horizon at mid-left, so that he does not leap out of the picture, but helps the movement into space in the opposite direction. The figures are simply blocked in, and their simple poses also help the timelessness of the scene. Constable, then, to [*sic*] a boundless feeling for nature and twenty years' experience of close observation has created a work which is as pure as he can make it, a memory of his Suffolk home. *The Hay Wain* owes much of its lasting success to the feeling that in this "Idyllium", this image of "rustic life", "the essential passions of the heart speak a plainer and more emphatic language", as Wordsworth justified his own work in a different context, but we should not forget that, equally, even more than in his Hampstead Heath scenes, it also looks back to the high art of the seventeenth century and, in particular, to Rubens [...].[9]

[8] Malcolm Cormack, *Constable* (Oxford: Phaidon, 1986), p. 132.
[9] Cormack, p. 133.

The painting is appropriated here solely in the formal terms which allow it to be abstracted from any determining social context: consequently it is made to signify what is "balanced", "timeless", "boundless", "essential". But if to these qualities the painting "owes much of its lasting success", they are also precisely what cause it to be "never looked at", "taken for granted". For these attributes are so indefinite, so abstract, that they cannot *be* seen.

Nor (if one studies Constable's picture) can Jack Frake, or anything that could be mistaken for him. But no one who reads Sharp's text will look again at *The Hay Wain* without feeling that he is *there* – without the suspicion, indeed, that he has been *deliberately erased*. One does not *see* anything new *in* the picture: rather, one is made to *confront* it in an entirely different manner. For Frake the scene is anything but "timeless". He is wondering whether to "make a break for it" or "wait for dusk", temporal calculations based on a visual activity ("Frake glances wildly back out of the window") which is the reverse of contemplative. He suddenly hears dogs:

> The cattle are gone, the ferryman's gone. The man with his sketchpad has folded up his little stool and is walking away along the riverbank path. He's bent forward, holding up his trousers, the sketchpad half-slipping from beneath his arm as he tries to keep the turn-ups out of the mud. Undisturbed by the sound which rivets Frake's gaze to the yard, the ferocious barking, brutes on leashes, brutes with studded collars, straining, slavering excitedly, towing behind them as they burst from around the back of the house half-a-dozen grim, burly constables. As they move towards the doorway below the artist on the far bank disappears from view. Now all Frake can see is the ferryman, back where he was before, punting across a bowed labourer who holds a scythe. (p. 124)

Life-enhancing bucolicism, seen from one bank, becomes death when stared at from the other, for what else can the scythe-bearing labourer, accompanied by his Charon, represent? That Frake's end is meted out to the accompaniment of "the grunts and curses of the heavy constables" amid a knell of "hollow reverberating chimes of a nearby church ringing noon" intensifies the passage's marvellous, terrible resonance. One starts to detect traces of blood in Constable's *Landscape, Noon*.

"The Hay Wain" seems to me one of the most powerful ideological deconstructions to be found in contemporary fiction. One can detect in it a persistent aim of historical materialism, the exposure of the truth, in the words of Walter Benjamin, that "there is no document of civilization which is not at the same time a document of barbarism".[10] *The Hay Wain* is a "myth" ripe for dismantling, as Roland Barthes takes to pieces bourgeois culture and the western consumerism it serves in *Mythologies*. In "Wine and Milk" Barthes points out that French national euphoria over wine is so habitual that it seems "natural", and the economic basis of its production ("deeply involved in French capitalism, whether it is that of the private distillers or that of the big settlers in Algeria who impose on the Muslims, on the very land of which they have been dispossessed, a crop of which they have no need, while they lack even bread") deliberately and outrageously ignored. Thus to link seemingly innocent everyday pleasures with the barbarities of imperial conquest is, of course, to shatter them: "wine cannot be an unalloyedly blissful substance, except if we wrongfully forget that it is also the product of an expropriation".[11] The "unalloyed blissfulness" which *The Hay Wain* represents in English culture proves equally brittle when it is invaded by working-class history.

But Sharp knows that there are proletarian myths as well as bourgeois ones. Peterloo (eleven dead) was a mere scrap by comparison with massacres on a modern scale: the vast magnitude of its *impact* on English radicalism routinely gets transferred to the event itself. But in a contemporary Britain in which the labour movement has been in retreat for three decades, such episodes from working-class history have become mythological in a much more damaging sense than this: that is, the nostalgic and romantic celebration of them has come largely to replace radical political action in the present. But there is no such living in the past for Sharp. *The Hay Wain* does not, he knows, belong simply to the nineteenth century. It is permanently in process, an image in ideological circulation along with those produced today:

> [...] a painting like *Top Gun*, all gloss, myth, fantasy. The judicious placement of flagpole or cart, runway or field, sunset or cloud,

---

10 Walter Benjamin, *Illuminations* (Glasgow: Fontana, 1973), p. 258.
11 Roland Barthes, *Mythologies* (London: Paladin, 1972), p. 61.

labourers or carrier in the Indian Ocean, until the two blur, and now that speck's a MIG fighter, beyond the house lurks a blonde in leather, all sunlight and honey, in which there's no place for agricultural depression, recession, squalor, poverty, the all-night wage slave, the women in the electronics factories of Korea, the tortured of Palestine, the black children with puffy bellies and skull faces and big teardrop eyes, the masses blotted out by the sugar of individual destiny [...] (p. 139)

This is from the second section of "The Hay Wain" (Frake's story occupies only eight of the story's thirty-one pages), the action of which takes place on 31 March 1990, the date of "The Battle of Trafalgar Square" in which 200,000 Poll Tax protesters staged one of the most insurgent demonstrations witnessed in Britain within living memory. [12] Sharp's roller-coaster description of this event is punctuated by "flashbacks" to historical disorders and protests (the Peasants' revolt, the Blanketeers, Peterloo itself), thumbnail philippics aimed at Establishment icons whose statues are met *en route* by the marchers (Richard the Lion Heart, Cromwell, "Sir Winston Twister Dardanelles-Disaster dulled-by-brandy dago-hating [...] Churchill", Earl Haig), and attacks on the media which have replaced Constable in providing reactionary representations of what is to be seen.

At the centre of this physical and textual vortex is Robinson, chased by the police into the National Gallery, who finds himself arrested, in more ways than one, before a familiar painting:

[...] much bigger than he'd imagined after seeing it all those times on biscuit tins and trays and calendars and hanging on the lounge wall of

---

[12] "The Hay Wain" is clearly indebted to *Poll Tax Riot: 10 Hours That Shook Trafalgar Square* (London: Acab Press, 1990), a virulently anarchistic pamphlet account of this demonstration, and itself a prose specimen worthy of study. There is a brilliantly surreal passage in "The Hay Wain" in which even the inanimate world becomes enlivened by the riot. A wooden chair suddenly appears "suspended in the air, about ten feet from the ground ... tilted, as if about to launch itself into battle. The chair bides its time, enjoying every moment" (p. 132). A photograph on p. 30 of the pamphlet depicts a chair, presumably hurled at the police by a protester, seeming to do just this.

remote dusty relatives along with the Reader's Digest Condensed Novels and the 22" TV and the hideous china country maids and cherry-cheeked grinning shepherds [...] (p. 137)

He steps towards the canvas to read the gallery description of the painting ("'represents a link between the idealism of Claude and Poussin, and the future empirical vision of the Impressionists'") and the police assault him, flinging him against the canvas, his blood "spurting in a bright unreal slash across *The Hay Wain* by John Constable R.A." He spends the following moments in a new vision of art – "seeing for the first time a ghost in the murky water" – that mingles with a foreseeing of political corruption (the Coroner's evidence concluding that he perhaps vandalises the painting out of his anarchistic impulses). Thus, as well as putting "real" blood on the picture, does Sharp defuse in advance reactionary readings or critical "inquests" of his text. In the precise image, also, of a violent collision between present and past, and between conventionally different realms of discourse (art and politics in particular), we have the master trope of his fictional method.

While reading *Lenin's Trousers* I was revising an undergraduate course I taught in modern and contemporary English Literature, and I decided to make it the "up-to-the-minute" prescribed text which I usually nominated on the eve of the course.[13] I thought I had better check with the publishers that sufficient copies were available for a large class, and so I wrote to them. My enquiry must have been passed on, because a few days later I got a call from a man with what I considered a rather refined voice, who said, "Hello, I'm Ellis Sharp." If he was surprised that his obscure book had been so instantly acknowledged and prescribed on a Literature course, he didn't sound it. I forget the brittle details of the call (just as I forget most of the detail of the three or four occasions on which we subsequently met) but the contact developed into a full-blown and very memorable correspondence – old style, printed on paper and sent through the post – his side of which occupies a large box file in my possession, another box file being occupied with publications, drafts and

---

[13] For the record, I seem to recall that Sharp's book left my students, with one or two enthusiastic exceptions, almost entirely baffled. Nearly all of them avoided writing about it. This was what I expected.

other literary (and much non-literary) material he forwarded. The correspondence extended over three or four years, on average at least once, sometimes twice a week, until Sharp – on paper a scintillating correspondent – became converted to email and our communications thereafter became briefer and more transactional, for reasons no more likely than the change of medium. It has been a curious friendship, conducted almost entirely through writing.

Its most unexpected consequence, for me, was that I ended up being co-author of Sharp's next book. I believe he had sent me drafts of stories about Nietzsche and Trotsky. Coincidentally, I had a story about Nietzsche tucked away in a drawer and I had recently published a satire involving Trotsky (the latter somewhat inspired, in fact, by the liberation of constraints I witnessed in Sharp's own stories). I sent him both and, as it ended up, we decided each to write two more stories involving hirsute mega-intellectuals, eventually choosing Engels and Freud. The resultant eight stories – each of us being sole author of four – was published as *Engels on Video*, so entitled because the year of publication, 1995, was also the centenary of Engels' death.[14] All of the Sharp stories in the volume seem among his best to me – he was, I think, at the height of his confidence and consistency at this time – and I have represented the book here with his two longest contributions to it, the stories involving Nietzsche and Engels. We felt especially grateful to *The Journal of Nietzsche Studies* for lacerating the book in review: it was about the only periodical to bother.

Many of Sharp's letters to me detailed his ongoing and intensifying political activity, which seemed to oscillate between the *Socialist Worker* newspaper and direct action of an anarchist kind, such as that involved in the anti-roads protests. He was, for example, regularly involved in occupations of land made in the course of a campaign against the M11 link road development near his home in East London (the occupied territory became known as "Wanstonia"). I once turned up at his house in my modest Triumph Acclaim and his greeting was a quite curt (although objectively correct) instruction to me to move my car off the kerb. His letters crackled with anti-automobile static. *To Wanstonia*, the

---

[14] Mac Daly and Ellis Sharp, *Engels on Video: A Joint Production* (London: Zoilus Press, 1995).

collection he published in 1996,[15] occasionally fictionalises these political activities, particularly in the title story, which is an experimental attempt to document (though Sharply) the M11 protest, and in the often hilarious "Scenes from the 39 Day Strike at Thrabb's". The collection on the whole, however, seems to me to lack the élan of Sharp at his best. For example, the stories sometimes repeat old formulae without improvement: the Jane Austen tale, "Spiders", is in some ways a repetition of the earlier, better Emily Brontë story, just as "One Morning Twenty-Nine Carp Were Caught", which identity-switches Lenin and Chekhov, is excelled by "Tinctures, Stains, Relics", a story in *The Aleppo Button* which much more bizarrely swaps the lives of Karl Marx and Charles Fort (of *Fortean Times* fame). "Paper Heart (a story in three albums)" is included here largely to let the "stream-of-consciousness" side of Sharp's fiction be heard; the albums concerned (onto which the possibly autobiographical protagonist's varying fortunes are implicitly projected) are Bob Dylan's relatively obscure *Planet Waves* (1974), the double platinum *Desire* (1976), and the rather poorly received *Hard Rain* (1976). Still, the impressionistic story does not entirely engage me in the way that many other Sharp tales do. But the collection continued to show Sharp capable of virtuoso performances, such as "A Rag", a story which poignantly revisits the scene of Antonioni's cult film *Blow-Up* (1966), and "The Henry James Seminar at My Lai", a text it is not wise to embark upon if one's sensibilities tend towards the comfortable.

In retrospect, I can now see that Sharp was always going off in a different direction from short fiction hereinafter. His stream-of-consciousness propensities (in contrast with his postmodernist leanings) had always seemed to me incapable of integration with his political obsessions in a satisfactory fictional form until I read *The Dump*, a slab of 50,000 paragraphless words, his first novel, written *à la* Samuel Beckett, a searing, grotesque parody of the Britain of the 1990s.[16] Stream-of-consciousness needs that larger canvas, it would seem. Arguably his finest single work so far, *The Dump* nonetheless competes with *Unbelievable Things*, an exquisite 500-page-plus epic published a mere year later, which blends the English "country house" genre with

---

15 Ellis Sharp, *To Wanstonia* (London: Zoilus Press, 1996).
16 Ellis Sharp, *The Dump* (London: Zoilus Press, 1998).

such incommensurables as science-fiction and, inevitably, the Bolshevik Revolution.[17] In 2007 appeared *Walthamstow Central*, an hilarious novel-length pastiche of cyberpunk plotting and prose.[18]

In the periods between publication of these three novels Sharp produced two further volumes of short fiction.[19] But the swerve of direction is now clear. The texts in both books are very short, sometimes squibbish: narrative mostly yields to lyricism or contrived humour. I have ignored the collection of 2004 entirely, as it yields nothing to compete with the merit of any single text herein, and is rather marred by a nasty tale which glories in the wanton murder of a TV personality (my objection is aesthetic rather than ethical). But among *Driving My Baby Back Home*'s stories of some substance there remain four which, for me, still demonstrate his powers in the short form, though on the wane – or perhaps, more correctly, on the wing. These four texts close this selection. The last words of the final story seem to me, in particular, in their epitaphic summing-up of a major element of Sharp's literary methods, an appropriate point at which to draw the curtain on his achievement in the short story.

It is very curious to write about an author whose talent is such that one considers he should have a large audience when, in fact, the number of those who appreciate his work is infinitesimally small. Of course Sharp's scalding up-front politics and the literary demands he makes on his readers will inevitably alienate him from a mass readership. But it has been my hope in preparing the present volume that it will prove to be a lasting introduction to a writer whose modicum of acknowledgment is long overdue. There is certainly no contemporary British writer quite like him.

2009

Postscript

When I edited *Dead Iraqis*, I assumed that Sharp had finished with the short story. It was where he had first made his unusual mark in the nineties, but by the new century his energy seemed entirely channelled

[17] Ellis Sharp, *Unbelievable Things* (London: Zoilus Press, 2000).
[18] Ellis Sharp, *Walthamstow Central* (London: Zoilus Press, 2007).
[19] Ellis Sharp, *Driving My Baby Back Home* (London: Zoilus Press, 1999) and *Aria Fritta* (London: Zoilus Press, 2004).

into novels, short and long, six of which he has now published. Indeed, I found nothing in his last book of short stories, *Aria Fritta* (2004), worthy of inclusion in the selection, and assumed there had been a definitive end, at that point, to any attempt he might make to encapsulate his fictional concerns in an abbreviated compass. Eleven years later, his sixth volume of short stories proved me wrong.

The Quin of "Quin Again", the novella which occupies the second half of *Quin Again and other stories*,[20] is the English experimental novelist Ann Quin, a writer almost as obscure and unknown as Sharp himself. But at first glance this 78-page seeming tombstone to Quin appears to put the collection into a state of obvious imbalance, casting a long and perhaps too substantial shadow over the fourteen much shorter stories which constitute the first half of the book. After *To Wanstonia* (1996), Sharp's stories, in gatherings like *Driving My Baby Back Home* (1999), became much more concise, in the mould of what has sometimes been termed "flash fiction", less prone to extending his particular obsessions into hilarious narratives with surreal, highly bizarre plots. The more lyrical, stream-of-consciousness dimension of his work came to the fore, in which the same riches of language were evident, but the deadly Swiftian irony of his finer earlier stories, not to say to the political satire which had become his trademark, seemed incapable of realisation in a diminished extent of four or five pages per story, often less.

Quin Again on first inspection threatens to be that kind of book until the reader realises that, if the name "Quin" is what unifies its second half, the first is also unified by a single character, who appears in nearly all of the shorter stories, and whose name is Douglas Elijah McMaster. We do not learn this "real" name, however, until "Ridiculous", the third last story of the book. We first meet him under the moniker "Doodles", an appellation which suggests his insignificance, his almost cartoon-like contours, his being a mere creation of the pen, his fictionality. In the first story, ironically called "Finished", we learn of Doodles and Hazel and their erstwhile love, including some gritty details of their pastoral frolics, only to have all the apparent facts of the story denied within two pages. The authorial voice – which we read as that of an older Doodles – commandeers the narrative and explains that the details are false,

---

[20] Ellis Sharp, *Quin Again and other stories* (London: Jetstone, 2015).

imaginatively conjured out of his immediate writerly surroundings. He then seems to hear the voice of Hazel herself, travelling down the years, pointing out that he has mixed her up with a different ex-girlfriend (words which he then denies having heard as he peremptorily finishes both with the story and with her, a mere four pages in). Thus is a Gerontion-like narrative consciousness concisely established, in which past memories are elegiacally recalled, but in which memory and imagination cannot firmly be distinguished, and therefore in which the presentation of the realist "facts" of the stories is always subject to internal attack from the narrator's ability to make things up, deny things, or rewrite them differently.

This narrator dominates most of the stories in the collection, and he is the teller of the Quin story too, a presence which binds both halves of the book together. In the second story, "The Writer", a febrile Doodles, high on Valium, goes on a walk which takes him around various points of London. This story too is broken-backed. It could end on its sixth page, but the authorial voice again intrudes with a series of stern correctives, refuting with forensic precision many salient features of the events just described (including the Valium-taking, which might otherwise realistically have been used to explain the discrepancies). He remarks bathetically, in conclusion, "But the route mapped out in this story is entirely accurate." This narrator casts doubt on almost everything, and verisimilitude in these texts is consequently like a small island regularly pounded by the hurricanes and crashing waves of an unpredictable imagination. ("I haven't had any verisimilitude for over two pages," one character complains.)

The turn and endless return to language of experimental fiction can often feel claustrophobic compared to "classic" or realist writing. Some experimental writers really do seem to write as if there is nothing but language and puritanically purge their work of many available affective and narrative elements. The result often reads like the arid production of a skilled machine, as the constant refusal to permit the reader suspension of disbelief gives the text the property of wishing to deny the reader certain time-honoured and dominant aesthetic pleasures. I have always considered Sharp's strength as a writer of fiction to derive from his unerring ability to deploy experimental techniques (in some cases inventing them) while never forgetting that fiction is not primarily read as a manual in post-structuralist linguistics. He used to ensure this, often, by the quite prosaic means of actually telling a story, though never very straightforwardly. Every new narrative was also laced with wit and humour. There were clear political and moral values underpinning (and sometimes overwhelming) his writing too, and these gave the stories their snapping satirical bite.

Quin Again is the work of an older man: Sharp was in his mid-sixties when it was published. The politics and the humour are never far away, but they recede a little before the unifyingly mordant tone of someone recalling fragments of a life mostly gone, putting half-remembered past joys into a collage with dreams and fantasies and the sense of diminution experienced in the present. As the narrator tells us in one of the stories, the past tense is not only desirable, it is inevitable. (With typical contradictoriness, several of the stories are actually written in the present tense.) There is an undeniably Proustian undertow of sadness and unfulfilled desire, but the writing keeps in check, with its expected vibrancy and verve, any propensities the reader may have for trite emotional indulgence. Sharp's writing is tremendously urbane and erudite in style, and it never attempts to elicit sentiment. In effect, the mordant tone reaches for your bowels rather than your heart strings.

The shorter stories are, however, genuinely overshadowed by "Quin Again", which further distinguishes itself from them by being punctuated, W. G. Sebald-like, with mostly desolating photographs of what appears to be an East Anglian coastal town in winter.[21] (The real Ann Quin drowned herself in the sea off Brighton in 1973.) This long mosaic-like narrative appears to be written (at times at least) by someone claiming to be an old lover of Quin, shocked into renewed consideration of her by news of her death. But the story, which it would be nearly impossible to summarise, is in no sense really about Quin, nor is it homage. It is at once profoundly serious and somewhat haunting, yet also howlingly funny and screamingly parodic. It contains, for example, a brilliant spoof of John Buchan's *The Thirty-Nine Steps*, as well as a paragraph in which the

---

[21] This visual allusion to Sebald's *The Rings of Saturn* appears to be corrective of its excesses, not imitative of its style: in a novella published in the same year, Sharp has his narrator witheringly condemn Sebald's text as an "arid, bloodless, evasive encyclopaedia of posturing indulgent narcissism" (see Ellis Sharp, *To Wetumpka* [York: Zoilus Press, 2015], p. 42).

reader must guess the words that have been deliberately omitted.

While *Quin Again* is technically a collection of short stories, its title story, also its longest by some measure, convinces me anew that Sharp's centre of gravity is now definitively the novella or short novel. No short story of Sharp's is ever likely to lack value, but since the publication of *The Dump* (1998) his investment of his creative gifts has been most rewarding in longer forms. "Quin Again", at a guess, is necessarily gathered with shorter pieces because it could not satisfactorily form a volume on its own. But it makes it clear that Ellis Sharp is less and less likely to paint miniatures.

2015

SHALL WE ARRIVE AT *NINETEEN EIGHTY-FOUR* FOR *CLOCKWORK ORANGE* REASONS?

To include (or to use) a future date in (or as) the title of a text would seem, at first sight, to risk imposing a sell-by date on the commodity form (or book) the text takes in social circulation. Prospective calendrical specificity of this kind almost inevitably invites, and arguably gives overwhelming importance to, evaluation of the text's predictive accuracy, whether or not its author was primarily or even secondarily concerned with speculative futurology. The date invoked provides a ready temporal touchstone against which, when it arrives in real historical time, the text's depiction of the once future society can be judged against conceptions of the actual contemporary circumstances in which its readers now live.

To take one obvious example of the phenomenon, Arthur C. Clarke's *2001: A Space Odyssey*, the novelisation of a film directed by Stanley Kubrick, seemed by 2001 to have been much more exaggeratedly optimistic about the possibilities of human space travel and communication with extra-terrestrial beings, after several decades in which there had been abandonment of and/or relatively reduced investment in international space and planetary exploration programmes, than it must have done at the time of the text's first publication in the heady months of the American Apollo moon reconnoitring missions leading to the eventual human landings on the moon of July 1969. Then, it must have seemed quite conceivable that, thirty-two years later, the technological advances and the social commitment to their use which Clarke's text posits would have been likely. But quite some time before the third millennium had even been reached in real time, readers knew that this likelihood had drastically diminished. Readers' orientation towards a text which finds itself in such a bind is in danger of altering drastically. The text may fall out of favour (or out of circulation altogether) because deemed a now superannuated prophetic folly. In the case of Clarke's text, which has little of aesthetic quality other than the prose of its quasi-theological conclusion to rescue it, this demise would probably have occurred, were it not for the fact that Kubrick's film – the "original" text, after all[1] – both continues to impress, aesthetically and technically, the former unsurprisingly, the latter surprisingly, because, generically, the global standard of the space movie is now the artistically weak but special-effects rich *Star Wars* saga. In other words, I would argue, for a date-bound text to escape the potential market extinction self-programmed in its title, some kind of "preservative" is needed: in the case of Clarke's novel, that function is performed by Kubrick's still aesthetically unsurpassed movie, which continues to tower above all others in the genre. Where such support is not present, the text's survival is usually merely archival. Who now reads Raymond Williams' discourse on a possible socialist reform for Britain, *Towards 2000*? The book is not currently in print.

George Orwell's *Nineteen Eighty-Four* – a text I first encountered as a teenager in the nineteen-seventies – is, like Clarke's novel, one which bucks this common trend. It never seemed in such danger, even then, just a few years before the sand ran out in its hour glass. Why this is so cannot be specified definitively, but we can dispense, I believe, with the notion that it has anything to do with its intrinsic aesthetic value, the satisfactions it may offer as an accomplished specimen of textuality alone. The fact is that few of Orwell's texts have ever been hailed as any kind of triumph of literary value. Orwell is one of those authors – in Britain, at least – who has not gained a foothold in anything that may be thought to be "the canon". There are those who simply consider his prose, or his narratological skills, or his imagination, wanting. [2] The formalist standards most commonly applied to police the canon of English Literature have seldom known how to accommodate that quite rare thing – the English novel of ideas – and the consequence is that British academic literary criticism has, in general, passed over Orwell without

---

[1] Matters were slightly more complicated than this phrase suggests: Kubrick commissioned Clarke to write the novel with the deliberate intent to use it as the basis for his screenplay. He then withheld permission for the novel to be published until after the release of the movie.

[2] Perhaps most witheringly, Vladimir Nabokov, in the 1963 Preface to his own 1947 satire on the Russian Revolution (Nabokov, 1974: 6): "automatic comparisons between *Bend Sinister* and Kafka's creations or Orwell's clichés would go merely to prove that the automaton could not have read either the great German writer or the mediocre English one".

comment. Writing about Orwell seldom starts with any considerations of an artistic kind at all: it is his politics, or his implied construction of Englishness, or his influence on other thinkers and writers, that usually offer the stimulus to discourse about him. But none of this affects his popularity, and Orwell enjoys a kind of popularity which the writers of gold-embossed paperbacks can only dream of. He may not be canonical to English Literature, but to this day he enjoys a privileged place in Britain as the most widely read English writer of serious fiction in a site that is (I would argue) much more ideologically potent than the university literature class: namely, the secondary school literature class, where his two most famous novels are to this day deployed in ways that he himself would deplore, in support of political positions he himself would abjure, and by means which would raise the ghost of Louis Althusser.[3]

Orwell was my favourite author in my teens, long before I encountered him in the classroom. But *Animal Farm* was compulsory reading for fifteen- or sixteen-year olds in the Scottish state secondary school I attended, and it was taught with plain ideological intent, namely as an illustration of the "pointlessness" of all revolution – not the "pointlessness" of the Stalinist Revolution in particular (which many of us would wish to distinguish from the Bolshevik Revolution), or of Mussolini-like Fascist coups, but of all revolutions, especially insurrectionary ones. The enhanced ideological advantage of teaching literature in this didactic fashion depends, as Althusser would point out, on pupils' verbal inarticulacy, cognitive limitations and experiential inadequacy, which are blatantly exploited to permit all manner of glaring contradictions to go unexplored and all kinds of frankly tendentious liberal or conservative political nostrums to be offered as decided truths. It would be satisfying to report that myself or my classmates counterposed to the "pointlessness of revolution" thesis the awkward fact that Hitler had come to power by sanctified Parliamentary democratic means, or that Orwell had himself taken up arms in the Spanish Civil War, but I regret to say that these insights (insofar as I ever witnessed them being expressed) were no more than *esprit de l'escalier* of some years'

---

[3] I am thinking, obviously, of the Althusser of "Ideology and Ideological State Apparatuses (Notes Towards an Investigation)" (Althusser, 1984), a text I would usually contest theoretically but have often found experientially persuasive.

belatedness.[4] Quite whether Orwell is still taught in such homiletic mode in British schools I do not know, but the fact is that one or both of his last two novels remain compulsory fare for thousands of British teenagers annually. For many – those who do not continue with the discipline of English Literature – *Nineteen Eighty-Four* may well be the most intellectually sophisticated novel they ever read or at least formally study.

Is, then, the continued currency of *Nineteen Eighty-Four* (a text which, if read as a prediction, got it woefully wrong) merely educationally enforced? Was its survival of the double blow which fell on 1 January 1985 (its implied "best read before" date) and 9 November 1989 (the date of the official "fall" of the Berlin Wall) a function of school teachers' inability to recognise that history had not gone the way Orwell forecasted? The answer is obviously no, not least because the novel continues to enjoy massive global sales in a multitude of languages, and demonstrably continues, in ways it is my aim to try to delineate, to have its finger on the pulse of some yet-to-be-defined elements of the *zeitgeist*. The reason why this is so is probably to be found in what also became evident, as the year 1984 approached, hesitated, and then passed: namely, that very metaphor which Orwell's novel had turned the year into was by then so culturally pervasive that the mere loitering of the four portentous digits for a twelvemonth was little other than a trivial blip on its – *Nineteen Eighty-Four*'s – more epoch-defining radar screen. It quite rapidly became clear that the novel held the whip-hand: the year would bow to it, not the novel to the year.

Whatever the state of international relations (and so on) may have been in the actual 1984 turned out to be immaterial to the fate of the novel, which by then had come to enjoy something of the status of what is now recognised to be a "brand" – it was dispersed throughout global culture and had a recognition value that made it proof against any light missiles

---

[4] Indeed – if I may risk one telling of one further revelatory personal episode – one year later, in 1980, with what must have been unquestioning concurrence to what I had been told *Nineteen Eighty-Four* was all about, and much to my father's chagrin, I packed a copy of the novel into my bag as a deliberate provocation to the Friedrichstrasse U-bahn station border officials as we set out on our only visit to the pre-unification East Berlin. Much to *my* chagrin, they paid no attention whatsoever to the Orwell book but spent an inordinate time contemplating the gauche juvenilia in a notebook I was also carrying.

the calendar or the real world might be able to launch at it.[5] There are few artistic works which enjoy this degree of security. There are no others I know of which are inescapably political in the traditional sense. There really is a case to be made for *Nineteen Eighty-Four* as the single most historically influential novel ever written, by which I mean us to consider it as a fictional text written expressly as a political act, taken up and used – often in shorthand or sloganising forms – by working politicians to adumbrate their ideological positions and justify their ideological antagonisms, and also mobilised within less "official" political groupings for different, but nonetheless comparably propagandistic ends, all of which informed very practical political decisions, of momentous import, taken throughout the Cold War. Is there another single fiction which an entire political generation, right and left, used as its compass?

But the high point of the novel's historical importance must now, surely, have passed, nearly a quarter of a century after 1984? This is a common-sensical assumption, yet I do not register a shift in opinion towards the novel which suggests that it is passé, important, but now only historically so, not any more. The text has gone on being mobilised in a variety of ways, despite the passing even of the century in which its fictional events take place (see, for example, Gleason et al., 2005). There is an interesting study waiting to be written on the cultural processing of

---

[5] With hindsight, the first implicit understanding of *Nineteen Eighty-Four* as being the cultural equivalent of a commercial "brand" was made by the American advertising firm Chiat/Day in a television advertisement commissioned by Apple Computers and first broadcast during a commercial break in the Superbowl of 22 January 1984. The advertisement depicted a scenario in which a "Big Brother" figure (projected onto a screen in monochrome blue and usually taken to signify "Big Blue", or IBM) speaks indoctrinatingly to a group of skinheads assembled in a cinema space. Suddenly a voluptuous and athletic young blonde woman, allegorically representative of the Apple Mac, breaks into the auditorium, swings a sledgehammer and smashes the screen. The commercial concludes with a male voiceover stating, "On January 24th, Apple Computer will introduce Macintosh. And you'll see why 1984 won't be like *Nineteen Eighty-Four*." This was the only occasion on which the full 60-second version of the advertisement was aired nationally in the USA. The Apple board of directors did not like the advertisement, but it came to have enormous popular appeal (Linzmayer, 1994). The advertisement itself can be viewed online at **http://www.theapplecollection.com/Collection/AppleMovies/mov/1984.mov** (accessed 22 August 2007).

Orwell's novel post-1984. But my own inclination here is to contribute to the fray rather than to adjudicate on it from outside. In short, I want to make a political argument and I wish to bring Orwell's novel to bear on that argument. From a certain literary critical point of view, it is irresponsible to use a text as a counter in an ideological debate like this. But I am not, here, engaging in literary criticism and, in any case, as we have already seen, literary criticism is hardly ever the discourse which engages with Orwell. I am doing what everyone always does with Orwell's book, which is grinding it to make politics. What else is to be done with it? What else keeps it alive and repeatedly readable?

The best writing on the novel has never adopted academic procedures, and has usually been consciously political. In my view the richest discussion of all – the first part of Anthony Burgess's *1985* – shows the necessity of abandoning traditional literary critical procedures in relation to it, although it is a text of Burgess's which remains very little known. First published in 1978, the book was, Burgess tells us, initially commissioned as a "reconsideration" of Orwell's novel, although it ended up as a broken-backed volume, half-critique (Part One), half-novella (Part Two). The novella is what one may call a right-wing riposte to Orwell: it depicts a Britain a few years in the future, ruled politically by trades unions and dominated culturally by Islam. If the plot seems prognostically inept, Burgess wryly notes further that history soon radically demolished his speculative narrative: "my own *1985*, which was written before the Thatcher revolution, must raise very sardonic guffaws when the nightmare is compared with the reality" (Burgess, 1994: v). Indeed, it was in the very year 1985 that the Conservative Thatcher government won its greatest battle in this arena, humbling the National Union of Mineworkers after a year-long national industrial dispute, virtually the last of its kind in twentieth-century British history. Despite these deficiencies, however, Part One of the book remains a long, wittily conceived and entertainingly executed series of discussions (sometimes "conversations" or "interviews" Burgess has with "himself") of Orwell's novel, which stand quite independent of the weakened novella which follows. Every student of Orwell's novel should read half of *1985*. But for my purposes the crucial connection Burgess there makes is between *Nineteen Eighty-Four* and his own novel, *A Clockwork Orange*, published in 1962.

A Clockwork Orange is Burgess's best-known novel, and one of the few novels of the past half century which comes close to the "recognition value" enjoyed by *Nineteen Eighty-Four*. It does so because it was adapted for the cinema by – again – Stanley Kubrick, who subsequently was to give both book and film mythical status by persuading Warner Brothers to withdraw it from circulation in the UK in the same year it was released (1971). The film could not be seen publicly in the UK for the next twenty-seven years, nor was it available on video: the nearest regular venue where British viewers could watch it was in Paris. I had just turned eight when the film was released, but I have a distinct memory of my mother and father returning from the cinema, having seen it. So the social controversy generated by the movie was real enough for it to register even on a child's consciousness. When the film was withdrawn, the novel, very much a weaker artistic product than Kubrick's – I agree with Burgess when he admits that it is "too didactic, too linguistically exhibitionist" (Burgess, 1994: 369) – filled the cult-shaped gap. Upon first reading it about ten years later I saw what it had in common with *Nineteen Eighty-Four* clearly enough, at least in the abstract: the common vein that runs through both novels is their exploration of the degree of power which the State does, can or should exercise over the individual, but also the methods it may employ to wield that power. But I did not become aware until seeing Kubrick's movie, as belatedly as the year 2000, quite what the concrete relation between *Nineteen Eighty-Four* and *A Clockwork Orange* might be, irrespective of the intentions or express claims of their respective authors. To be more precise, I was beginning to understand what kind of political dynamic there might be made to be between them and why this might offer an explanation of a developing political reality. I shall return to this matter after a short but necessary detour: this essay is something of an intertextual excursion.

The intertextual nature of my dawning understanding gets increasingly complicated. But without another film intervening in this process – a film ironically much weaker than its novel original – the dynamic between *Nineteen Eighty-Four* and *A Clockwork Orange* is less clear to see. This film was *1984*, in which Richard Burton, as O'Brien, made his last movie appearance, alongside John Hurt as Winston. I saw it upon its release late in 1984, and found that the attempt to render visual Orwell's verbally depicted world inevitably flattened the intellectual content of the novel but, worse, pointed up many of the weaknesses of Orwell's imagination. For example, any reader of the novel knows that Winston has to rewrite past editions of *The Times* to bring them into line with the latest Party orthodoxy, but few readers of the novel can have a strong sense of *The Times* as a palpable, physical object. Actually to see, on the cinema screen, paper copies of a newspaper, and to witness Winston "delete" old photographs by placing something as technologically primitive as brown adhesive tape over them, makes one acutely aware of the unlikelihood that the degree of social control seemingly exercised in the novel could be maintained in such a technologically backward society. In other words, the film discouraged suspension of disbelief by highlighting visually the kind of improbabilities Burgess had already noted in reading the novel: "we may ask why separate copies of *The Times* are allowed to exist, since the collection of them for destruction must be a great nuisance" (Burgess, 1994: 324).

When I first saw Kubrick's *A Clockwork Orange* sixteen years later, unexpectedly it was Michael Radford's disappointing film which came primarily to mind. Again surprisingly, the correspondences were not primarily thematic, although they stimulated speculation that such perceived similarities might lie beneath. The notable correspondences were, on the contrary, visual, very much to do with the *mise en scène*, often engrained in the framing choices made by the latter director. I have no idea whether or not Radford consciously quoted Kubrick in these matters (possibly he did not), but it hardly matters if he did because, for me at any rate, the latter film, visually, was drawing itself onto a track oddly parallel to *A Clockwork Orange*, whatever other evident differences there may be, and it was the political implications, not the aesthetic ones, that exercised me.

Let me enumerate some of the more patent intertextual echoes between these two films. *A Clockwork Orange* opens with Alex and his Droogs hanging out delinquently in the Korova Milkbar just as, in a similar wide shot, 1984 ends with the disconsolate Winston drinking in the Chestnut Tree Café. The pedestrian subway in which Alex's gang discover and beat up the supine wino seems echoed by the underground tunnel in the Ministry of Truth in which Julia feigns a fall so that she can surreptitiously pass Winston a note. Alex is beaten by the police, before his incarceration, in a white-tiled interrogation room: Winston is analogously punched in the stomach and shown with a bloody face in a white-tiled room in the Ministry of Love. During his imprisonment, Alex is "taken under the wing" of the prison chaplain, quite literally, the chaplain at one point extending an arm protectively around his left shoulder as he sits in the library – a gesture repeated in one of Winston's fantasy sequences when O'Brien places a hand paternally on his right shoulder. Both Alex and Winston are strapped and restrained so that "therapeutic" measures can be enacted upon them, Alex watching violent film excerpts under drug treatment until his enjoyment of violence makes him physically ill, Winston suffering electric shocks until O'Brien is satisfied his will is thoroughly extinguished: indeed, the famous close up of Alex with his eyes forcibly prised open is shot at exactly the same angle as the moment at which we see Winston's facially enacted horror as the rats approach him through the cage mounted on his head in Room 101. After Alex's ordeal, a government minister is seen half-embracing him in his hospital bed, a sign of false affection replicated in the holding of Winston in his arms by O'Brien (a member of the Inner Party) during an interval in his torture.

In view of these similarities, and despite being aware that Burgess himself did not, in *A Clockwork Orange*, mean to propose that the State set about rehabilitating criminals by the medical and psychiatric methods it uses experimentally on Alex – the very paradox of his title indicates that the product would be a morally repellent perversion of nature – I found myself hypothesising that the average British Conservative (and probably many a New Labour) voter would be likely to feel much more ambiguous about the treatment of Alex than they would about the treatment of Winston, similar though they are, close though the moral purpose of these two "parables" of the State versus the individual happen to be, imaginable side by side (and ethically on the same side) as my comparisons above invite the reader to think them.

This ambivalence arises because the figure of Alex, unlike the figure of Winston, remains very much alive and strongly socially mythologised in early twenty-first century Britain – albeit, in the contemporary imagination, he may take the form of a paedophile, a drug dealer, one of a gang of sinister youths wearing hoodies, an accumulator of Anti-Social Behaviour Orders, a football hooligan, an asylum seeker, or a potential

Islamic terrorist. Indeed, Alex is arguably worse than any of these – his violence is motiveless, he is nihilistic, he is a murderer and a rapist – yet for the apprehension or prevention of the activities of those lesser (or only potential) wrongdoers the extension or supervention of technological methods has been acceded to with only very weak opposition in Britain in the last two decades. I refer (not even invoking the many forensic developments and naming only a handful of examples) to CCTV, telephone tapping, email surveillance, monitoring of web activity, anklet tagging, prospective programmes for individual identity cards carrying biometric data, exploitation of global positioning satellite technology in mobile phones and other devices, increased arming of the police, and, more recently, legitimation of the limited use by the police of Tazers.

My point here is not to bewail these developments or engage in a futile discussion as to their political rightness or wrongness: as Orwell once said of the D. H. Lawrence who yearned for a simplicity of life such as that represented by the Etruscans, "it is difficult not to agree with him, and yet, after all, it is a species of defeatism, because that is not the direction in which the world is moving" (Orwell, 1957: 26). Arguably, it is not so much that the citizens of Britain (and other affluent democratic countries) have willingly accepted these developments, more that they have been pacified into acquiescence by the lullaby of security these technological possibilities have been made to sing, a melody replete with sweet reason – mainly that primary "Clockwork Orange" reason, the keeping of Alex and his like from the door. Yet the current state of our technology and the extreme capacity for tracking and surveillance, control and punishment of individuals it offers raises in me a wry smile at *Nineteen Eighty-Four*'s totalitarian prognostications: the idea that a State which cannot maintain a power supply could exercise such far-reaching domination of its citizens by technological means is frankly risible.[6] But any Western State could do so now, and without the need for the misery and penury endured by Winston Smith: for example, all of them already mediate surveillance, to a greater or lesser degree, through the devices we ourselves buy to enhance our pleasure, our happiness, and our convenience.

---

[6] Cf. Burgess (1994: 300): *"The electricity has been cut off, but the telescreen is braying statistics to an empty apartment. It's hard to accept the notion of two distinct power supplies."*

Concern that computational evolution, for example, threatens to provide the direst technological potential for totalitarianism is hardly new. But the real argument does not devolve on technology – it is a question of moral and political values – and in the present historical moment the greatest danger would seem to me to lie with those who are deluded enough to consider those values to inhere in the technology itself. My final intertext, Peter Huber's *Orwell's Revenge*, which I first read in 1995, demonstrates for me the extreme political danger of this presumption. Formally, Huber's book owes a great deal to Burgess's *1985*: he offers both a literary critique of Orwell's novel (in which, essentially, his laboured point is that Orwell was too pessimistic about computer technology) and rewrites the plot (so that a character called "Blair" discovers the diary of a character called "Orwell", previously vaporised because he developed the cellular potential of the telescreen, thus transforming it into a potentially liberatory technology). In other words, Orwell's telescreen has become the personal networked computer, and all's right with the world because the cellular nature of the net is designed to undermine any centralised control. Huber is only occasionally aware of the abyss of technological determinism on which his central argument occasionally teeters, and he eventually falls into it directly because this argument is firmly tied to a very heavy weight in the form of a somewhat simplistic need to defend (seemingly *a priori*) free market principles. It is possible to accept the limitations of Orwell's technological thinking while considering it highly unlikely that his ideas, driven to a rational conclusion, would imply so enthusiastic an embrace of even the most regulated forms of capitalism.

But it is precisely Huber's project to confine Orwell to his Procrustean bed of right-wing libertarian ideology. When Huber, refusing simply to discourse in the abstract about the vast potential of the PC, demonstrates it by feeding Orwell's entire works through an optical scanner, he empowers himself to search and plunder them in the most thorough manner imaginable. But he seems unaware of the monstrous contradiction implied by this action: his resultant footnotes reveal a virtually totalitarian command of Orwell's oeuvre, but his new technological capacity to query the digitised text can as little be called reading as the data it has become can be called writing. By this means the critic becomes a kind of self-congratulatory O'Brien, literally interrogating Orwell's texts until they yield up meanings Orwell would have considered perversions of his intentions and beliefs and – having Orwell's complete work now entirely at his disposal – Huber performs the violation he knows to be, in the world of *Nineteen Eighty-Four*, one of the greatest taboos: he rewrites Orwell's narrative. This enslavement of Orwell's work is done in the name of its and our freedom – a joke Huber would probably enjoy.[7]

Burgess – a very different kind of right-wing libertarian – had already pointed out in *1985* the dangers of the political complacency of the growing horde, which Mark Slouka has come to call our present day "technoevangelists", such as Huber: in short, at any time a certain kind of political interest may assume power – perhaps even by sanctified Parliamentary democratic means – which finds the potential for control of those it governs in the technology at its disposal too tempting to resist, particularly if it sees in them a mass of oranges in need of clockwork regulation. Cyberoptimists like Huber, in thrall to the notion that properties inherent in the same technology will of themselves save us from the *Nineteen-Eighty Four* that could follow – those who believe, as he does, that the cellular nature of the net, for example, ensures our "freedom" – are little more than sirens of technological determinism, at whose sound we should indeed take alarm. It is not too late, but there may come a time when we are no longer able to find on someone's shelves texts which will explain the intellectual bankruptcy of their faith and intimate the peril of permitting it to spread unopposed. One might start with Raymond Williams' *Towards 2000*, for example.

---

[7] It is therefore a pity that Lawrence Lessig, contributing an essay stimulated by Huber's book to a very mixed American collection on the import of Orwell's novel for the future, although making a similar point to mine about the non-deterministic nature of technological forms, evacuates his criticism of all its potential political content by annulling it with reference to something he is happy, trivially, to call "a fundamental aspect of humanity: the principle of bovinity" (Gleason *et al.*, 2005: 221).

References

Althusser, Louis (1984). *Essays in Ideology*. London: Verso.

Burgess, Anthony (1962). *A Clockwork Orange*. London: Heinemann.

Burgess, Anthony (1994). *Future Imperfect: The Wanting Seed/1985*. London: Vintage.

Clarke, Arthur C (1968). *2001: A Space Odyssey*. London: Hutchinson.

Gleason, Abbott, Jack Goldsmith and Martha C. Nussbaum (eds.) (2005). *On Nineteen Eighty-Four: Orwell and Our Future*. Princeton, N. J.: Princeton University Press.

Huber, Peter (1994). *Orwell's Revenge: The 1984 Palimpsest*. New York: Free Press.

Kubrick, Stanley (dir.) (1968). *2001: A Space Odyssey*. MGM.

Kubrick, Stanley (dir.) (1972). *A Clockwork Orange*. Warner Brothers.

Linzmayer, Owen W. (1994). *The Mac® Bathroom Reader*. San Francisco: Sybex.

Nabokov, Vladimir (1974). *Bend Sinister*. Harmondsworth: Penguin.

Orwell, George (1957). *Inside the Whale and Other Essays*. Harmondsworth: Penguin.

Radford, Michael (dir) (1984). *1984*. Virgin Films.

Slouka, Mark (1995). *War of the Worlds: Cyberspace and the High-Tech Assault on Reality*. New York: Basic Books.

Williams, Raymond (1983). *Towards 2000*. London: Chatto and Windus.

2007

I

It is well known that the phase following the October Revolution in Russia in 1917 (of which Trotsky, my eponymous protagonist, was one of the principal agents), Russia's exit from the Great War at the Treaty of Brest-Litovsk in 1918 (at which Trotsky was the Soviet Union's chief negotiator), and the eventual Soviet victory in the Civil War which ended in 1921 (throughout which Trotsky was the leader of the Red Army), was one of extreme cultural ferment in the new-born USSR. My interest at the time I first engaged with this period was rather narrow: I was concerned with how it affected the future course of Marxist literary and cultural criticism in Western Europe, particularly, such of it as there was, in England. Today I remain interested in what another look at this period can tell us about the way we negotiate the issues of culture and conflict here and now, in an England that is certainly different, but one that, like almost everywhere else, has even less interest in Marxism than was the case in the nineteen-twenties and 'thirties.

The two decades or so after the October Revolution are commonly characterised as a period which began with notable artistic experiment-ation. There is no need to go into any great detail about these developments here. Let the image reproduced as Figure 1 stand synecdochically for them.

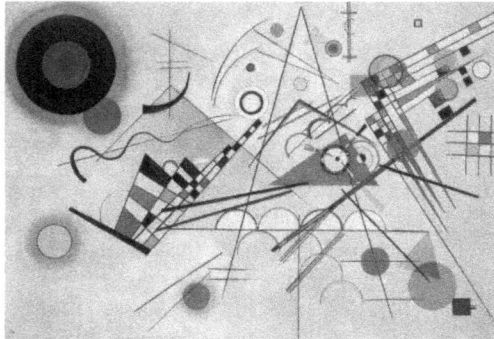

Fig. 1. Wassily Kandinsky, "Composition VIII" (1923)

After the death of Lenin in January 1924 and his supersession by Stalin, this phase of modernist efflorescence gradually turned into its opposite, the rigid, sterile, ideologically slavish practice known, and understandably universally reviled, as Socialist Realism. Let the image reproduced in Figure 2 stand for that.

Fig. 2. Arkady Shaikhet, "A Komsomol Youth at the Wheel" (1936)

I do not dislike this photograph or consider it particularly comparable to the painting, excepting the fact that the obviously experimental painting renders any particular reading of meaning or representation ambivalent while the photograph proclaims its own (no doubt) prescribed obviousness: here we have Soviet youth literally turning the wheel (through a revolution). This perceived shift away from relatively unhindered experimentalism towards enforced ideological dogmatism typifies the received view of Soviet post-conflict culture of the nineteen-twenties and 'thirties, and it is not my intention to challenge that view here, but to indicate what cultural (as opposed to political or military) part Trotsky played in the period. But I also want to articulate, to join up, what I have to say about Trotsky with attention to something closer to home in both place and time.

Whenever one contemplates the dramatic and varied life of someone like Trotsky one cannot help but reflect that contemporary times throw up hardly any examples of his seeming combination of man of action with man of aesthetic inclination and intellectual ability – certainly not in Britain. Here, politicians don't even write their own memoirs, which are ghosted for them (compare Trotsky's *My Life*); at best they produce pulp novels (one thinks of Jeffrey Archer, Douglas Hurd, or Edwina Currie); Gordon Brown, the former Prime Minister, has a little advertised Ph.D. from the University of Edinburgh (1982) and wrote a semi-respectable biography (1986) of James Maxton, the Scottish Socialist labour leader, but it hardly ranks with Trotsky's three-volume *The History of the Russian Revolution*, which was published in English in 1932-33. You have to go back to Churchill before you get anything like that from a British statesman but, although Churchill oversaw a noted multi-volume history (*The Second World War*), he did not also have a lot to say about the state of contemporary literature, art and criticism. Trotsky did: and in what follows I shall compare him unfavourably in this regard to some typical contemporary British Parliamentarians. But before I adjust to these twin foci, I wish to air some more general thoughts, to which I shall return finally, on the relation between conflict and culture.

Trotsky is a proponent of post-conflict culture proper: for him, the culture which might be made possible by the cessation of the conflicts he participated in would be the ultimate triumph over those conflicts. To quote from the introduction to *Literature and Revolution*:

> [...] even a successful solution of the elementary problems of food, clothing, shelter, and even of literacy, would in no way signify a complete victory of the new historic principle, that is, of Socialism. Only a movement of scientific thought on a national scale and the development of a new art would signify that the historic seed has not only grown into a plant, but has even flowered. In this sense, the development of art is the highest test of the vitality and significance of each epoch. (Trotsky 1960, 9)

Coming as it does from the Soviet Commissar of War, that statement seems a refreshingly congenial endorsement of art and its social importance. It is harder to find a name for what contemporary British Parliamentarians see as the relation between conflict and culture. As we shall find out, they largely envisage "culture" (or a certain kind of "culture") as a means of preventing conflict. It would be nicely symmetrical if we could call this "pre-conflict culture", but as, ideally, culture in this view prevents conflict from occurring, there is no "pre-", there is only an "instead of". However, both positions share a certain structural notion of conflict and culture, in which there is a very obvious culture/good, conflict/bad binary opposition.

Thus, neither party would entertain the extremism of the notorious adage, "When I hear the word 'culture' I reach for my gun." Such a statement entirely reverses the terms of the opposition I have just described (it is now culture/bad, conflict/good), and it will come as no surprise that the statement has a Nazi provenance. [1] I flag up the quotation here because we shall hear an echo of it, in significantly modified form, from the mouth of a British noble, a little later. What can we call this attitude except "anti-culture conflict"? It is not uncommon. When certain Islamic groups hear the words "American culture" they may indeed reach for their firearms or their *fatwahs*. Others may harbour a less militant but otherwise similar antipathy. But, again, this is in the realm of the specific. It is very rare to find antipathy to culture *as such* in the abstract, and even philistinism is not quite that (it is simply a failure to see the point of culture in general or specific manifestations of culture in particular: it is not necessarily principled opposition to culture). Likewise, hostility to American culture is hardly ever opposition to that culture *per se*, but it indicates a conflict between cultures – what used to be called "culture clash" – in which formulation, I would point out, the opposition between conflict and culture is in fact dissolved: here, culture is the arena of contestation, or it is what you have conflict over. Thus, for example, you are not meant to be able to procure Coca-Cola in Cuba or Havana cigars in the USA. Of course, one opposition is here abandoned

---

[1] "Wenn ich 'Kultur' höre, entsichere ich meinen Browning!" is a remark usually attributed to Hermann Göring , but in fact it is a quotation from Hanns Johst's *Schlageter*, a play first performed in celebration of Adolf Hitler's forty-fourth birthday: see Johst (1933).

only for another to be instated, *viz*: our culture is good; theirs is bad, let's fight it out, by the pen or the sword or, in the case of my last example, by resort to economic sanctions. But "clash of cultures" is a phrase that seems largely to have dropped out of contemporary parlance, replaced by "cultural difference", a term which attempts to restore all cultures to an equivalence (i.e. non-opposed, non-conflictual), *viz*: we have our culture; they have theirs; they are different, but equal or incommensurable.

The other body of thought I can identify as contributing to this constellation is the Marxist one. It argues that culture, in a capitalist economy, does not deliver us from conflict. We are *always* in conflict, and there will be no true culture until we are beyond conflict. It does not matter what you think of this position. My point is that, logically, it renders the term "post-conflict culture" tautologous. Culture is the reward we shall enjoy only after the cessation of conflict, and conflict is virtually coextensive with capitalism. Not surprisingly, this Marxist note signals the true entry of Trotsky into my discussion.

Literature and Revolution is seen by many as a bizarre and indeed politically irresponsible aberration of Trotsky's. Why? Isaac Deutscher, Trotsky's most famous biographer, sets the scene:

> In the summer of 1922, when he refused to accept the office of Vice-Premier under Lenin and, incurring the Politbureau's censure, went on leave, he devoted the better part of his holiday to literary criticism. The State Publishers had collected his pre-revolutionary essays on literature for republication in a special volume of his *Works*; and he intended to write a preface surveying the condition of Russian letters since the revolution. The "preface" grew in size and became an independent work. He gave to it nearly all his leisure but failed to conclude it. He resumed writing during his next summer holiday, in 1923, when his conflict with the triumvirs, complicated by the expectation of revolution in Germany, was mounting to a climax; and this time he returned to Moscow with the manuscript of a new book, *Literature and Revolution*, ready for the printer. (Deutscher 1959: 164)

In other words, Trotsky failed to seize the political position which might have enabled him to achieve the official adoption of the cultural policies implied by *Literature and Revolution* (had he become Vice-Premier it would have been automatically easier for him to succeed Lenin) and instead absented himself from the intense political fray so that he could adumbrate those very policies. As a political miscalculation, this is second in notoriety only to his later weekend wild duck-shooting trip, taken in November 1923, when Stalin's machinations against him were at their height. The adventure laid him up with a malarial infection that rendered him largely *hors de combat* during the crucial following months, leaving the field virtually clear for Stalin to assume the succession.

Nonetheless, the implied cultural policies of *Literature and Revolution* remain on record. They are not at all complicit with what eventually took place under Stalin – intensifying censorship, rigid prescriptivism for writers who were prepared to toe the line, and systematic liquidation or geographical banishment of those who were not. In Trotsky's *Literature and Revolution* all the best possibilities of artistic tolerance were promoted alongside the recognition that "it is silly, absurd, stupid to the highest degree, to pretend that art will remain indifferent to the convulsions of our epoch" (Trotsky 1960, 12). Unreservedly suspicious of philistine attempts to reject the achievements of bourgeois art, to impose a "proletarian culture" in its place, and to exercise widespread repression in the cultural field, Trotsky undertook a vigorous and trenchant survey of the contemporary state of Russian literature from his undeniably partisan position as one of the architects of the revolution. Insofar as government was concerned, he stated:

> Our policy in art, during a transitional period, can and must be to help the various groups and schools of art which have come over to the Revolution to grasp correctly the historic meaning of the Revolution, and to allow them complete freedom of self-determination in the field of art, after putting before them the categorical standard of being for or against the Revolution. (Trotsky 1960, 14)

The position may seem characteristically contradictory. Once writers have "come over to the revolution", and once they have been helped to "grasp correctly" its historic meaning, they will be allowed "complete freedom of self-determination". But what if they do not "come over", or what if they do but fail to "grasp correctly" the revolution's "historic meaning", or, even if they do both, what if their allegiance to and "correct" understanding of the revolution later flags or is otherwise found wanting by those who consider themselves empowered to judge? The implications are obviously anxiety-provoking to liberal democratic sentiment. Yet Trotsky's position goes to the heart of the debate about literature and politics. If literature has no political effectivity, but is merely a concern of hobbyists, then it can be left well alone by the state. But if it does indeed have an appreciable role in shaping a society, it would be a foolish government that did not keep an eye on and attempt to control its workings – and, indeed, many liberal democratic governments have imposed censorship and repression precisely out of a recognition of literature's perceived social effectivity. If it happens that the best known cases in the "free world" are to do with the sexual rather than political content of literary texts – from the bowdlerisation of Shakespeare to the banning of *Lady Chatterley's Lover* – all that is demonstrated thereby is that liberal governments have considered public discussion or dramatisation of sexual mores to be a powerful social force requiring their vigilant control in much the same way as the Soviets came to consider expressions of political "deviance" a threat to October. Inimical as all writers and most readers understandably are to such control, where it is present it is clear that literature is not politically underestimated.

It is simply not true in any case that democratic governments do not prohibit literary texts which depart from what one might call the "political bottom line". How many are aware that Joseph Goebbels, that other notable statesman who was a man of action and a man of aesthetic inclination and intellectual ability, wrote a novel called *Michael* (published in 1929)? The answer is probably not many, because for a long period in modern democratic Germany, particularly during the immediate post-war period of denazification, it was suppressed along with many other thousands of "poisonous" texts (the most well known case is of course Hitler's *Mein Kampf*, whose copyright the state government of Bavaria acquired in 1945, and whose reprinting it thereafter refused to license; it was not published again in Germany until 2016, after the copyright had expired). Largely on account of Goebbels' later actions when in power, rather than its gauche content, the novel was considered not to toe the post-war "democratic bottom line", and few people lost any sleep over its state-sanctioned repression. Closer to home, and closer in time, Edward Bond's anarchic play *Early Morning* was refused a public performance licence as recently as 1968 because, among other things, it depicted Queen Victoria as a lesbian, a murderer and a cannibal.

If these comments enable us to put the somewhat bothersome problem of potential textual censorship and repression on political grounds in brackets, then Trotsky strikes me as the only twentieth-century politician of major historical importance who has shown anything like a grasp of the indispensability and potency of cultural production and a willingness, given those propensities and capacities, to encourage it to flourish as freely as possible. One has to remember the tremulous fragility of the October Revolution almost up to the eve of his writing the book, as well as the stormy political environment in which he moved (note his qualification that his remarks applied only to the "transitional period" of the revolution: they were not meant to apply to an established and consolidated state of affairs). It is somewhat easier, in times of peace and plenty, for ruling liberal bourgeois politicians to let artists say whatever they like, not least because, under examination, they ironically turn out, in my view, to be more thoroughgoing materialists than Trotsky ever was. That is to say, whereas the Trotsky who wrote *Literature and Revolution* was the one who argued that the acid test of an economic revolution was whether or not it ultimately delivered in the realm of culture (which in my view, contrary to all popular conception, is the classic Marxist position), the acid test of culture, for liberal bourgeois politicians, is whether or not it delivers in the realm of economics. This latter conclusion I hope to demonstrate in the remainder of this essay, and so I now turn, as promised, to what I have called those "less fortunate" statesmen.

II

Late one evening in the January of 1989, I learned that the familiar and time-honoured term "Cultural Relations" had been replaced in official British political discourse by the phrase "Cultural Diplomacy". I was listening to the BBC radio programme *Today in Parliament*, which reported that the House of Lords had debated a motion calling for increased government funding for the British Council and the BBC's external services (particularly the World Service, which broadcasts to foreign territories world-wide). These are two main agencies of Britain's overseas cultural representation, and both had recently suffered financial cuts in real terms under the Thatcher government. The entire (and entirely astonishing) debate can be found in the official Parliamentary record.[2]

To be fair, some of the noble Lords expressed dislike for the new designation – Lord St. John of Fawsley (then better known as the Rt. Hon. Norman St. John Stevas, Conservative ex-Minister for the Arts) thought that "Cultural Diplomacy" had a "forbidding ring" – but they grudgingly took it up. Lord Bonham-Carter, the Liberal peer proposing the motion, wasted no time in launching a strategic military metaphor, referring within five minutes to the external services of the BBC as "an essential weapon in our armoury". He gave a stirring example of how, shortly before the Falklands War, the BBC's broadcasts to Spain had been cut, with the result that Spain's coverage of the War came almost entirely from Argentinian sources. The amount saved by this cut had been £230,000 – "rather less," he ventured, "than the cost of a single Exocet missile". All around Lord Bonham-Carter, parliamentary minds started to whirr into characteristic British warspeakmode. The Earl of Stockton, then Director of the Macmillan Publishing Group, which has always profited greatly from the British Council's promotion of British books overseas, said that in supporting calls for increased government funding he was "speaking from the sharp end of the publishing salient" (a salient is a military fortification or line of defences which points outwards). Lord Weidenfeld (another publisher, of Weidenfeld and Nicolson fame) piped up with the idea that cultural diplomacy was "an excellent conduit for reconciliation and peace" in the hostilities he seemed convinced Britain was involved in: "it heals wounds and builds bridges". He ardently hoped that, by the 'nineties, assuming increased funding for the British Council, Britain's involvement in belligerence around the globe would be at an end and that our motto would be, "If I hear the word 'gun', I reach for my

---

[2] *House of Lords Weekly Hansard*, no. 2379, cols. 209-46. Unless otherwise indicated, all quotations in this section are taken from this text.

culture" (a quaint inversion of the Nazi *bon mot* we encountered earlier, although the noble lord wrongly attributed it to Göring because he probably dredged it up from the *Penguin Dictionary of Quotations*). Lord Moore of Wolvercote also hit the target when he repeated what nearly every other peer had said, namely that the universality of the English language gave Britain a ready-made market: "from that base we have various weapons with which to press our cultural offensive".

In this fashion, the Lords harangued the government for two-and-a-half hours, like Generals come back from the field to sort out the bureaucrats who were holding up supplies. It became clear that there was indeed a foreign war of sorts going on, which had to be fought on two fronts. There was the Influence Front, on which a Britain sadly dispossessed of Empire must scramble anew for cultural colonies, in the teeth of fierce competition from the other Western capitalist nations and from the "unfree" world (which then meant Communist countries). The Influence Front had to be secured if Britain was to be successful on the Trade Front, where there was (and no doubt still is and for any foreseeable future always will be) a frenzied struggle going on to flog everything from aeroplanes to zoom lenses in foreign markets.

An obvious instance raised in the debate of how the Trade Front cannot neglect the Influence Front is in the markets created abroad when foreign students educated in Britain return to take up influential positions in their countries of origin. But how can you get people to come and study here when they haven't learned English because the British Council hasn't enough resources to teach them; when they can't hear BBC broadcasts demonstrating how marvellous Britain's culture is, because of poor signals, outdated relay equipment, or sheer absence of a service; when the number of scholarships offered to overseas students is inadequate, and their tuition fees are going through the roof?

And so on. This is where the "civilising" quality of "British culture" is usually deployed, because, naturally, it would not do to advertise straight out what a commercial coup you stand to effect on foreign nations who allow themselves to fall under your influence. At this point in the debate was heard a tactically evangelical maiden speech by the said Conservative ex-Minister for the Arts. Cultural diplomacy, he averred, is simply "the increase of British influence in the wider world", and yet:

This increase is not pursued principally for commercial or economic reasons, but because we believe the long, continuous, extraordinarily rich and varied experience of this nation constitutes a unique contribution to the welfare of mankind, and we are therefore under a duty to make it as widely available as possible.

If I were asked what had been this country's three greatest contributions to world civilisation I should reply unhesitatingly: the common law, parliamentary government, English language and literature, and at the heart of all three lies the idea of liberty. I do not believe that we can export our institutions indiscriminately, but by informing people of how they work and flourish, by imparting thoughts about them, we can enhance the chances for freedom elsewhere.

Listening to this on radio – so boundlessly confident was the delivery – one was almost tempted to disregard the strangeness of the argument. Our legal, political and cultural institutions are all about liberty, so we have a duty to press them on everybody else. To force people to be free Britain cannot use gunboats as it used to, so it has to resort to convenient arks such as "English language and literature". We should count ourselves lucky, because we invented English, and know how to use it:

The benefits of the universality of that language are truly incalculable. I often reflect on the extraordinary disposition of Divine Providence that a language spoken originally by a few thousand savages trapped on a fog-encrusted island on the edge of the North Sea should, in the fullness of time, and in the era of communications, become the common language for the entire world [...]

Culture may seem a frail boat to embark on the tempestuous waters of great power and international diplomacy. What has that quiet, nuanced voice to say in the world of telegrams and anger? – I think rather more than one might suppose [...]

Let me say this in conclusion: worldly powers, dynasties, empires rise and fall, culture and learning abide. They are the achievements by which future ages looking back assess the value of previous generations. Power in the 19th century sense has passed from us, never to return. But it has been replaced by something perhaps even more important – influence. Through the dissemination of our culture that influence can be exercised for the good.

This was a hybrid tale of the fertile Noah (the frail boat), delivered in the cadences of Ecclesiastes ("empires rise and fall, culture and learning abide"), told by St. John the Divine. Whatever one's political persuasion, it would be difficult not to admit that the sentence, "What has that quiet, nuanced voice to say in the world of telegrams and anger?" approaches the condition of the poetic. It is arguably two lines of iambic pentameter blank verse. Most of the noble assembly no doubt attended in hypnotised wonderment.

But the proposing Lord (Bonham-Carter) had not asked for poetry: he only wanted cash for the British Council and the BBC. Perhaps he was aware (unlike St. John) that God, actually, was responsible for the confusion of the tongues in the first place (Genesis, xi). At any rate, the only bibliolatry he was interested in was the kind that would profit the Earl of Stockton and Lord Weidenfeld. Sadly, English will not reach foreigners along the effortless route of Divine Providence any more. We have to teach them it. And if we do not, there are American cowboys who will: their Lordships were reminded by Lord Bonham-Carter that "there is a battle going on about the teaching of English English and American English" because, "believe it or not, the Americans claim to be able to speak English":

If you are taught English English you are likely to buy books and other goods from this country: if you are taught American English you are likely to buy books and other goods from the United States of America. Cultural diplomacy is therefore an important commercial consideration and one which should not be forgotten.

This was a blunt and belated formulation of a sense of demise. We may have invented English, but the patent ran out years ago, and we perhaps need to remind ourselves that Britain builds very few boats these days. So, alas, the plea was to no avail. Naturally, in that straitened post-credit-boom heading-towards-the-Thatcher-sunset year of 1989, the cash just was not on the table for Lord Bonham-Carter's cause, no matter how ardently he argued the case for overseas cultural representation being part of the diplomatic service.

It seemed to me at the time, and it still does, that it was a sign of the increasingly frank recognition of the inescapably political nature of cultural work that Whitehall should have accepted the re-designation of "Cultural Relations" to "Cultural Diplomacy". Of course, it always was starkly political, even when it was called "Cultural Relations". But the new term caught on very rapidly in the immediately ensuing years. Perform a search today on Google for "cultural diplomacy" and you will come up with an appreciable number of Masters programmes offered by British and American higher education institutions. Its other recurrent surfacing is in the pages of *Hansard*, the publication of the proceedings of the two chambers of the UK Parliament. For example, as recently as 19 March 2001, there is an exchange like this:

> *Lord Puttnam*: My Lords, is the Minister aware of the fact that in 1995 a conference was held in London under the title "Britain and the World", at which the Foreign Secretary, Mr Cook, the then Foreign Secretary, the noble Lord, Lord Hurd, and the then Prime Minister, Mr John Major, all confirmed unequivocally that cultural diplomacy represented the best value for money in presenting Britain to the rest of the world? Has anything happened in the past six years that would allow Mr Cook to think that that is no longer true?
>
> *Baroness Scotland of Asthal*: My Lords, absolutely not. It is incredibly good value. Britain's creative sector, including music, design and advertising, generates more than £112.5 billion each year and employs more than 3.3 million people. It is growing faster than the economy as a whole: in 1997-98 it was growing at 16 per cent a year. Exports total £10.3 billion. It is a very vibrant sector, of which we are rightly and justly proud.

This exchange not only demonstrates that British Parliamentarians are impressively telepathic (Baroness Scotland was able to read Robin Cook's mind, despite the fact that he was not even a member of the House of Lords, and thus was not present during this debate): more sinisterly, note how Puttnam's "cultural diplomacy" is simply equated by Baroness Scotland to "Britain's creative sector" and that the only terms in which it is lauded are economic.

Ultimately, such overseas culture-mongering has always been directed towards the process of consolidating the already powerful economic position of Britain in the global economy. Even before the 1989 Parliamentary debate as I have summarised it, the late Sir Anthony Parsons (former Foreign Policy adviser to Margaret Thatcher), had stated this without disguise, and had been quoted with approval by the British Council, in terms which can conclude any case for the thoroughgoing materialism at the heart of the British political establishment:

It is really dazzlingly obvious. If you are thoroughly familiar with someone else's language and literature, if you know and love the country, the arts, the people, you will be instinctively disposed to buy goods from them rather than a less well-known source, to support them actively when you consider them to be right and to avoid criticizing them too fiercely when you regard them as being in the wrong. (British Council 1988, 7)

III

The juxtaposition of an individual of world renown and his capacious views on literature and culture and their potential for human liberation with a comparatively indifferently talented bunch of unelected politicians and quango-masters mouthing pious nationalist banalities on the relations between trade and commodifiable cultural artefacts is, no doubt, the throw of a loaded dice. Can anyone who truly believes in the social value of culture consider Trotsky the loser from this comparison? This we can ask even before we draw attention to the ironies which result from the contrast, such as the spectacle of Trotsky, the thoroughgoing communist, recommending what one might call a "regulated free market" approach to culture, while apparently liberal bourgeois lords try desperately to pressgang cultural endeavour into the narrow service of enhanced balance of trade figures, a manoeuvre that makes them seem a little Stalinist, in the sense that Stalin also attempted – much more successfully than they – to extend state patronage to culture as long as it knelt at the feet of narrow economic and ideological dictates.

However, such observations are far from my main purpose in here co-locating these ostensibly disparate attempts to construct and project cultural policies. To juxtapose them may raise questions and prompt conclusions about the general relations between conflict and culture. I suggest that a predictable dialectic of supply and demand is at work between them. Conflicts of the kind that Trotsky and the nascent Soviet Union had survived at the time he was writing were deeply privative. Russia in the years before the Great War was already a materially poor peasant society, whose culture (in the sense of high or artistic culture) was accessible only to a very restricted élite. The War, the February and October Revolutions, and the subsequent Civil War all put culture (in this specific sense) into a suspension even more extreme – who can engage in artistic pursuits or pleasures or enjoy their potentially edifying consequences amidst an absolutely shattered material infrastructure and within a mercurial polity (from which the culturally inclined classes understandably, if they could, tried to escape)? What may explain Trotsky's apparent irresponsibility in turning to literary debates in 1922 was his sense that only with reference to cultural practices and their potential benefits did the privations suffered in the immediately preceding years seem worthwhile: *Literature and Revolution* may have been intended as a timely clarion call (from someone to whom everyone, friend or foe, would certainly have to pay attention) to see the point of it all.

One might feel, by comparison, rather sorry for well-fed-and-feathered politicians plying their trade in times of apparent relative material plenty and peace. Few grand gestures seem possible in such un-Renaissance-like circumstances, when there is an uninhibited plethora of cultural choices and practices to choose from. At best, all that seems possible then to the official political mind is petty calculation. If anything, such a situation seems to lead politicians implicitly or explicitly to turn the important question on its head, to ask what the point of culture is, and to come up with justifications for it which are stultifyingly pragmatic (it wins us friends abroad) or banally economic ("an important commercial consideration and one which should not be forgotten"; "the best value for money in representing Britain to the rest of the world"; "growing faster than the economy as a whole"). Culture is at such a moment even susceptible, as we have seen, to redesignation in econospeak as the "creative sector" to which one can apply income generation figures and with reference to which one can calculate a national contribution to gainful employment.

References

British Council. (1988). *The British Council Overseas Career Service* [British Council staff recruitment brochure]. London: The British Council.

Brown, G. (1986). *Maxton*. Edinburgh: Mainstream.

Brown, Gordon. (1982) *The Labour Party and Political Change in Scotland, 1918-1929*. Unpublished Ph.D. thesis, University of Edinburgh.

Deutscher, I. (1959). *The Prophet Unarmed: Trotsky: 1921-1929*. Oxford: Oxford University Press.

Goebbels, J. (1929). *Michael: ein deutsches Schicksal in Tagebuch-blättern*. Munich: Zentralverlag der NSDAP F. Eher Nachf.

Johst, H. (1933). *Schlageter, Schauspiel*. Munich: A. Langen/G. Müller.

Trotsky, L. (1960). *Literature and Revolution*. Ann Arbor: University of Michigan Press.

2007

One of the self-proclaimed *raisons d'être* of the organised study of the media is that it is serves to make media consumers more "critical". Such is virtually always articulated as an aim in the mission statements of departments in schools, colleges and universities which teach about the media. In such documents, the invocation of the word "criticism", although it can hover between two alternate meanings, decidedly tilts towards one of them rather than the other. "Media criticism" tends not to be understood in the way that "literary criticism" or "film criticism" usually are, namely as the organised rationalisation of one's response(s), more often positive than negative, to a valued literary or cinematic text. By contrast, "criticism" of the media is more frequently conceived of as an oppositional interrogation of the media text in order to demonstrate one's objection(s) to it, with the explicit or implicit conclusion that it should not be accorded value.

It is this proclaimed "critical" ambition, above all others, from which the study of the media derives a sense of moral seriousness and implicitly seeks social legitimation. Yet few people ordinarily turn to the media in order to criticise it. It is hard to imagine tuning into BBC Radio 4's "Shipping Forecast", or one of its comedy sketch programmes or documentaries primarily to exercise one's critical faculties. The media consumer is more usually in practical search of information, diversion, emotional stimulation or aesthetic pleasure: "criticism", where it arises spontaneously, usually signals that the consumer has been disappointed in that search. The most inarticulate but decisive form it takes is typically switching television channels or turning the radio off. Arguably, the educational drive to make viewers or listeners more "critical" comes from a benign intent to render such a negative impulse more susceptible to elaborated analysis, on the assumption that such critical tendencies are of value even if their object (the TV or radio programme) is not.

Let us take a media source I wrote an entire book about (Daly 2016), and therefore can claim some extensive knowledge of: BBC Radio 4. In that book I quoted the following exchange between the presenter of the morning "Today" programme and the then Shadow Chancellor of the Exchequer, Labour MP Ed Balls:

JUSTIN WEBB: Part of what you're announcing today is that you're going to go to the Office of Budget Responsibility, or you'd want to be able to, and have them look at all your plans. That is a stunt, though, isn't it, because you know it's not gonna happen?

ED BALLS: Well, I not only want it to happen, I think it will happen –

JUSTIN WEBB: It can't happen. It would have to go through Parliament and the Conservatives won't agree to it.

ED BALLS: Oh, I see, so, because the Conservative Party will play party politics with trying to give the public reassurance that all parties' manifestoes add up, to rebuild trust in politics, then it won't happen? Well, that's their choice, but I don't think that that's what they'll do [...]

JUSTIN WEBB: All your big announcements, though – and here's the sort of wider criticism of you – all your big announcements are about spending more or reversing cuts that there have been. You don't make big announcements about the kind of really big cuts or tax increases that will be necessary if the deficit is to be brought down.

ED BALLS: The last time I was on your programme and we did an interview together, I said to you that in difficult times we couldn't justify paying the winter allowance to the richest pe–, pe–, pe–, pe–, pensioners –

JUSTIN WEBB: That's tiny, though, isn't it, tiny?

ED BALLS: [Inaudible] we debated it at the time.

JUSTIN WEBB: [Inaudible but challenging] [?] say?

ED BALLS: Look, it's a big deal for Labour to say that, and I've said that. What I'm going to say to the Labour Party –

JUSTIN WEBB: But it doesn't come up with the kind of money you've gotta come up with –

ED BALLS: What I'm going to say to the Labour Party conference today [...][1]

---

[1] "Today", BBC Radio 4, 23 September 2013, interview commencing 7.36am. Note that Balls has a slight natural stammer. The symbol "[?]" indicates inaudible words.

Bearing in mind the usual circumstances of practical listening, we can offer a range of exemplary possibilities as to how listeners might react to this exchange, in which Webb is certainly highly critical of Balls. Listeners might share Webb's criticism, they might react critically to that criticism, or they might have no critical reaction at all. It is conceivable that listeners might be:

(1) critical in a merely superficially reflexive way ("Oh, Ed Balls is Labour, so I am unlikely to agree with what he says");

(2) vicariously reliant on the presenter to be their surrogate critic ("Go on, Justin, give it to him!");

(3) selectively critical depending on what is being said or not being said ("Let him speak, Webb, he was answering your question!");

(4) critical in a manner that reaches beyond mere content and extends to querying the *forms* of radiophonic discourse ("I am unable to find out much about what the Labour Party's new policies are because the sceptical manner of the interviewer seems designed more to ridicule them than to allow them to be explained");

(5) not critical at all but merely summarising what they have heard ("Hey, honey, did you hear about that stunt the Labour Party is trying to pull?");

It is my view, however, that these reactions are mostly so predictable that it is certainly not worth the expenditure of time, energy and money involved in having a band of media audience researchers investigate them empirically. The reason is that we can probably all recognise these reactions readily from our own personal experience as follows:

(1) is our reaction, for example, when we have an emotional or ideological or similar predisposition towards the subject under discussion;

(2) is our reaction, for example when we are in a relatively thoughtless frame of mind but nonetheless are pleased to have our "gut reactions" voiced for us;

(3) is our reaction, for example when we are genuinely open-minded and have not already arrived at a firm opinion;

(4) is our reaction, but this seems less likely than the other possibilities, because even when, for example, we are well informed about a subject under discussion and aware how poorly it is being discussed, we would need also to reach a judgment that the problem is not simply deficiency of content but a problem with the *form* or *manner* in which it is being presented;

(5) is our reaction, for example when we simply concur with what is being said or at least accept the authority with which an opinion or fact is stated.

In short, we are sometimes critical and we are sometimes uncritical listeners. The degree of critical attention we give to any text is dependent on the kinds of dispositions indicated in the examples above, not to mention other possible circumstantial influences such as being tired or even simply in a good or a bad mood. Just as we are credulous or incredulous, pleased or displeased, engrossed or detached in variable ways in response to variable stimuli, how critical the responses of any individual are will be conditioned unpredictably by the prior knowledge or quantum of interest s/he brings to bear at the point of consumption of the particular media text, not to mention other contingent features of the moment, such as the physical environment in which it is consumed, what else we are doing as it is consumed, or even the sheer accident of who else might be present with us as we consume it. No amount of empirical audience research, as far as I can theoretically divine, is going to tell us anything very decisive in general as to whether the mass audience is more or less critical of the media it processes.

It is obvious, but commonsensically obvious in a way that does not readily require formal academic confirmation, that (all extraneous factors aside) we tend to be more critical of some media textual genres, such as those focusing on politics, than we are of others, such as cookery shows, precisely because some genres invite us more readily to evaluate given opinions than do others. To that extent, then, the form of encoding is likely to have *an influence* on the manner of decoding, because we are seldom merely hearing random sound or language, but listening to make sense of deliberately organised discourse. I think we can accept from these observations that the core of Stuart Hall's classic theoretical thesis nonetheless seems unassailable, namely that our decoding of the media text is not simply determined by the forms in which it has been encoded, and that a critical response is always practically possible, however authoritative or persuasive or even "innocent" the encoding seems to be.[2] How much a critical response is *likely,* however, often depends on its perceived appropriateness to the genre under scrutiny.

For example, although the two programmes have an almost identical format and duration, it would be strange to propose to investigate seriously whether or not listeners tend to react with as critical an opposition to the horticultural views expressed on Radio 4's "Gardeners' Question Time" (Friday, 15.00; repeated Sunday, 14.00) as they do to the politically saturated opinions aired on "Any Questions?" (Friday, 20.00; repeated Saturday, 13.10), because we already know the answer.[3] Indeed, the Saturday repeat of the latter is followed immediately by a companion phone-in show called "Any Answers?" (14.00), which effectively enables listeners to voice their personal disagreements with the views expressed in the earlier broadcast. This is so not because gardening is without controversies (presumably it has them), but that we know without any detailed audience research being required that its likely controversies do not tend to excite a mass audience the way political differences do.

It does not follow that all audience research is negligible or that the educational over-emphasis on a "critical" study of the media is entirely

---

[2] Hall (Ryan 2008: 907-16) identifies three broad types of response to the media text ("dominant-hegemonic", "negotiated", and "oppositional") to designate symmetry, partial symmetry or asymmetry between the institutional encoding of the media text and listeners' decoding of it. This does not preclude the observation that the range of possible decodings can be more finely graded.

[3] This is not to say that a programme like "Gardeners' Question Time" is immune to adverse criticism, but simply that it is formally less susceptible to it. In February 2008, for example, the BBC issued an apology after it received several complaints from listeners about the humour and ribaldry with which, during an edition of the show the previous year, panelists discussed a plant, *Rhodochiton Volubilis,* vulgarly known as "the black man's willy". The corporation accepted that the item was potentially offensive on racial grounds, although it "did not agree with listeners who said it was inappropriate to air the segment at a time when large numbers of children might be listening, as youngsters only formed a small proportion of the audience" (Anonymous, 2008). Clearly, therefore, audience criticism of a programme even of this generally "innocent" nature is always possible, but the mode of response to it of most listeners for most of the time is unlikely to be "oppositional".

misguided. Hard, factual, quantitative audience research of the kind conducted by media and industry institutions into the size of audiences, for example, is unignorable: it not only tells us about the mass reach (and thus the magnitude of potential influence) of particular programmes, but it explains in large part why we have the programmes we have (namely, those which can sustain appreciably sized audiences); why they are scheduled when they are scheduled and why they are the length that they are (that is, to maximise the size of the likely audience available in and at that time); and it strongly affects the price of commercial advertising which, although this does not apply to the BBC, pays for the programmes on the multitude of commercial channels with which it competes for listeners and viewers. Nuanced, qualitative academic research into real audiences of the kind conducted by Morley (1980, 1992) undoubtedly increases our understanding of how actual listeners actually process (critically and/or otherwise) particular media broadcasts, although such studies may be more labour-intensive and methodologically complex than their rather limited conclusions justify, and those conclusions tend to be less reliable the more they are offered as generalisations about audience responses to the media as a whole rather than to the particular programmes under scrutiny.

But a great deal of audience research (and research which encourages us to be more "critical") still seems posited on a willing ignorance of or refusal to accommodate Hall's theoretical position, in that it seems to assume, quite contrary to what he argues so convincingly, that forms of encoding determine manners of decoding. This is nowhere more evident than in that branch of audience research which investigates "media effects", most frequently the effects of media representations of sex, violence, crime and "bad language". This approach often tendentiously sets out to prove the harmful social effects of those representations and is usually allied to: (1) an assumption that the audience, or a significant portion of it, is unable to distance itself from those representations and hence reproduces or imitates "uncritically" in real life the kinds of harmful or offensive behaviour or prejudices therein depicted; and (2) a conclusion that such representations ought to be restricted, censored or prohibited. So, for example, much public money is spent (especially in the United States) on quasi-scientific research which examines, using test groups, the physiological and/or psychological "effects" of the consumption of certain kinds of media. For example, a group of adolescent boys might be wired up to various scientific instruments which, as they are allowed to play various (violent and non-violent) video games, monitor their heart rates, perspiration, reflex responses, pupil dilation, brain activity, and more.

The results of these experiments and the conclusions drawn from those results are almost always the same. In the example given, the boys will tend when playing the violent games to display more of the physiological and psychological effects typified by anger or rage than they will when playing the non-violent games. The recommendations which issue from these observations are usually along the lines that adolescents should be restricted or prevented from playing video games with such violent content, either by their parents or by the law, on the assumption that, because experience of the games has a propensity to stimulate physical or mental conditions associated with real-world violence, there is a corresponding risk that (at least some of) the boys' actual behaviour outside the games may consequently be violent if they are allowed to play them. The general presumption seems to be that the boys are so unable or unlikely to be sufficiently "critical" of the game's content that they (or at least some of them) may in some way fail to distinguish between the imaginary world of the game and the real world, and that therefore their guardians need to be "critical" (that is, censorious or prohibitive) on their behalf.[4]

"Audience research" of this nature in respect of this and other likewise suspect media tends to have a generous amount of approving exposure in the popular press, and in many countries is the rationale for a number of legislative, domestic and retail initiatives (age-related censorship or outright legal prohibition, parental dissuasion concerning or parental withholding of the material assumed to be potentially harmful, withdrawal of the same content by some shops and rental stores) which effectively try to implement its social recommendations.

---

[4] Loath as I am to encourage the reader to visit any of this research, who am I to protect you from its negative intellectual effects? For one review of the relevant academic literature, written by two subscribers to its general prejudices, see Anderson and Bushman (2001). Dismissive as I am of this approach, it should nonetheless be acknowledged that it has an enormous band of assenting followers, including feminists, anti-racists, mothers, fathers, and schoolteachers.

These restrictions also have consequences for what is deemed permissible in broadcast media content. Even Radio 4, which one might *prima facie* consider somewhat immune from this kind of censorship by virtue of the station's entirely auditory nature, is subject to many of the same constraints as the visual media, summarised by *The Ofcom Broadcasting Code*:

> 1.1 Material that might seriously impair the physical, mental or moral development of people under eighteen must not be broadcast.
> 1.2 In the provision of services, broadcasters must take all reasonable steps to protect people under eighteen. [...]
> 1.3 Children must also be protected by appropriate scheduling from material that is unsuitable for them.
> 1.4 Television broadcasters must observe the watershed.
> 1.5 Radio broadcasters must have particular regard to times when children are particularly likely to be listening.
> 1.6 The transition to more adult material must not be unduly abrupt at the watershed (in the case of television) or after the time when children are particularly likely to be listening (in the case of radio). For television, the strongest material should appear later in the schedule.
> 1.7 For television programmes broadcast before the watershed, or for radio programmes broadcast when children are particularly likely to be listening, clear information about content that may distress some children should be given, if appropriate, to the audience (taking into account the context). (Ofcom 2013, 7-8)[5]

These are just some rules in a panoply of constraints on media content imposed by UK legislation (compliance with which it is the function of the *Code* to ensure), and many of the restrictions do not apply solely to children or those under eighteen. Most are aimed at preventing harm or offence (that is, designed to minimise certain "effects"), a considerable

---

[5] In guidance included in the same passage of the *Code* from which these rules have been excerpted, children are defined as "people under the age of fifteen years", "the watershed" (which applies to TV only) is specified as "at 2100", and "times when children are particularly likely to be listening" (which are relevant to radio only) are clarified as referring to "the school run and breakfast time, but might include other times".

amount of which seem to be based on a political consensus that certain groups, especially young people as contrasted with adults, have as yet insufficient interpretative (or "critical") skills to be able to process certain kinds of broadcast material without risk to their well-being.

Despite these many legal constraints, the climate in which broadcasters in the UK work remains relatively permissive and liberal when compared to the situations in many other countries, and we perhaps need to remind ourselves that media censorship on the whole is today much lighter in most countries than it was, say, even just thirty years ago. Nonetheless, many scholars within Cultural Studies stand aghast (as do I) at the fact that the greatest success in the very real world of public legislation that the study of the media can claim should derive in large part from a general acceptance of the conservative findings of populist, intellectually vulgar research into "media effects" on audiences. The usual response from Cultural Studies to the experimental psychology lobby is to point out that its position is broadly based on (1) a fundamental argument which is simply not demonstrable, namely that, exposed to certain kinds of media material, at least some members of an audience are so "uncritical" that they either believe entirely what is said, or are unable to distinguish what is possible in fictionally represented conduct from what is appropriate in real-world behaviour (or, put in simpler terms, unable to tell fantasy from reality); and/or (2) an unjustified prejudice against the media which blames it for a number of social ills which, in actual fact, have quite other origins (for example, in the poor mental health, or low levels of education or socialisation, or even the simple innate or developed social psychopathy, of those who commit violence). The debate as conducted by these opposing camps using polarised conceptions seems to me condemned forever to stalemate, and I suggest, before returning to the possible significance of the "critical listener" to Radio 4 in all of this, that we might consider whether or not any compromises can be made between the two positions.

To begin with, we all know, because it is perfectly obvious, that the media can exert powerful psychological and physical effects. Comedy can make us laugh out loud; a horror movie can raise goose bumps or cause us to start in shock or fear; coverage of a sporting event can bring us to our feet, exclaiming with joy or dismay; we can find ourselves weeping at a range of media material, from tragic drama to moving documentaries;

erotica and pornography can (quite literally) give rise to a desired effect which it is hard not to notice. Few of these results last very long, however, and while they may have observable repercussions on the body or the mind, they do not usually have very noticeable effects on subsequent real-life behaviour. We do not go on laughing for hours after the comedy has ended; we do not sleep with the lights on three nights straight after watching the horror movie; we do not go into a profound depression, take to bed and not go to work for a week because we watched our team lose; we do not find ourselves becoming uncontrollably and continually lachrymose for a fortnight after watching a "weepie"; we do not spend the next month attempting to rape members of the opposite sex, even if we have seen the same thing simulated in a hardcore porn video. The reason this is so is that we have acquired "critical" (or discriminative) mental functions which allows us to differentiate the conventions of organised (or staged) media representations from the quite different conventions which govern everyday real life.[6] This is why (however unpleasant it may be to acknowledge that this is true) consumers of pornography can take pleasure in watching a simulated rape while genuinely abhorring the real crime. It is no doubt even more uncomfortable to contemplate, although it is essentially what Aristotelian concept of *catharsis* has sometimes been used to argue,[7] that the disinclination of some men to rape may be related directly to the possibility of being able to take vicarious pleasure

[6] The "we" in this paragraph is meant to designate adults with, as indicated, "average" mental health, cognitive understanding and levels of emotional affect. Clearly there are people in certain categories, such as those with a mental illness or disability, the very elderly, and children, who might not be so classified. Curiously, however, no one can prevent a senile or mentally ill person from consuming whatever media is available in circulation: such prohibitions apply only to children, even if they are "normally" functional.

[7] In his *Poetics*, Aristotle uses the concept *catharsis* to explain the powerful effect on the audience of tragic drama. Although he himself does not so define his metaphorical use of the term, it was bandied about by subsequent interpreters to argue that the violence of tragedy permits a purification or purgation of the emotions of pity and fear. By experiencing pity and fear vicariously by means of the dramatic simulation, runs this interpretation, the audience is restored to a real-life state voided of these powerful emotions. Whether or not this was Aristotle's actual meaning, one can easily see how the concept, so formulated, can be applied to argue that modern media representations of sex, violence and crime have effects, but in fact benign, socially pacifying effects.

in watching media simulations of the act. Experimental psychologists will no doubt continue to use the blunt instrument of stimulus-response theories to try to establish that certain kinds of media directly cause social harm, but in doing so they will wittingly ignore, as they always have, the fact that most people are usually able critically to distinguish simulation from reality. While most experimental psychologists working in this field are unlikely to accept the *catharsis* argument, those who do accept it can easily accuse *them* of contributing to social harm by their wish to censor or prohibit material useful for cathartic purposes.[8]

On balance, I am with the Aristotelians. If in fact we do experience long-term adverse effects on our conduct subsequent to consuming certain kinds of media, it is likely to be because we are suffering some more profound mental or bodily disturbance than could possibly be attributed to the media text as a cause. Even when we continue to consume particular kinds of strongly stimulating media, even to become in some way "addicted", say, to representations of violence or sex, the law of diminishing returns often kicks in, and the stimulus tends to lead to less and less potent reactions. Where this does not occur, or where our judgment or our mental health become degraded in the process, to the extent that we try consciously to "live out" these kinds of fantasy in our actual lives by becoming, say, a stalker or a serial killer, the cause cannot really, it seems to me, be said to lie in the nature of the material itself, but in our obsessional "choice" (if such a word can be used of a compulsion) to consume it to the point where we have lost our usually operating "critical" functions with regard to it. A person who drinks even too much water may be killed by it, but it would be absurd to say that his death was caused by the fatal properties of water.

This is not to deny that the media *does* demonstrably have effects on our everyday conduct. Indeed, it is precisely and largely because what we see and hear through the media does affect our behaviour that so many lobbyists, politicians, business-people, social activists, moralists, char-

---

[8] These experimental psychologists therefore tend to be aesthetic Platonists, not Aristotelians: they share Plato's suspicion that artistic *mimesis* overwhelms our usually rational state of mind by arousing powerful and uncontrollable emotional states. Like Plato in the *Republic*, who wished to exclude poets from the ideal State, their solution (at least to what they consider the most destructive forms of media representation) is prohibitive.

ities and more seek strenuously for access to it. But where we can convincingly claim these effects to have been brought about, it is usually not by means of simulated representations, but by the provision to us of data or opinion about the real world. If a Radio 4 weather bulletin tells me that there has been early morning flooding in the centre of Birmingham, this data will have the effect that I avoid Birmingham today, although I was planning to travel there. This decision of mine is not made out of gullibility or because I fail to take a "critical" attitude towards the weather bulletin, however. I would have to be suffering from a peculiar form of paranoia if I believed that the weather report was broadcast out of a deliberate intent to deceive, not least because it comes from a source (the BBC) not known predominantly for hoaxing the nation. My conduct is therefore influenced because I believe the information given to be true or at least trust it to have been given in good faith: it is not simulated, nor is it about an imaginary or fictional world, but about the world in which the city of Birmingham actually exists and in which I am actually intending to travel there. If I avoid Birmingham I have the weather report to thank for helping me make a decision beneficial to myself.

Likewise, the usually extensive Radio 4 coverage of a general election campaign has a great deal of potential to affect my conduct. I may use the contents of that coverage to help me decide how to vote, or not to vote at all; the coverage will almost certainly affect the kinds of conversations I have with relatives and friends; I may refer to it when I harangue any local politician who dares darken my doorstep; and so on. I will not be "uncritical" of that coverage, because I am aware that its content does not have the status of straightforward "data" but is a complex admixture of data and opinion, that its discourse is not one that can be judged by standards of simple veracity but is, in fact, largely pervaded by rhetoric. But, although I shall not have the same degree of accepting trust in such coverage as I might have in a weather report, if it is one of my principal sources of election-related comment it is highly likely to influence how I act in relation to that election.

One could reproduce dozens of similar likely scenarios. If "Money Box Live" (Wednesday, 15.00) tells me about some new rock-bottom mortgage interest rate on offer, I may call up to begin changing my mortgage provider before the programme has even ended. If I have a visual impairment and "In Touch" (Tuesday, 20.40) informs me of an extremely useful new iPhone or Android app which helps me better negotiate railway stations, I may purchase it and find my mobility transformed. If I discover from "You and Yours" (weekdays, 12.00) that a new fee will be levied from 29 July for lodging an employment tribunal claim, it is highly probable that I will act to take a case against the employer who recently fired me before that date rather than after it.

In short, where the media discourses to us about the actual (rather than an imaginary) world, it seems to be that the case for probable "media effects" on our course of conduct is at its strongest, because the referent of that discourse, what it claims to describe or analyse, is not the fictive or the enacted, but the very world in which we breathe and move, here and now – the world of "Today". It therefore seems to me extremely odd that "media effects" propagandists have chosen largely to pitch their tent on the rocky ground of media simulations when, in fact, there is much more grip in the soil of media discourses which purport to tell us what is happening, and explain how and why it may be happening, in the current world of the socially real.

Radio 4 is a station which largely, though not exclusively, sets out to do just that, for many hours a day, by means of its myriad news and current affairs programmes, documentaries, round-table discussions on politics and the arts, and magazine-type features on business, science, economics, culture, consumer affairs, and more. The scope for influencing (or "affecting" or even changing) individual and collective behaviour is enormous for such a station by comparison with the rather pitiable influential possibilities of the BBC's other terrestrial radio channels, devoted as they are (with the exception of the World Service) almost exclusively to monolithic genres of output (music on Radios 1, 2, and 3, sport on 5 live). If one seeks a pressing reason for the importance of an audience being informed, critical, discriminating and sceptical, it is in relation to a station with such potential ideological influence: indeed, it is hard to think of another radio station in the world with such concentrated discursive status and power.[9]

This is why, although the BBC's independence from government is an essential element in its valued freedom from any simple editorial or ideological alignment, it is nonetheless properly subject to a degree of

[9] The World Service, very similar in character to Radio 4, is by virtue of its global reach probably the radio station with the greatest *dispersed* status and power.

liberal democratic control in the form of legislation, regulation and publicly codified constraint. It also explains why there is considerable professional agreement within the BBC itself that a station like Radio 4 should be accountable to government and listeners for its output and that it should be diverse, pluralistic and, for want of better words, "balanced" or "impartial" in ideological terms. It is why Radio 4 even invites criticism of itself by means of a regularly scheduled slot like "Feedback" (Friday, 16.30; repeated Sunday, 20.00), which happens to be one of many of its programmes commissioned from production companies independent of the BBC.[10] None of this means that Radio 4 is beyond criticism, or that listeners may incautiously throw down their critical defences before its acknowledged editorial integrity. But there is good reason to suppose that a station with such high professional standards and undeniable culture of editorial integrity might make us feel encouraged to criticise it less in the manner of typically negative and dismissive "media criticism", and more in the positive and affirming "literary critical" vein.

References

Anderson, C. A. and Bushman, B. J. (2001). "Effects of violent games on aggressive behavior, aggressive cognition, aggressive affect, physiological arousal, and prosocial behavior: a meta-analytic review of the scientific literature". *Psychological Science* 12, 353-9.

Anonymous. (2008). 'BBC apology for 'rude' plant chat". BBC News, 5 February. **http://news.bbc.co.uk/2/hi/entertainment/7229041.stm** (accessed 12 October 2013).

Daly, M. (2016). *Reading Radio 4*. London: Palgrave Macmillan.

Ofcom. (2013). *The Ofcom Broadcasting Code (Incorporating the Cross-Promotion Code)*. London: Office of Communications.

Ryan, M. (ed.) (2008). *Cultural Studies: an Anthology*. Oxford: Blackwell.

2013

---

[10] "The Media Show" (Wednesday, 16.30) also regularly scrutinises BBC policies and practice. Indeed, Radio 4 ever aired a comedy show which entirely poked fun at BBC radio, and especially at the station itself: "Listen Against" ran in a weekday 18.30 slot for four series between 2007 and 2011.

"ANTI-TABLOID PARANOIA"? *THE SUN*, LABOUR, AND THE 1992 UK GENERAL ELECTION[1]

Labour and the Tory Press

Announcing his intention to resign as Labour leader on 13 April 1992, Neil Kinnock chose to blame his party's election defeat, in the first instance, on the Tory press:

> There will be many opportunities to consider the causes and consequences of last Thursday's election result. I will not dwell on them here. I will content myself, for the moment, with drawing attention to the words of the former treasurer of the Conservative party, Lord McAlpine, in yesterday's *Sunday Telegraph*: "The heroes of this campaign," said Lord McAlpine, "were Sir David English [editor of the *Daily Mail*], Sir Nicholas Lloyd [editor of the *Daily Express*], Kelvin MacKenzie [editor of *The Sun*] and the other editors of the grander Tory Press. Never in the past nine elections have they come out so strongly in favour of the Conservatives. Never has their attack on the Labour Party been so comprehensive [...] This was how the election was won, and if the politicians, elated in their hour of victory, are tempted to believe otherwise, they are in very real trouble next time."
>
> Lord McAlpine could not be expected to acknowledge the degree of misinformation and disinformation employed in the attacks on the Labour Party, but in all other respects his assessment is correct.[2]

This claim was consistent with the other main explanation offered for the Tory victory by Labour, namely that opinion polls showing a clear Labour lead throughout the campaign were correct, but that there was a swing in

---

[1] This is a written version of a lecture for May Day, 1992, delivered at the University of Nottingham. I would like to thank Gordon Riddell, Sydney Daly and Chris Davies for assistance with material, and Chris Wright for discussion on some of the issues raised herein. I would also like to register my especial gratitude to Mark Pursehouse for kind permission to quote from his unpublished research on *Sun* readers.
[2] "'My Decisions Require Rapid Change'", *The Independent*, 14 April 1992, p. 1.

support to the Conservatives in the three days prior to the election as a result of the mainly tabloid bombardment. To point the finger at the Tory press thus exonerated the Labour campaign, the party's policies, and Kinnock's leadership itself, from responsibility for electoral failure. It also permitted Kinnock to avoid admitting that it was the Tory campaign, Tory policies, or John Major, which won the election for the Conservatives. Indeed, Kinnock expressly dismissed these possibilities in his condemnation of the press:

> [...] the Conservative-supporting Press has enabled the Tory party to win yet again when the Conservative Party could not have secured victory for itself on the basis of its record, its programme or its character. The relationship between the Conservative Party and those newspapers which Lord McAlpine describes as being edited by "heroes" is a fact of British political life.
>
> I did think that it would be possible this time to succeed in achieving change in spite of that. Clearly it wasn't. Success will therefore have to wait.[3]

Labour subsequently decided to make representations to the Press Complaints Commission and the Advertising Standards Authority regarding "flagrantly misleading factual statements" in a variety of tabloid and broadsheet newspapers.[4]

The pros and cons of this argument were debated, in somewhat familiar terms, on succeeding days. *The Guardian* in particular devoted many columns to the controversy. Roy Greenslade felt that "to listen to party members closing ranks to revile evil press barons is to hear prison doors clanking shut on their minds".[5] John Ezard, however, found two Labour

---

[3] *Ibid.*

[4] John Ezard, "Party Calls in Media Watchdogs Over 'Onslaught'", *The Guardian*, 18 April 1992, p. 3. Moreover, in June 1992, the Labour Party's National Executive Committee endorsed a report identifying a "tabloid factor" which, it was claimed, lost Labour 381,000 votes, more than half of which it attributed to *The Sun*.

[5] "Partial Reasons", *The Guardian*, 14 April 1992, p. 23. I am sympathetic to Greenslade's general position, but he is concerned only with the tabloids' explicit content and hardly with how readers negotiate it. It ought also to be noted that Greenslade's career has consisted almost wholly of spells with the *Sunday Mirror*,

canvassers, one in Waveney and one in Basildon (that crucial marginal), who claimed that, in the last few days of the campaign, appreciable numbers of sympathetic voters were announcing on the doorstep that they had decided not to vote Labour after all because of what they had read in the tabloids about Labour's tax plans.[6] *The Guardian's* correspondence columns were equally divided. Employees of News International, the group which owns *The Sun*, made criticisms of Kinnock's position which were not only institutionally partisan. Paul Connew, Deputy Editor of the *News of the World*, made a case for the tabloids as primarily agents of entertainment rather than news:

> [...] the truth is that a tabloid newspaper's political stance is fairly low on the totem pole of reasons why the majority of its readers buy it. General affinity with the style of a particular title, plus the popularity of an individual columnist, racing tipster, astrologer or cartoonist, usually rank higher.[7]

This suggested that the debate might more profitably be moved onto the ground of what readers do *with papers* rather than what papers do *to them*; but its author was more concerned to proceed to pillory Labour's "anti-tabloid paranoia" than to investigate how readers in fact negotiate the relationship between the priorities of leisure and politics which he had invoked. The fatal weakness of this perspective, furthermore, is that it views a paper's politics as separable from its "style [...] individual columnist, racing tipster, astrologer or cartoonist". As we shall see, such a distinction is invalid: most of these elements are demonstrably integrated into tabloid politics. Conversely, then, there may be something to be said for Labour's "paranoia". One correspondent was anxious to counter the notion that, even if it is only the Tory converted who buy the tabloids in question, these are not the only people who read them: for instance, "The *Mail* has a promotions campaign whereby anybody buying a McDonalds breakfast

---

the *Daily Express*, the *Daily Star*, and *The Sun*; from February 1990 to March 1991 he was editor of the *Daily Mirror*: see S.J.Taylor, *Shock! Horror! The Tabloids in Action* (London, Bantam Press, 1991), pp. 262, 266.

[6] John Ezard, "Labour Counts Cost of Tabloids' Bombshell", *The Guardian*, 18 April 1992, p. 3.

[7] Paul Connew, letter to *The Guardian*, 17 April 1992, p. 20.

receives a free copy of the paper: these are not all Tory converted."[8]

This is true. A large number of readers of right-wing newspapers are not Tories by conviction (many are not Tories at all), and no one disputes that some voters must be influenced to some degree one way or another by what they read in the tabloids. But one of the problems with the election post-mortem arguments is that they depend on far too many unexamined assumptions about how readers respond to tabloid texts. Readers are envisaged as either wholly assenting to or dissenting from elements of a particular paper's political line (e.g. what it says about tax), and their voting preferences are assumed to be directly related to this assent or dissent. The assumption fails to take into account all kinds of variables, such as, to name only two, their recourse to other sources of news, and their participation in political discussion within households and workplaces. In these and other contexts the content of the tabloid press is often the subject of critical reflection and scrutiny. The essential redundancy of the "election by tabloid" case, then, is not that the tabloids are uninfluential, but that their direct influence, its degree and extent, can only remain a matter of speculation rather than knowledge. There is no ready means whereby this supposed persuasive capacity can be observed or measured. The Labour argument thus comes to take on the appearance of an article of faith, and Kinnock's complaint was easily refuted as sour grapes by the editorial writers of *The Guardian* and *The Independent*,[9] as well as the Tory tabloids in question.

One of the inadequacies of Kinnock's statement is its blinkered focus on "misinformation and disinformation". From this angle, the tabloids are seen simply as *deceiving* their readers into voting Conservative, by telling deliberate lies, half truths, or lies of omission, about Labour policies. While the election campaign threw up many examples of falsehood and factual

---

[8] John Pollard, letter to *The Guardian*, 17 April 1992, p. 20. The misguided "preaching to the Tory converted" argument had been put by an employee of News International, Andrew Knight, in a letter to *The Guardian*, 15 April 1992, p. 20. Surprisingly, Knight's rather negligible letter provoked a curiously pointless reply from Kinnock himself (*The Guardian*, 16 April 1992, p. 22). There were many more letters on this issue in *The Guardian* throughout April than I cite here.

[9] See "Mr Kinnock's Bitter Farewell", *The Independent*, 14 April 1992, p. 18, and "Beyond the Smoke of Tabloid Battle", *The Guardian*, 18 April 1992, p. 22.

licence (not to mention ingenious muckraking), [10] it seems to me that concentration on these elements of tabloid *content*, without corresponding regard to the tabloid *form*, tabloid *conventions*, and tabloid *culture*, is unlikely to help us to understand with any fulness how tabloids might, indeed, manage to win over the public to a particular political cause. For what the sole emphasis on "misinformation and disinformation" fails to do is address the issue of the range of techniques which the tabloid press has at its disposal. These are by no means restricted to deliberate lies and calculated deceptions, and they reveal a great deal about the tabloids' understanding of their readers.

In what follows, I intend to examine some of the formal strategies exhibited by *The Sun* during the 1992 general election campaign, under three main headings:

(a) tabloid visibility;
(b) the enlistment of celebrities;
(c) political exploitation of "Page 3".

Finally, turning to content rather than form, I shall consider *The Sun*'s problematic political allegiances. Having observed *The Sun*'s coverage as it happened, day by day, and bearing in mind the memory of its rampantly pro-Thatcher campaign of 1987, I hope to be able to offer some indications as to the likely effectiveness of this particular tabloid in influencing its readership during the recent campaign. My basic conclusion, quite contrary to Neil Kinnock's, will be that *The Sun*'s coverage, by comparison with 1987, was lacklustre and unconvincing in the extreme. I will try to

---

[10] Two consecutive front pages give a flavour of the *Sun* style in these modes.

The first, on 31 March 1992, reported that "A Labour government would revert to hard-line socialism as soon as it got into No 10, says Leftie Tony Benn". This proved to be a complete falsehood. Tony Benn neither said these words nor anything approximating to them during the television interview from which they were purportedly quoted. He argued nothing more unreasonable than that trades unions ought to enjoy a relationship with a Labour government similar to that which big business has with the Tories (*Star Chamber*, Channel 4, 1 April 1992).

Secondly, as a typical (but not, despite the date, jocular) example of muckraking, see the leading article of 1 April 1992, whose headline ran: "I'M ALRIGHT JACK: Shadow Education Minister lectures us on the scandal of private education from the luxury of his £300,000 cottage, his £200,000 town house and his £40,000 flat!"

show that *The Sun*'s difficulty in this election was that the bedrock belief in Toryism which has hitherto inspired its political rhetoric has evidently been shaken; and that, in any case, and in a quite strict sense, the political allegiances of the paper itself are not, as we shall see, as clear cut today as they were five years ago. This conclusion will then form the basis for some brief speculation as to what Labour can learn if it reconsiders the case of "election by tabloid".

Tabloid Visibility

The Sun's editor, Kelvin MacKenzie, was one of the first to pounce on Kinnock's resignation statement. According to him there had been no abuse of information in the paper and Kinnock was simply demonstrating what had always been evident, that he was a "whingeing politician" who could not accept defeat.[11] However, the two do not seem to have been in fundamental disagreement with specific regard to the question of the paper's influence: the message blazoned on the front page of *The Sun* two days earlier had been 'IT'S *THE SUN* WOT WON IT", the accompanying article stating, in typically over-the-top terms, the tabloid's pre-eminent rôle in securing victory for the Conservatives.[12]

[11] Kelvin MacKenzie, soundbite on ITN's *News at Ten*, 13 April 1992. MacKenzie's antagonism is unsurprising. Kinnock had himself issued a libel writ against the paper on 26 March (see *The Sun*, 27 March 1992, p. 5).

[12] *The Sun*, 11 April 1992, pp. 1-2.

Particular self-praise was lavished in this leader on *The Sun*'s election day issue, which featured the plea, in white lettering on a blue background, "If Kinnock wins today will the last person to leave Britain please turn out the lights".[13] According to the leader, "hundreds of readers hailed our polling day front page – showing Neil Kinnock's head in a light bulb – which alerted people to the dangers of Labour rule".[14] The remainder of the article purportedly reproduced items from this shower of applause:

> Tory MP Matthew Banks, who won back Southport from the Lib-Dems, could not thank *The Sun* enough.
> He said yesterday: "Wherever I went on polling day everyone was talking about *The Sun*'s front page.
> "We even stuck a huge blow-up of it on to the noticeboard in our campaign centre."[15]

> Shadow Environment Secretary Bryan Gould said 50 per cent of people in Basildon, Essex, are *Sun* readers.
> And that was "one of the factors there" that kept the marginal seat Tory – and made Labour realise their mistake.
> Winning Basildon MP David Amess got a majority of 1,480, a swing of only 1.3 per cent from Tories to Labour.
> He told us yesterday: "It was your front page that did it. It crystallized all the issues. People in Basildon were so impressed with *The Sun*'s front page that they stuck it in car windows."[16]

Anecdotal details imparted in the insomniac euphoria of election triumph should be treated cautiously, but what both of these extracts unconsciously draw attention to is *The Sun*'s *visibility*. It was not the informational content of the front page of 11 April that was seen as important. What was crucial about it was that it could be used as an electioneering flier. It was a poster rather than a tract. Three elements contributed to its eye-catching quality: the use of colour; the large and contrasting typeface; and the dimensions of the paper itself. Here the major and obvious formal

---

[13] *The Sun*, 9 April 1992, p. 1.
[14] *The Sun*, 11 April 1992, p. 1.
[15] *Ibid.*
[16] *Ibid.*

difference between tabloid and broadsheet – size – demonstrates the advantage, for such purposes, of the tabloid. *The Sun*, unlike *The Guardian* (which, as well as, amazingly, the *Financial Times*, had come out in favour of Labour), can indeed be placed in the window of a car. Furthermore, because of its more compact size one story can be allowed to dominate the page. On account of its smaller dimensions, therefore, *The Sun*'s front page was able to reach an audience far beyond merely its buyers and readers, particularly in newsagents' shops where, increasingly, the dailies are displayed in racks with tabloid-sized shelving, and the entire front pages of the tabloids thus face customers as they search for the paper they wish to buy. Broadsheets, by comparison, are folded in half and must be turned through ninety degrees to be accommodated in such shelving. Even if they did carry such front page slogans (which they do not), they are much less immediately noticeable and much less easily displayed. The essential difference here, then, has nothing to do with "misinformation and disinformation" and everything to do with the contrasting formal properties of tabloids and broadsheets. *The Sun* exploited its tabloid dimensions to full effect to maximise the visibility of its election day front page.

So pleased was *The Sun* with this leader that it printed a large souvenir poster of it which readers could obtain freely by writing to the paper explaining why they liked it. [17] But its influence, which has to be distinguished from its appeal, was more probably a figment of *The Sun*'s editorial imagination. The "light bulb joke" is obscure and inept. There was no frame of reference established at any moment in the campaign which would have directed readers as to how to "read" the light bulb or the placement of Kinnock's head within it. The decapitation effect no doubt aimed to make him look absurd, but the Kinnock physiognomy fits the light bulb rather too well, and the latter thus acts as a kind of halo around the former: if anything, Kinnock emerges from this skilful photomontage with the appearance of a saint rather than a demon (there is, indeed, a somewhat visionary cast about the eyes). The image graphically prophesies the political possibility the page is attempting to undermine, so that the cover's high visibility is potentially more ambiguous than it seems at a first glance conditioned by prior knowledge of the paper's political loyalties. The

[17] *Ibid.*

headline itself fails to provide a stable frame in which to read the photograph, its tenor being, on second thought, extremely defeatist. The message at best is an incitement to vote in protest against Kinnock rather than an affirmation of the merits of Major. This failure to declare any strong faith in John Major hung over *The Sun*'s entire election coverage; the comparison with its long-standing adoration of his predecessor is almost embarrassing. The reason for such lack of commitment was quite simply belief in the general accuracy of the opinion polls. Inside the same edition an editorial noted, with an evident air of wishful thinking, that "victory for John Major would be the most spectacular comeback since 1970 when the Tories won despite trailing 12 points behind Labour up to polling day".[18] Unlike 1987, when its interventions really did seem to matter, *The Sun* in 1992 was generally as half-hearted, lacking in invention, and defeatist as this front page, on analysis, turns out to be. Even the morning edition on the day after the election (printed late the previous evening but appearing when everyone knew the actual result) was a proclamation of disbelief in the possibility of an overall Tory majority: "DEAD HEAT: It's a Hung Parliament".[19]

The Enlistment of Celebrities

The Sun had made a much more positive start to the campaign. Its front-page headline on the day after the announcement of the election read "BOTHAM BATS FOR MAJOR: Cricket Ace Joins Tory Poll Battle":

> England cricket hero Ian Botham is to help Premier John Major hit Labour for six in the election.
>
> Botham, a close friend of cricket-mad Mr Major, is expected to announce his full support for the Tory campaign after he returns from the World Cup in Australia.
>
> His backing is a sensational catch for the Prime Minister, who yesterday announced Britain will go to the polls on April 9.
>
> It will also stump Labour leader Neil Kinnock in his bid to mop up the support of big-name sports stars.[20]

[18] "Photo Finish", *The Sun*, 9 April 1992, p. 2.
[19] *The Sun*, 10 April 1992, p. 1.
[20] *The Sun*, 12 March 1992, p. 1.

An article like this encapsulates what broadsheet readers find confusing and risible about the tabloids, their unerring talent for highlighting the trivial and ignoring the momentous. Such readers fail to understand a tabloid culture which can accord a cricketer political status equal to that of a Prime Minister (and in this instance perhaps even more). Mark Pursehouse, in his research on *The Sun* – on which I will be drawing later – has memorably described its culture as one in which

> [...] a very ordered, limited and serious ideological view is presented as a full, dynamic, entertaining representation of the world. Populist interest in individuals, personalities, sex, scandal, violence, sport and amusement are presented in a lively, identifiable language and format which makes the ideological layer of reinforcement for a heterosexual, male, white, conservative, capitalist, British world elusive.[21]

In other words, there is an important connection between the ideology of *The Sun* and its style, but this connection is not readily perceived by readers. I would argue that, on account of evident political imperatives, this relation is more obvious in the metaphorical "wartime" of an election than the "peacetime" of government. The curious eruption of a sporting hero from the rear pages to the front page of *The Sun*, when there was news of seemingly much greater moment to report, can be shown to demonstrate the link rather well.

The intention of the story is to associate two kinds of campaign: that of the England cricket team to win the World Cup, and that of the Conservative Party to gain victory in the General Election. The cricketing enterprise (at this point in time it was looking extremely promising) is a struggle which can be relied upon to have considerable support across the populace; a support, significantly, which is widely offered irrespective of class, profession and status (although not, perhaps, irrespective of sex or nationality). John Major is depicted as fervently lending his weight to that loyalty, and Botham as passionately declaring his favour for John Major, the two campaigners thus becoming mutually reinforcing symbols of

---

[21] Mark Pursehouse, "The Discourse of *The Sun*" (unpublished dissertation, Centre for Contemporary Cultural Studies, University of Birmingham). Part of this thesis is now available as "Looking at *The Sun*: Into the Nineties With a Tabloid and Its readers", *Cultural Studies from Birmingham* 1 (1991), pp. 88-133.

national commitment, implying that the logical extension of support for one is support for the other. The success of both, the article goes on to predict, would probably revivify a dispirited citizenry:

> A friend of "Beefy" Botham said last night: "He thinks John Major is marvellous."
> *Other England team stars could follow the all-rounder's lead by batting for the Tories.*
> Support from the World Cup side would be a huge boost for the Major campaign.
> England are favourites to win the final in Melbourne on March 25 – two weeks before polling day.
> Victory would be a massive morale-booster during the economic gloom.[22]

The enlistment of this particular celebrity, therefore, is made in an attempt to transfer an already operative allegiance for one patriotic venture (England in the World Cup) into active endorsement of another (the Tories in the election). There was considerable mileage in it, one would have thought, up to the point of the England team's failure to win in Australia, but in fact the device was never repeated. The reason was simple:

> Ian Botham, the cricketer, has issued a High Court writ claiming damages for malicious falsehood against the editor and publishers of *The Sun* over a report on 12 March under the headline "Botham Bats for Major".[23]

False information, then, is an element here, but hardly the prime one. Botham's Tory sympathies are not at issue, for they are public knowledge. The falsehood consists simply in the fact that he made no specific endorsement of Major of the kind claimed. The persuasive potential of the article does not essentially reside in this fiction, but in the careful yoking together of sporting loyalty and political preference, by the assimilation of

---

[22] *Ibid.* (italics in original).
[23] Rachel Borrill, "They Had Them on the List But Some of Them Were Miffed", *The Independent on Sunday*, 22 March 1992, p. 19.

two disparate national icons. Botham's litigious action seems to have spoiled the party just as it was getting started. This was the cleverest thing *The Sun* did in the entire month of its election coverage.

The broadsheet reader's difficulty with *The Sun* is essentially caused by bringing an invalid explanatory model to bear on the interaction between tabloid reader and text. Pursehouse's interviews with four *Sun* readers demonstrate that the purposes for which they turn to it make the term "newspaper" something of a misnomer. Information and discussion about the public worlds of politics, culture and commerce are not high on their list of priorities in their choice of daily reading. On a purely informational basis, sports news and television schedules are of greater interest. Moreover, *The Sun*'s "entertainment" value is its main attraction. It provides amusement, pleasure in gossip, and (for many of its male heterosexual readers at least) erotic stimulation. These elements are delivered in a format which is linguistically brief and undemanding, allowing the paper to be frequented at various points in the day, and thus the paper accommodates itself effectively to the working routines of many people. Pursehouse's interviewees were generally able to recognise and hold at arm's length *The Sun*'s partisan politics. The weight of evidence he assembles suggests that explicit political content is not the major factor in *The Sun*'s formation and mobilisation of political belief and action. Of greater importance is the "ideological coup" effected from within the "entertainment" ethos of the paper.

The main "news" of *The Sun* consists of gossip about the private lives of public figures in television, film, popular music, sport, and royalty, preferring a scandalised tone of a usually sexual complexion. *The Sun* thus addresses its readers, in the main, as *leisured* subjects. Its content is derived, by and large, from the actions of the *dramatis personae* of the mass media with which its readers occupy many of their non-working hours. It is through this "populist interest", to cite again Pursehouse's description, that *The Sun*'s "very ordered, limited and serious ideological view" is channelled. For election purposes, the inevitably Tory sympathies of many of the affluent stars featured regularly in its pages are trumpeted loudly and clearly, the advocacy of Conservatism resting not so much on arguments articulated in defence of the party's policies or record, as on an emotive emphasis to the effect that pleasure and Toryism are co-extensive.

The Sun's enlistment of celebrities in the forging of this emphasis is, of course, extremely partial. In comparison to Botham, its treatment of another of its heroes, Brian Clough, the football manager whose Nottingham Forest team was preparing for the Rumbelows Cup Final at Wembley, had to be much more politically reticent. Articles about and interviews with Clough remained in the sports pages only, and although he was described as a "self-confessed millionaire",[24] his Labour loyalties were not mentioned. Bearing this in mind, however, all was essentially business as usual in the celebrity *Sun*, party politics generally being left aside. The frequent domination of front pages by stories which had no party political overtones – for example, Hulk Hogan's alleged cocaine snorting, Mandy Smith's pre-menstrual tension and suicide bid, Fergie and Andy's divorce, Earl Spencer's death, Graham Souness's heart operation – suggests a desire to use the celebrity card as an exit pass, an escape, from a difficult and perhaps boring election campaign.[25] Even on 9 April *The Sun* was reluctant to devote the entire cover to politics: beside Kinnock in the light bulb ran a column headed "TENNIS CHAMP ASHE HAS AIDS".[26]

When celebrities were linked with politics, the effect was often potentially ambiguous. The anti-Labour remarks of another sportsman, the boxer Chris Eubank, could hardly have had the mobilising capacity of the Botham story:

> "I can manage now to pay 40 per cent tax. But if Neil Kinnock is the next Prime Minister we will be paying 50, 60 or perhaps 80 per cent tax. Even on a million pound purse I would end up with less than I need to live."[27]

The slippage from "I" to "we" in this comment is, of course, extremely misleading, but if voting intentions were altered by Eubank's described financial plight it is hard to believe that the change worked in John Major's favour. Likewise, the presentation of William Roache (the actor who plays

[24] John Sadler, "On to Year No. 28 – and Defeat Still Hurts Brian", *The Sun* ["GOALS" Section], 6 April 1992, p. 5.
[25] See, respectively, the front pages of *The Sun* for 13, 14, 19 and 31 March, and 6 April 1992. The excess of newsprint devoted to Souness on 6 April and succeeding days was particularly spectacular, given the imminence of polling day.
[26] *The Sun*, 9 April 1992, p. 1.
[27] "EUBANK: I WILL QUIT BRITAIN IF NEIL WINS", *The Sun*, 7 April 1992, p. 4.

the *Coronation Street* character Ken Barlow) as a Tory exemplar might have given the wrong message altogether. As every *Sun* reader knows, the paper considered Roache "boring, self-satisfied and smug" last year, for which comment he successfully sued it to the tune of £50,000.[28]

Political Exploitation of "Page 3"

The strategy of identifying pleasure and politics is nowhere more flagrant than in *The Sun*'s electioneering attempts to do for Toryism what a glance at the Conservative Cabinet would suggest was impossible: to make it seem sexy. One way that it attempts this is to have some of its topless "Page 3" models avow that they intend to vote Conservative. In all essentials *The Sun* recycled its strategy of 1987 in this respect, but with amazing incompetence. It opened a series of "Page 3 Vote Winners" three days before polling with a twenty-two year old from Northampton, whose only item of clothing, apart from arm-length gloves, was a rosette on her left thigh urging the viewer, in rather small lettering, to "VOTE Conservative", the accompanying caption, in *The Sun*'s customary pun-a-microsecond style, explaining, "TORY be! Rosette-wearing Rachel Garley can't wait for election day – she's a de-voted fan of John Major and wants to show her true-blue colours."[29] The picture, however, was black-and-white, which was a major problem with Rachel's successor on the Tuesday, whose rosette didn't bear any words and, in monochrome, could easily have been red or blue. We had to read the caption, which did not cry out for immediate attention, to discover that "SUPER Sami is backing Tory chairman Chris Patten. The Lincoln lass, 21, will vote for him any time – she thinks he's a bit of all Right."[30] (Bearing in mind Patten's failure to be re-elected two days later, the case for tabloid influence is perhaps here starting to wear somewhat thin!) It wasn't, seemingly, until the Wednesday

---

[28] Roache fell ill with a perforated ulcer on 24 March "hours after meeting former PM Margaret Thatcher" during his "battle for the Tories in the North West" ("KEN BARLOW IN HOSPITAL WITH ULCER'", *The Sun*, 27 March, 1992, p. 19). "Staunch Tory Bill received get-well cards from John Major and Margaret Thatcher" as well as using the opportunity to say, "The NHS saved my life – it's a wonderful institution. I would not hear a criticism against it" ("TV Ken: I Lost Half My Blood", *The Sun*, 31 March 1992, p. 6).
[29] "Rachel is Polls Apart", *The Sun*, 6 April 1992, p. 11.
[30] "Sami is Right Behind Chris", *The Sun*, 7 April 1992, p. 7.

that someone in *The Sun* office put two and two together. A major technical difference between 1987 and 1992 is that *The Sun* now has colour, and black-and-white "Vote Winners" should thus have been consigned to the past. Accordingly, the picture editor's choice for the Wednesday arrived adorned in blue rosette and panties:

> TRUE Blue Tracey Coleman is hoping for a Tory landslide tomorrow – or she'll be more than a little cross.
>
> The 22-year-old Sheffield lass has enough X appeal to produce a winning swing. After all, she's already a couple of points ahead in the opinion polls.[31]

It is easy to ridicule or take offence at "Page 3", but the important thing is to try to understand what *Sun* readers make of it. Pursehouse's two female interviewees tended to ignore it, but not to be opposed to it: "it don't do nothing for me" and "if you don't want to look at it you don't have to" are representative reactions. If the "Page 3 Vote Winners" did actually win any votes, it is unlikely that these were from women. By contrast, the two male readers interviewed by Pursehouse found "Page 3" an absolutely constitutive element of their pleasure in *The Sun*, perhaps the greatest single pleasure of all. Here is the opening of Pursehouse's interview with Adrian, a twenty-year-old qualified bricklayer who left school at sixteen. Pursehouse informs us that Adrian "has a 'labour' background, with his father a member of N.A.L.G.O." (M = Mark Pursehouse; A = Adrian):

M.   Describe what you do on your working day.

A.   Well, it consists of getting up around 6.45. Down at work for 7 o'clock, going from the yard in Cannock at 7 to the job. Arriving there, unlocking, going to the cabin, having a quick cup of tea and a glance at the paper – at this stage only the back page.

M.   That's the first look?

A.   That's the first look of the day – not even when I buy it – I've got to be in the cabin first. Then it's never opened – it's only the back page, due to the quick rush of having a quick cup of tea and going straight out – just a quick read.

---

[31] *The Sun*, 8 April 1992, p. 17.

M. You've got to do some work then?

A. Yes, well, until half past nine, breakfast time.

M. Is there another look at the paper after breakfast?

A. Yes we do. We get to breakfast; at this stage it's straight to the front. Then it's a read of the front page and then the highlight of the day, turning to page 3. Just a quick glance, like, opening it up – never before. If anybody asks me, "What's on page 3?", which some do, like in the morning as soon as we get there, I always open it and never show me, so they can see and they'll comment – I don't look myself. Very, erm, specific point, that is, to save that 'til breakfast.

Pursehouse's other male interviewee, Keith, "a middle-aged unqualified worker at [a] paint and varnish factory [...] married with two young children and living on a modest housing estate" referred to "Page 3" five times in a short interview without once being specifically asked to comment on it. At work, he explained, "we always – no matter how many's in the room – we always stop at page 3 – sort of spread it round, you know, 'Who is it today?' – it's either a 'ugh' or 'phew'".

For these readers, "Page 3" is bound up with certain daily routines and communal experiences with other men. It is a regular feature of the day and produces conversation among a group. One can only speculate as to whether a political message when incorporated with this erotic stimulus is more effective (that perhaps depends, among other things, on whether the woman depicted registers an "ugh" or a "phew"), but one can imagine their disappointment when the stimulus is unexpectedly withdrawn. *The Sun* did this on 2 June 1987, when a blank space appeared on page 3 and readers were informed that this was how the page would look in future if Labour got into power. Exploiting a current issue – Clare Short's proposals to have photographs of topless women prohibited in daily newspapers – *The Sun*'s attempt on that occasion to press the sexual anticipations of its male heterosexual readers into political service demonstrated a shrewd intelligence.

But it was a masterstroke that could be used only once. *The Sun* in 1992 made a colourful and all too predictable attempt to reproduce something like it, this time on the day of the election. The 9 April edition presented readers with Pat Priestman, a fifty-three-year-old "former flab-o-gram", in a red off-the-shoulder swimsuit:

> There are really B-I-G changes for Page Three if Neil Kinnock gets to No. 10, *The Sun* can reveal today.
>
> Roly poly Pat Priestman would be the shape of things to come under a killjoy Labour government.
>
> It's not just taxes that will be heavy. It's not just the economy that will sag.
>
> Kinnock's opinions will not be the only things wobbling.
>
> Lefties like Clare Short want to ban pretty girls from the nation's favourite page. She has already tried once to bring in a bill stopping girls from going topless in papers.
>
> Labour has no plans, however, to stop the whole country going bust.[32]

This was one of the features hailed later by *The Sun* as an example of its electoral influence, but this claim is only a product of the paper's self-obsession. Clare Short's proposals were simply no longer current enough to make this more than a parody of *The Sun*'s previous election "Page 3" gimmick. The issue was too much of a dead letter, and its resurrection here more likely to produce a base amusement than the sexual anti-climax of its 1987 stunt. A crucial consideration is that male readers cannot now have a secure sense of anticipation regarding "Page 3", because it is no longer a *Sun* fixture. On the previous three days, indeed, the "Page 3" girl had actually appeared on pages 11, 7 and 17 respectively, and on the odd occasion (such as 14 March 1992) she does not appear at all. "Page 3" fans of the 'nineties have to hunt through the first half of the paper to find her, and are more used to disappointment nowadays in any case.

The Problematic Politics of the 1992 *Sun*

Much more could be said about the formal strategies exhibited by *The Sun* during the election. Its uses of humour and fantasy, for instance, might be worth analysing. A large cartoon appears daily, adjacent to the editorial column, and often acts as a humorous gloss on it. In the month of campaigning, virtually all of these cartoons were anti-Labour. The point to make about this is not that it is especially objectionable (Steve Bell's daily "If..." strip in *The Guardian* is much more vehemently anti-Tory), but that

---

[32] "HERE'S HOW PAGE 3 WILL LOOK UNDER KINNOCK!", *The Sun*, 9 April 1992, p. 3.

it shows how the paper's politics are strongly integrated with its "entertainment" ethos. The self-conscious silliness of an article in which a psychic revealed how famous dead people would vote if they had the chance was, moreover, genuinely funny, but this, like so much *Sun* output of 1992, was a repeat from 1987.[33] By and large, analysis of these features would simply confirm what has already been argued. In short, *The Sun*'s attempts to mobilise its readers through the "entertainment" channel were usually uninspired, heavy handed, inept or repetitive.

Turning to its explicit political allegiances, one has to acknowledge immediately that *The Sun* is not as much of a Tory monolith as those who read only the "quality" press seem to believe. There was a great deal more anti-Tory than pro-Tory advertising in *The Sun* during the election period. As well as many "Vote Labour" advertisements, *The Sun* carried a series of blasts against the Tories sponsored by the trades union N.A.L.G.O.,[34] and a page strongly criticising Major's taxation record, placed by the Inland Revenue Staff Federation.[35] Of course, it might be said that the reason for this predominance of anti-Tory purchased space is that *The Sun* itself is, every day, an extended free advertisement for the Conservative Party, which therefore hardly needs to buy pages in the paper to have its voice heard.

However, a "Jilted Wife's Election Call", three days before polling, publicised the campaign of a divorced woman to persuade her local Tory party not to adopt her ex-husband, Tony Pratt, as a Council candidate. Pictured with a placard stating "DON'T VOTE FOR A PRATT", Hazel Pratt's complaint was that she had been "dumped by Tony in favour of his 23-year-old secretary two years ago" and wished to offer an "election message" as to the moral unsuitability of her ex-spouse to represent the people.[36] It is curious that a seemingly virulent Tory tabloid should choose

---

[33] "IT'S MAO OR NEVER FOR NEIL: Mao Tse Tung Backs Labour From Beyond Grave", *The Sun*, 8 April 1992. Labour emerged from this post-mortem poll as the largest single party, but with no overall majority, primarily because Adolf Hitler, Sir Francis Drake and Ghengis Khan voted Monster Raving Loony, Anti-Federalist and Don't Know respectively.

[34] See, for instance, *The Sun*, 25 March 1992, p. 14; 30 March 1992, p. 12; 4 April 1992, p. 14.

[35] *The Sun*, 6 April 1992, p. 23.

[36] "DON'T GIVE YOUR X TO MY EX, HE'S A PRATT", *The Sun*, 6 April 1992, p. 26.

precisely this juncture to run an article showing a Conservative candidate in such a bad light, even if the candidate in question was not a contender in the general election. The episode demonstrates that *The Sun* has certain "entertainment" priorities. If a scandal is juicy enough, it will run it regardless of politics.

But the most extraordinary political development was *The Sun*'s decision to back the Nationalists in Scotland. The extent to which it did so is graphically epitomised in its Scottish edition's polling day editorial, which presented an array of the Scottish *Sun*'s front pages since 23 January 1992 inside a St Andrew's cross with the accompanying words, "ENOUGH SAID: VOTE SNP".[37] The Scottish edition adopted the slogan "FIGHTING FOR INDEPENDENCE", which ran throughout the election period directly beneath its (bethistled) masthead. While the English *Sun* the day before polling was still gnawing its fingernails with uncertainty (its cover asking "WHO WILL BEST RUN BRITAIN?" and declaring that this was essentially "A QUESTION OF TRUST"), the front page of the Scottish *Sun* was telling its readers how to act: "DO IT FOR SCOTLAND: Vote SNP and We'll Be FREE".[38] The contradiction, it ought to be said, was not simply one of conviction. Here was a regional edition of a newspaper committing itself to a political party whose policy on the British constitution, an absolutely crucial election issue, is diametrically opposed to that of the party supported by the paper's parent edition. The Scottish *Sun*'s secession from its English master could hardly have been more spectacular. It also gives the "election by tabloid" theory its *coup de grâce*.

Cynical responses to the *Sun*'s Scottish strategy see it as a clever Tory plot. By urging readers to vote SNP, runs this argument, the Scottish *Sun* was splitting the Labour vote in Scotland, and thus frustrating Labour's advance. If this was so, the SNP could have been expected to perform much better than it did. In fact, it emerged with only three seats in the new Parliament. Yet Scotland was the only region in Britain in which there was

[37] "The Scottish *Sun* Speaks Its Mind", *The Sun* [Scottish edition], 9 April 1992, p. 6. Naturally, it was not simply on its covers that the Scottish *Sun* spoke its mind. A comparison of inside pages would show how widely and consistently it was at variance with the English edition. The Scottish *Sun* is separately edited and printed in Glasgow, although it duplicates a significant amount of material in the London-produced *Sun*.

[38] Cf. *The Sun*'s English and Scottish editions, 8 April 1992, p. 1.

a swing (of 3%) *to the Conservative party*. This occurred despite the fact that not one of the independent Scottish tabloid dailies urged its readers to vote Tory! These facts utterly confound Kinnock's "election by tabloid" argument, unless it is to be subject to an unvoiced and preposterous qualification which assigns greater gullibility to tabloid readers in England. The Scottish *Sun*'s approach to the election should be seen, rather, as an example of readers' limited power over the medium. This was a clear instance of negotiation with a potential readership threatening not to buy if the explicit ideology of the paper remained in conflict with the readership's conscious political sentiments. It is obvious to those who know the country that a Tory tabloid in Scotland cannot hope to commandeer a high circulation. When a newspaper's political line is in such flagrant contradiction with its commercial aspirations, the former goes out the window. For *The Sun* to compete in Scotland for the market dominated there by the Labour-supporting Mirror Group's *Daily Record*, the dead weight of its Toryism has had to be jettisoned.[39]

Insofar as an analysis of *The Sun* is helpful, then, there seems in Neil Kinnock's argument that the election was won by the tabloids to be little of

---

[39] I have been unable to obtain independent data on the daily circulation of The Scottish *Sun*. Its advertising desk (telephone conversation, 5 May 1992) claims a daily circulation of 300,000 and rising (the circulation for February/March 1992 was said to be approximately 284,000). The Audit Bureau's figure for the *Daily Record* in the second half of 1990 was 777,879 (*Benn's Media Directory (United Kingdom) 1991* [Tonbridge, Benn Business Information Service, 1991], p. 251) and its advertising desk cites a current figure of 760,003 (telephone conversation, 5 May 1992). Given its almost exclusively Scottish distribution, the *Daily Record* has a larger share of its market than any other British daily, and no Tory tabloid could hope to challenge it. The Scottish *Sun* has seen itself as directly challenging the *Record* since at least 11 May 1987, when its news editor, Steve Sampson, sent a circular to freelance journalists explaining his newly acquired control over the content of its "English" pages. Sampson's letter requested that the journalists offer the Scottish *Sun* the same service that they gave the *Daily Record* and stated that he was prepared to pay more and faster than the latter. Quotation gives a flavour of the directness of the challenge and the willingness to change the paper's content to meet it: "I stress – we are in the market for *Sunday Mail/Daily Record* features type material that you would not hitherto have associated with *The Sun*" (the *Sunday Mail* is the sister Sunday of the *Daily Record*, and is also owned by Mirror Group); Steve Sampson, circular to freelance journalists, 11 May 1987 (copy in my possession).

substance and much of convenience. The tabloids do, indeed, "misinform and disinform" their readers, habitually and deliberately. But, as I have been attempting to demonstrate here, this is not the only, or even the primary, manner in which *The Sun* attempts politically to persuade its audience. *The Sun*'s "entertainment" ethos is much more instrumental in this process, but readers accustomed to broadsheet culture often relegate this ethos to the category of "trivia", thus fatally neglecting its importance. Crucially, however, what *The Sun* was attempting to win its readers over *to* in this election was not the single political cause it advocated in 1987: its endorsement in 1992 was much more ambiguous and self-contradictory. And finally, most of *The Sun*'s political stunts during this campaign misfired or were bungled because of its fundamental lack of commitment to John Major and disbelief in the possibility of a Conservative victory.

Blaming the tabloids, however, lets Kinnock off the hook far too conveniently. It forestalls questions about his own leadership, although these have in any case become irrelevant since his resignation. But the illusion of "election by tabloid" disguises much more alarmingly the issue of the utter failure of the Labour policy review to secure more votes for the party. Despite the immense rightward drift of Labour – the many controversial and contested policy revisions of the past five years, behind which Kinnock was the main driving force – the party failed signally to increase its proportion of the popular vote. The theory of a press barons' conspiracy is the rabbit out of the hat which explains away that failure away much too patly. If Labour believes this illusion it is in danger simply of repeating its error; that is, of spending the next five years in a similar revisionary wilderness, vainly searching for the promised land of electoral success. That success, I would argue, is not going to come through what is in many Labour quarters already being prepared, a further drift to the right. It is only going to come by offering a distinct alternative. Reflection on tabloid performance in the 1992 election does, I think, prompt thoughts as to how that alternative might be constructed. It is by offering some of those thoughts that I wish, briefly, to conclude.

A New Labour Populism

Mark Pursehouse sums up the responses to *The Sun* of his four interviewees as follows:

It is not read without criticism. Nobody is impressed with its record for accuracy and the "scandal" element is not as welcome as the keener interest in more honest, human stories, which *The Sun* does not adequately cover. These features can detract from the success of the "fun" persona. There is also a dislike of the "hard sell" boasting of *The Sun* and a call for less strong political hammering. This suggests some of the bludgeoning directness of *The Sun* may induce opposition rather than attract support. There is a similar criticism of the overworked "corny" phraseology, which is never mentioned as a source of amusement. It is also interesting that the excess of royalty coverage gets heavily criticized, which suggests that the media institutions are more interested in royalty than their readers and that if royalty is being used as a symbol of ordered, traditional Britain overkill may bring a rejection rather than reinforcement.

These observations run counter to many of the presuppositions about tabloid readership made by those who do not understand or feel imaginatively able to participate in tabloid culture. Neil Kinnock's case against the tabloids, for instance, suggests a view of a readership simply swamped by right-wing propaganda and unable to exercise its critical faculties. Pursehouse's work explodes this illusion and instead emphasises that the success of *The Sun* depends upon the fact that readers such as his interviewees, while critical of the paper, are limited by its agenda because they "cannot receive an alternative view of the world in the newsagents on the way to work each morning". His final thought, which he is not concerned to develop, is that "some of the discoveries about the readers' reception and awareness show it may be necessary that the same means which got *The Sun* on the 'other side of the fence' are required to get the 'Left' on the popular side of the fence".

The discussion so far has suggested that the high noon of *The Sun*'s Conservative populism was virtually co-extensive with Thatcher. While the paper's general election coverage demonstrated that such populism is still alive, it is certainly not kicking the way it used to. Major's leadership has so far failed to elicit that deep tabloid commitment which came almost instantly, and lasted so long, with Thatcher, although his electoral victory may well presage a resurgence in Tory tabloid confidence. Labour, conversely, has no evident plans to struggle on the ideological ground of "populist interest" catered for by *The Sun*. Its own sympathetic tabloids, such as the *Daily Mirror*, are not really in competition with *The Sun* for readers: Adrian, for instance (see above), expressed a lack of interest in the *Mirror* because it offered what he considered serious news coverage of the kind he could get on television bulletins. A more alarming consideration is how much support Labour, with some of its current policies, can expect even from tabloids such as the *Mirror*. A recent Sunday broadsheet article which asked "Can hard-pressed hacks struggling by on £50,000 a year keep their tax coverage impartial?" outlined the nature of the problem:

> Journalists, highly paid to educate the public on election choices, did some frantic arithmetic last week as a test of their professional objectivity.
>
> "Bloody 'ell," cried a £55,000-a-year man in the *Daily Mirror* office. "I'm going to lose thousands."
>
> On his desk was the *Mirror*'s editorial on John Smith's budget proposals for a Labour government. "At last, after 13 years of fool's gold and empty promises, we can have a Chancellor who puts country before party," it said.
>
> The journalist spoke: "This newspaper shouldn't be supporting people who are taking money out of my effing pocket!"[40]

One can appreciate how a variety of self-interested pressures of this kind, even from within Labour's natural constituency, might contribute to a rightward breeze acting on any future policy flotation.

I have already asserted my view that a renewed rightward drive in policy is unlikely to solve Labour's problems. As well as the choice of a new leader, which is currently being deliberated, Labour ought to be thinking how to ensure that its voice is heard among those whom, for the last thirteen years, it has not been reaching. It might make a beginning by attempting to redefine and rearticulate the vocabulary of its politics. The word "socialism", for instance, has taken on wholly negative connotations in our culture only since the advent of Thatcher. It was not the revolutions in Eastern Europe which made the concept a source of embarrassment to the

---

[40] Cal McCrystal, "Grub Street is Hit Where It Hurts", *The Independent on Sunday*, 22 March 1992, p. 21.

Labour front bench, as they blushed at mention of it long before then. The history of the changed general associations of this word in the past decade and a half is also the history of a party which lost faith and pride in its guiding principles and faltered in the processes of thought and imagination required to keep them alive. A renewed sense of belief in and understanding of the power and rightness of socialist economics, socialist values and socialist culture needs urgently to be fought for: at the moment the only politicians using the word with any conviction, other than a few principled figures on the Left, are Conservatives. In particular – this has been the startling achievement of the Tories with regard to their political principles – a new Labour populism is needed which will link socialism with *pleasure*, demonstrating that socialism can command not only the moral high ground of communal life but also the moral low ground of private leisure. Politics is a serious business, and Labour's earnestness in conducting that business is, in many ways, commendable. But political trade is engaged with a wide range of clients and earnestness doesn't work with them all. Of course, a Labour populism would inevitably reject the crudity, seediness and prejudice of our present Conservative tabloid culture. One does not expect to see that kind of ugliness reproduced in the name of socialism. A successful Labour populism would, on the contrary, make political meanings for its audience which are, in the ideologically restricted condition of our times, unimaginable. Socialism, then, is where we ought to begin again. We should place our faith in it, unashamedly, once more.

But it is not my intention here to offer a general sketch for Labour's advance. The more pertinent question, given what has gone before, is, *how* is Labour to do this? On which sites will this struggle for a new Labour populism be waged? Is it only media institutions which offer favourable ground for constructing it? One has to note that tabloid publishing has hardly ever been a fertile plot for Labour. It isn't in direct competition with the likes of *The Sun* that Labour will make new political meanings. Labour's recent efforts have mainly been directed at the relatively more open and regulated institutions of television broadcasting, and these efforts must be sustained. The complaint from many party members on this score in recent years, however, has been that Labour's attempts to get its media image right have substituted rather than complemented more traditional political procedures. This dependence on image has often led to an abandonment of less mediated forms of political persuasion. Labour has seemed reluctant of late to take its case directly into the community.

One prescription, then, is that Labour ought to be much more willing to appeal to the people, as it were, over the heads of the media. This means developing strategies to address audiences in the places where Labour, traditionally, has always done it best: in workplaces, in educational institutions, at local meetings and organised events, and in the streets. There are many ways for a political party to talk *to* people in their homes: radio, newspapers, television. There is only one way to talk *with* people in their homes, and that is by knocking on their front doors. These more direct forms of communication have, of course, never stopped happening in local communities nationwide, but the impulse to maintain them in the past decade has hardly been coming from Walworth Road. They have always, in the past, formed the site of Labour populism and, along with the media, their importance as such ought to be acknowledged once again.

Coda

There was a *Sun* reader called Ken
Who worked somewhere close to Big Ben.
When he wanted the news,
And some up to date views,
He gave *The Sun* ten out of ten.

Neil Kinnock (of Kenneth Baker, mover of the Queen's Speech),
House of Commons, 6 May 1992

Labour's contempt for the tabloids has possibly never been greater. Yet the Labour mind, with regard to what should be done about the dailies and Sundays which it finds so risible and odious, has certainly never been emptier. The policy vacuum concerning the tabloids was evident from Kinnock's resignation speech of 13 April 1992, in which he acknowledged the relationship between most of the tabloids and the Tories as being simply "a fact of British political life" which he had hoped "it would be possible this time to succeed in achieving change in spite of". I have argued already that the "election by tabloid" case was a convenient smokescreen for the failure of Labour's policy review to secure the votes which might have put the Party into power. However, even when this became the official Party line – Labour's National Executive Committee in June endorsed a report identifying a "tabloid factor" which putatively lost Labour 381,000 votes – the stark absence of any proposal as to what kind of policy Labour should now adopt towards the tabloids was bewildering.

Nor did anything more concrete emerge in the subsequent summer. The nearest we got to a comment on the issue from a member of the Shadow Cabinet was Robin Cook's reply to a question posed on BBC1's *Question Time* on 17 September 1992. Asked whether or not he thought royalty should survive in its present form after tabloid revelations about royal marital tensions, he answered:

> The question that arises for me out of the last few months, actually, I have to say, is not so much "Should royalty survive in its present form?" but really "Do we want our present popular newspapers to survive in their present form?" Because as I look back over a summer in which there have been so many serious international stories – both in Somalia and in Yugoslavia, and Iraq – when we have seen the very serious economic situation that we've had in Britain, and again throughout Europe, to discover that more front pages have been given over to whether or not Princess Di had a conversation on a mobile 'phone with somebody in a car who may or may not have been somebody else who may or may not have been named, and whether or not Princess Fergie has done the right thing with her financial adviser, I find that offensive, frankly, to the intelligence of the great majority of the British people, and I do believe one of the things we should put on the table is not the royal family, but whether or not we can change the popular press of Britain.

Hardly a policy statement, and perhaps no more than a personal opinion, this nonetheless comes close to hinting that some kind of governmental regulation of the popular press might be what Cook would favour were Labour in power. Notice that he does not invoke "invasion of privacy" as legitimation for this potential move, but is making the rather more political point that the tabloids are neglecting what he sees to be their duty – the circulation of "serious" news – in favour of nugatory gossip about the private lives of public individuals. This is a respectable left-wing position with a long history. Elaborated, the argument is that the tabloids are capitalist institutions, owned by capitalists, with an obvious interest in the perpetuation of capitalism. Unsurprisingly, almost all of them therefore back the Conservative Party. More insidiously, they are also engaged in depoliticising their readers, hence their obsession with frivolities rather than serious news.

Whatever one's sympathies with this view (and I must say, as a member of the Labour Party,[41] that my own are numerous), what follows from it in terms of policy is unclear, and there are complexities about the popular press and its readers which it ignores. To take the first issue, that of policy, it is understandable that Labour should have steered clear of making any explicit formulation with regard to regulation of the press. To do so would be to ensure that what the NEC report calls "the particularly vicious anti-Labour" torrent of most of the tabloids becomes a Niagara. The rhetoric of the "free" British press has still not met with a sufficiently eloquent and concerted challenge to its persuasiveness for this to be a risk worth taking. The most politically expedient strategy would be to have a covert policy – one that did not become known until Labour assumed power – to regulate the tabloids, perhaps most particularly through legislation governing the conduct of general elections. The honourable tradition of open and collective policy making within the Labour Party militates against this, but in any case it is irrelevant to a much more urgent question. What can Labour do *now*, in the coming four years when it does *not* hold power, to challenge tabloid Toryism?

The answer to this depends partly on what conception one has of the relationship between the tabloids and their readers. It is quite clear that Labour's understanding of this matter is inadequate and, in its implied disdain for the reading habits of millions of working-class people, deeply objectionable. For example, Robin Cook's feeling that tabloid trivia is "offensive, frankly, to the intelligence of the great majority of the British people" sorts oddly with the fact that 300,000 readers *who did not normally take it* bought the *Daily Mirror* on the day that it revealed all about Fergie and her financial adviser. Here is an instance of what Colin

---

[41] A membership which I terminated upon the later ascension of Tony Blair to Leader of the Party, whose undeniable and successful populism turned out to be the reverse of what I suggested in this essay: he seduced *The Sun* and other tabloids to support him (retrospective editiorial comment, twenty-eight years on).

Sparks, in a trenchant discussion centring on this issue, has called the discomforting fact that "the vast majority of citizens [...] choose a press which systematically prioritizes other matters over and above political life".[42] Granted that it was probably not the public's intelligence that the *Mirror* was appealing to, Labour's failure to account or allow for the enormous popularity of this kind of journalism is a serious problem for it in tackling the entire issue of tabloid hegemony. For one thing, it dangerously underestimates the degree of public support for (and pleasure in) this kind of popular discourse, and hence the probable massive resentment at legislation against it. For another, Labour typically emerges from this debate looking boring, middlebrow and moralistic, leaving the volcano of populist hedonism in the tabloids capable of political eruption only in Conservatism. How then, should we understand the mass consumption of tabloids, and what strategy might Labour adopt in the face of this understanding?

Tabloid readership – that is, what readers actually do with and get out of tabloids, as opposed to simple analysis of their vast numbers – is an area in which no major research has been undertaken. The only recent (and extremely valuable) study I know is a small-scale, qualitative piece of research conducted with readers of *The Sun* in 1988 by Mark Pursehouse at the Department of Cultural Studies at the University of Birmingham. By means of interviews with a range of ordinary readers and analyses of *The Sun* itself, this investigation confirmed but also partly explained why readers, especially working-class readers, prefer tabloids. They are not particularly interested in *The Sun*'s political news, but prefer its "entertainment" elements. Linguistically undemanding, the paper can be resorted to briefly at several points throughout the day, particularly during breaks in a working routine, thus often providing a focus in which workmates can come together in discussion. The most surprising discovery made by Pursehouse is perhaps that the common notion of passive, uncritical, individualised consumption of tabloids is an illusion: reading of them is active, much less credulous than is usually supposed, and their content is continually debated and discussed among readers. The lack of hard political content does not mean that *The Sun* is unideological. As

---

[42] Colin Sparks, "The Popular Press and Political Democracy", *Media, Culture and Society* 10, 2 (April 1988) p. 216.

Pursehouse persuasively argues, the paper's ideological conservatism is more effectively mediated by means of its entertainment ethos than explicit political coverage, and he concludes by pointing out that the Left might learn a great deal from the techniques of this flagship of Tory populism.

The design of a popular socialist alternative, then, ought perhaps to be high on Labour's agenda. It does not follow that such an alternative has to be a new Labour tabloid (the *News on Sunday* disaster is sufficient warning against that) or that Labour's attempts to acquire a "respectable" media image are futile and ought to be abandoned. However, it is clear that those forms of political communication which, historically, Labour has always had to rely on – I mean the relatively unmediated dissemination of the Labour message in workplaces, local meetings, on the streets, and door-to-door – are being given less and less priority by Walworth Road.

Be that as it may, the problem of the trivial Tory press is perhaps soluble only by more radical measures than the provision of such an alternative. Colin Sparks proposes that the real question, in a society such as ours, may not be why people bother to read tabloids, but, on the contrary, why large numbers still read the "quality" press:

> A much more satisfactory explanation for this state of affairs is that political and economic power in a stable bourgeois democracy is so far removed from the real lives of the mass of the population that they have no interest, in either sense, in monitoring its disposal. The infrequent rituals of elections apart, there exist few if any channels whereby any opinion that anyone might hold can be implemented or even heard. [...] If it is indeed the case that the amount of political and economic information available is decreasing in the mass press, then this would tend to confirm the hypothesis that as people have more and more experience of their place in the bourgeois democracy they display less and less interest in it. [...] We might advance the proposition that the more stable and established a bourgeois democracy is the less interest the mass of the population will have in its workings and the more apolitical and "trivial" the popular press will become.[43]

As Sparks concludes, if this hypothesis is correct, "it follows that all the legislative tinkering and noble alternative dreaming is doomed to failure so

---

[43] Sparks, p. 217.

long as these social and political conditions persist".[44] In other words, when people's private lives are the only social arena in which they can see their views and decisions as having any concrete effect, it is hardly surprising that they choose to read mainly about the private lives of others. A politically informative mass press is only likely when readers sense that they have a stake in the public world about which "newspapers" are meant to inform them. If it is that kind of press which Labour would like to see, it needs to address seriously the project of increasing popular participation in and commitment to political life. There are four powerless years ahead in which to prepare and present such a project.

But, of course, no such proposal has emerged from the shambles of the post-election aftermath, and it does not look as if it will. The one senior Labour politician, indeed, who has been saying any of these things (he did so a week after the election defeat) is Tony Benn:

> It is no use blaming the media, the pollsters or the image-makers, for they were all responding, in their own way, to their clear and accurate perception that Labour had consciously decided to limit its appeal to those who wished to see the political, economic and social status quo better managed, but not fundamentally altered.[45]

Unless such words are heeded, Labour's bitter recriminations against the tabloids will ring progressively more hollow, for it will become more and more clear that the Party's own lack of commitment to a truly democratic socialism is partly responsible for their awfulness.

1992

---

[44] Sparks, p. 222.
[45] Tony Benn, "Facing the Real Agenda", *The Guardian*, 20 April 1992.

ACADEMIC FREEDOM AND THE UNIVERSITY OF NOTTINGHAM[1]

> And last, the rending pain of re-enactment
> Of all that you have done, and been; the shame
> Of motives late revealed, and the awareness
> Of things ill done and done to others' harm
> Which once you took for exercise of virtue.
> Then fools' approval stings, and honour stains.
>
> T. S. Eliot, *Four Quartets* ("Little Gidding", II)

> No reputable scholar would argue that academic freedom includes freedom to falsify or suppress evidence.
>
> Bill Rammell, Minister of State for Higher and Further Education and Lifelong Learning[2]

On 14 May 2008, two men were arrested at the University of Nottingham and held for questioning for six days under the provisions of the U.K. Terrorism Act (2000). The men – one an MA student in the School of Politics and International Relations and the other an administrator in the School of Modern Languages and Cultures – were then released without charge, only for the latter immediately to be re-arrested under immigration legislation and subsequently held in detention for a further twenty-six days, under threat of deportation, until 16 June 2008, at which point – following a powerful campaign on his behalf – he was bailed

---

[1] Written jointly with Sean Matthews.
[2] "The last shadow of liberty?: Academic freedom in the 21st century", a talk delivered to the Fabian Society, 27 November 2007 (**http://www. dius.gov.uk/speeches/rammell_fabiansociety_271107.html**, accessed 13 July 2008).

awaiting a court appearance. In March 2009, having been found guilty of "avoidance of enforcement action [by Immigration Authorities] by deceptive means", Hicham Yezza was sentenced to 9 months' imprisonment by Judge Charles Wide QC, who told him: "I find that your guilt in this case involved the deliberate, extended manipulation of the system for immigration control, which involved deliberate and serious deceit".[3]

Our interest in this case is not simply a matter of working in the building (or, in the case of one of us, the academic School) in which the arrests took place, or the fact that we knew personally and professionally many of the people who were involved in what was the most controversial and internally divisive issue in the University's recent history. We had spent a great deal of the preceding decade in trades union activity, both for substantial periods having been President and Vice-President of local associations of the University and College Union (UCU), and in those capacities were frequently vocal critics of the senior management of the University of Nottingham. We were immediately drawn into the affair by colleagues who sought our advice and support and called for us to act.

Our dealings with senior managers had predisposed us to believe that they would deal with the "terror arrests" in a manner primarily mindful of the University's reputation and market standing. We suspected that senior management's determination would be at all costs to minimise damage to its public image caused by high profile reporting of the events. This suspicion seemed initially to be confirmed by the University's public comment on the arrests, in which the press were informed that one of the two men detained was simply a "former student", which while *technically* true ignored the fact that he was a *current* employee.[4] Our first direct involvement in the matter, two days after the arrests, was thus to write in our trades union capacity to the University's External Affairs officer, Jonathan Ray, suggesting that the University come clean about the

[3] **http://www.thisisnottingham.co.uk/news/University-worker-Yezza -jailed-months/article-752889-detail/article.html** (accessed 13 April 2009).
[4] "Two men in campus terror arrest", BBC News online, 16 May 2008 (**http: //news.bbc.co.uk/go/pr/fr/-/2/hi/Uk_news/7403654.stm**, accessed 17 June 2008).

employed status of one of the arrested men.[5]

We were, of course, far from being the only members of staff at the University of Nottingham troubled by these events, though we put ourselves at some remove from the epicentre of the campaign that emerged in their wake. In the School of Modern Languages, during the two days preceding the arrests, staff had witnessed significant police and security presence focussed on the search of a (generally well-liked) colleague's office, to which access was now prohibited. In the School of Politics and International Relations, there was obvious concern at the detention of one of its postgraduate students and a desire to know the grounds of such an arrest. There was proper anxiety about the welfare and treatment of the two individuals in custody. Curiosity, worry and anger resulted in a febrile atmosphere of speculation, fear and alarm. The story rapidly passed around campus and beyond as the student body and the blogosphere became aware of the arrests. University management and the police offered little further clarification: statements for students and staff were identical to those for the press. The language was euphemistic, self-interested, and obfuscatory. The irony of that position is of course immediately apparent: those in possession of the information – and subsequent personal discussions with senior managers suggested that the Vice-Chancellor and the Registrar alone were determining the University's position, without consultation with Management Board or even those charged with responsibility for managerial oversight during the Vice-Chancellor's absence abroad – were unwilling or unable publicly to share it, but at the same time slighting of those who reacted angrily to the limited facts available.

The statements provoked anger and a plethora of secondary questions which were as unanswerable (and went as unanswered) as the first (why can't you say anything? what have you got to hide? don't we have a right to this information?), accompanied by a host of newer, more morally exhortatory statements and claims (e.g. this would never have happened

---

[5] Macdonald Daly, email correspondence with Jonathan Ray, 16 May 2008. It was not until a week later that the truth about the man's employment status became public: *Times Higher Education*, 23 May 2008 (**http://www.times highereducation.co.uk/story.asp?sectioncode=26&storycode=40212 5&c=2**, accessed 17 June 2008). Ironically, by this time the report was not even true, as the employee had been formally dismissed.

if the employee or the student had been white). An anonymous press release headed, "Nottingham University Students and Staff Express Serious Concerns about Recent Use of the Terrorism Act on Campus and Demand Academic Freedom" was circulated internally by email on 21 May 2008. This document must be seen in the context of the ignorance, the control of information, against which it rails, but in its more exaggerated and sensational allegations it set important precedents and trends for the media campaign which followed. It claimed the authority of academic status and perspective, whilst at the same time neglecting two fundamental principles of scholarly practice. First, its evidential basis was at best tendentious, at worst purely speculative, even false. Second, its authors were anonymous, refusing to associate their names, status or credentials with the very case they were making.[6] In short, the statement – which was quickly taken up by media outlets nationally and internationally as representative of the positions of (some) academics – lacked the basic elements of verifiability and accountability that are meant to be the essence of the academic profession. As the controversy unfolded, these alarming failures of professional responsibility were to become increasingly, worryingly, prevalent. The following is indicative of its tone and form of this statement:

> One of the officers involved in interviewing academic staff openly stated that: "This would never have happened if the student had been white." It seems that the over-zealous nature of the operation, causing great injury and distress to the students, their family, and friends, was spurred on by the ethnicity and religious background of the students involved. Police behaviour during the operation, including the apparent targeting of ethnic minorities for questioning, also suggested institutional racism.[7]

---

[6] We do not wish to imply that all public statements were issued anonymously: a letter to the Vice-Chancellor of 29 May 2008 carried the names of 67 signatories.
[7] The student was a British Pakistani and the administrator was an Algerian national. This document, which shoots wildly in all directions in the dark, constituted the first press release of the campaign which was subsequently launched in defence of the re-arrested administrator. Its unrealistic demands formed the basis for a petition which began to circulate on campus (and further afield) within a few days.

As with the email traffic at this time, which was further fuelled by this text, the dominant discourse was becoming sceptical, inflammatory and accusatory; the absence of authoritative detail in the public domain ensured that speculation and assertion not only filled the vacuum but were soon being reproduced as fact.

Although concerned for the fate of the arrested individuals (we helped draft a supportive resolution which was passed at UCU Congress), we were increasingly troubled by the conduct of the campaign on their behalf. As union officers, we were very conscious of the difficulties the University faced: there are perfectly good (moral and legal) reasons why an employer *cannot* make public details relating to individual employees or, in this case, students (and not simply those which may be deemed of a non-professional or private nature). The Data Protection Act (1998) affords important protection to us all in this regard, and few of us would wish its protections to be ignored in respect of ourselves. Yet divulgence of these personal details was what was being demanded of the University. Its proper refusal to accede to the requests was met, however, with vehement indignation on the part of a vocal group of staff and students. Following the re-arrest on immigration charges of the administrator – both men having been released without charge following six days in custody while the terrorism investigation ran its course – a website dedicated to obtaining his liberty, and related Facebook groups, were established. They soon boasted many thousands of adherents, and their press releases were widely reported in mainstream and independent media alike.

Analysis of the changes to participatory democracy and the Fourth Estate which have resulted from the extraordinary expansion of the internet over the past two decades – the important benefits but also the particular challenges – is beyond the scope of this essay. As the case unfolded, however, our concern at what the case was revealing about the left-liberal consensus with which, for many years, we had been readily aligned practically and politically as union activists and scholars, came to be uppermost in our thinking. The treatment of the arrested individuals, and the verifiable detail of their cases, became so rapidly and inextricably absorbed into a broad anti-establishment orthodoxy – an orthodoxy centred on principled opposition to the wars in Iraq and Afghanistan, the homeland terror legislation, and the security services' conduct in the enforcement of that legislation – that the representation of the case, and debate about it, became wholly disconnected from its inexorable unfolding on the ground.

On 24 May 2008 *The Guardian* ran a story under the following headlines:

Student researching al-Qaida tactics held for six days
- Lecturers fear threat to academic freedom
- Manual downloaded from US government website

The article revealed that the student had sent an electronic copy of "the al-Qaida training manual from a US government website for his research into terrorist tactics" to the administrator so that the latter, a personal friend who had access to an office printer, could print it out for him for free. Another member of staff, the report ran, had discovered the document on the administrator's computer and reported it upwards, which ultimately led to the police being called in. The article quoted Dr Bettina Renz, of the University's School of Politics and International Relations, the personal tutor of the student: "'He's a serious student, who works very hard and wants a career in academia. This is a great concern for our academic freedom but also for the climate on campus.'" It further reported that 'students have begun a petition calling on the university to acknowledge the "disproportionate nature of [its] response to the possession of legitimate research materials".'[8] The reporting was based largely on the text of the anonymous press release of 21 May 2008. The petition refers to "'radical material'", of which the individuals were in possession "for research purposes", and calls for the University to show that it "guarantees academic and political freedom on campus" and expresses the view that this incident constitutes "a serious violation of academic freedom".

The defence of academic freedom, it was clear, was to be the rallying cry for the campaign. After all, who would *not* want to defend such a

---

[8] Polly Curtis and Martin Hodgson, "Student researching al-Qaida tactics held for six days", *The Guardian*, 24 May 2008 (**http://education.guardian. co.uk/higher/news/story/0,,2282408,00.html**, accessed 11 July 2008). The text of the petition is available at **http://freehichamyezza.wordpress. com/resources/** (accessed 17 May 2009).

thing? There is, however, an Obstinate Fact. However and wherever it is defined and enshrined by law and statute, academic freedom is exclusively the attribute and privilege of *academic staff*. It does not extend to students, not even postgraduate students, and it certainly does not extend to university administrators. It is true – indeed, it is to be hoped – that the *culture* of particular institutions is more inclusive than such a fact may minimally dictate. It is also true that there are many places in the world where UNESCO reports grave concerns about the restrictions and threats to academic freedom.[9] And it is certainly the case that a moral and political paradox of the present time is the way that the *defence* of freedom and democracy, of rights established over generations, seems to involve significant *threats* to those freedoms from the very legislature and executive charged to protect them. However, in this case the Obstinate Fact remains of supreme importance. Academic freedom was at issue, we must assume, because the campaigners believed that academic freedom *did indeed* extend to students, and *perhaps even* to university administrators. Believing that it *should* extend to these people is, as we shall argue, another matter altogether. The relevant University of Nottingham statute stipulates very clearly the categories of University members who do have academic freedom.[10] Moreover, like most of its kind, it specifies that the freedom it grants is for research conducted "within the law". But this fact was obscured and then, we would argue, wilfully ignored, as rhetoric of "academic freedom" saturated the entire public discourse, with ultimately lethal effects for the credibility of the campaign.

As mainstream and independent media took up the story, we found ourselves increasingly at odds with our colleagues who were speaking out in defence of academic freedom. The *trahison des clercs* took place on several levels. Our colleagues seemed ignorant of academics' reponsibilities and status before the law. Their improper and damaging extension of the category, the fundamental confusion between high ideals of human rights and free speech and the realities of statute and law, was a serious and compromising flaw. If we do not conduct ourselves as

[9] See **http://www.unesco.org/iau/he/af/afreedom_ instrument. html**.
[10] See **http://www.nottingham.ac.uk/registrar/calendar/statutes/stat ute-35.pdf**, accessed 17 June 2008.

scholars and academics, then we put at risk the freedoms and protection that status confers. The case for academic freedom is weakened if those who claim it consider it an unbridled freedom (which it is not), or a freedom which carries no corresponding responsibilities (which it does), or a freedom which is not conditioned by competing liberties, rights and obligations (which it must be).

"Within the law"

Academic freedom in the U.K. is a matter of law: the Higher Education Act (2004) requires the Director of Fair Access to Higher Education in England "to protect academic freedom including, in particular, the freedom of institutions – (a) to determine the contents of particular courses and the manner in which they are taught, supervised or assessed, and (b) to determine the criteria for the admission of students and apply those criteria in particular cases" while having "regard to any guidance given to him by the Secretary of State". [11] Many in the academic profession seem to be unaware that academic freedom is so carefully enshrined in legislation, and assume rather that it is a "civil society" matter of institutional tradition and culture. Indeed, it is clear that many of our peers do not accept the legal determination of the concept, and insist on an altogether more capacious *principle* which might be invoked to protect students and even, perhaps, the entire University community.

At Nottingham, the particular statute undertakes "to ensure that academic staff have freedom within the law to question and test received wisdom, and to put forward new ideas and controversial or unpopular opinions, without placing themselves in jeopardy of losing their jobs or privileges". Like the legally protected freedom, the institutional freedom is only so protected as long as it does not come into conflict with other laws. So a professor does not, for example, enjoy the academic freedom openly to incite racial hatred, although she is and should be free to research, publish and speak on race and racism. A university researcher on sexuality and sexual practices is *not* automatically thereby permitted to acquire legally prohibited graphic material, even should it be readily available by means of the internet. Access to such material must be made

[11] Section 32 (**http://www.opsi.gov.uk/acts/acts2004/ukpga_20040 008_en_4**, accessed 17 June 2008).

in consultation with the appropriate internal and external authorities. Thus, the academic freedom to research and express on *any* subject with reference to *any* materials is always contingent upon the provision of the law in general. While it may be the case that one has antipathy towards laws which restrict freedom in this way, this is, after all, what laws usually do, and one's antipathy to a law does not put one beyond it.

Recently introduced prevention-of-terrorism legislation makes, in our view, alarming reading. [12] The severe restrictions on civil liberties, curtailment of freedom of expression and damage to inter-cultural/racial relations which these laws cause are deeply undesirable and even repellent. But, while we are free to criticise laws we consider ethically unacceptable, we are not as individuals free to break them or to ignore them (although, needless to say, we accept that the collective transgression of particular laws in specific contexts is often a necessary and effective form of protest), and we imagine that few people would consider it a proper thing for a publicly funded institution such as a university to do so.

When three of the most vocal critics from the campaign argued that "University managers are narrowly interpreting intellectual freedom to [*sic*] authorised academics and registered students"[13] by calling in the police, they conveniently overlooked the fact that the University managers were responding to a situation which, at the point of discovery, did not involve academics *or* students. Faced with a document promoting terrorism on an administrator's computer – a place it had no reason to be – in a room in the University's densely populated main administrative building (situated directly above the office of the Vice-Chancellor), the individuals concerned, from School Manager to Head of School to Registrar to Vice-Chancellor, most probably did not "interpret" anything in respect of "intellectual freedom". They considered their duty of care to 6,500 staff and 36,000 students and their legal obligations under anti-terrorism legislation. They reacted with alarm and discretion faced with a document which, *on the balance of the available facts* (which, we might

---

[12] We refer primarily to the Terrorism Act (2000) and the Terrorism Act (2006).
[13] Alf Gunvald Nilsen, Vanessa Pupavac and Bettina Renz, "The Nottingham Two and the War on Terror: which of us will be next?", *Times Higher Education*, 5 June 2008, p. 26 (**http://www.timeshighereducation.co.uk/story.asp? sectioncode= 26&storycode=402258**).

be sure, *included* an assessment of the recent conduct and character of the co-worker most nearly involved *in the context* of his place of work), and chose to consult the appropriate external authorities – namely, the police. It may have been a different matter had the document been on the computer of someone who enjoyed academic freedom, but the administrator, contrary to his own claims and the claims of his followers, was not and never has been an academic. We should note also that the document came to light solely because of the administrator's unexpected absence from work (though not altogether unusual: he had been warned about his absenteeism in the period prior to these events), which necessitated his line manager entering his office and accessing his computer.

Anti-terrorism legislation is aimed at preventing acts of terrorism: there is serious debate to be had about the reality and extent of this threat, and still further debate about the potentially counter-productive nature of the legislation itself. However, the invocation of the spectre of the police state, islamophobia and institutional racism in this case, and the continuing insistence (to this day) that academic freedom was under threat, served to generate, in accordance with what Edward Said once called a "dialectic of reinforcement",[14] the very tensions the campaign claimed to deplore: the fact of the ethnicity and religion of the arrested men was sufficient to corroborate, for those so pre-disposed, the fact of a repressive state apparatus. This is not to "blame the victim", but to note that the administrator's case – which ultimately hinged on inadequate documentation – became the rallying point of a left-liberal consensus horribly ill-informed about the details.

The manual in question is a document which gives advice on the execution of terrorist acts. The law, as we discuss further below, legitimises arrest on *suspicion* (not firm knowledge) of conduct even *preparatory* to such acts. The managers' decision to call in the police could scarcely be expected to consider the niceties of debates over the ethics of the legislation: it related to dubious, indeed distressing, materials and an employee whose behaviour and state of mind had already generated concern.

[14] Edward Said, *Orientalism: Western Conceptions of the Orient* (Harmondsworth: Penguin, 1998). p. 93.

It is further significant that the decision to call in the police was likely to maximise public attention to the University, attention that was likely only to do harm to its image, although no one could have anticipated the furore that ensued. It is also important to note that the police spent two days investigating the matter – an investigation initially concentrating solely on the administrator, as there was no immediate connection to be made with the MA student – before making arrests, and the arrests themselves were provoked by the realisation that a further person was involved and had contacted the administrator to warn him of events on campus. The idea that these were "wrongful arrests" is thus an odd one; they seem rather to have been something of a last resort, precipitated by the anxieties and actions of the very men under suspicion. An arrest is only wrongful if it is conducted in such a way as not to conform to the law. It is not wrongful simply because it does not lead to a charge. Although some of us may not like the relevant laws, the arrests and subsequent investigations were in accordance with them.

One would not expect academics, *in their capacity as or claiming the authority of* academics, to make pronouncements about a law in ignorance of its facts or its particular wording. U.K. legislation, proposed legislation, and related government advice on the implementation of legislation, is these days only ever a few mouse clicks away. If one wishes to check for the potential "wrongfulness" of particular arrests under section 41 of the Terrorism Act (2000), under which the "Nottingham Two" were detained, one can obtain the text with ease. Close acquaintance with both pieces of legislation is certainly disturbing, but that close acquaintance also makes clear that, in the Nottingham case, the actions taken were legitimate, no matter how distressful, unpleasant or Kafkaesque (a favoured epithet) those actions were for the two individuals involved (and their families and friends). The two men were quite properly arrested and then quite properly released without charge. In some ways, indeed, the proper functioning of the legal process in this affair might be taken as a matter for, if not celebration (the law in this matter is an awful piece of legislation), then at least relief.

When one dislikes a piece of legislation, whether it is contrary to one's own interests or one has disinterested ethical objections to it, one can, as a citizen, legitimately criticise it or combine with others (in protest groups or trades unions, for example) to campaign for its abolition or reform.

Academics, like members of other professions, can do so in their professional capacity, and share the additional privilege of the protections of academic freedom in such a case, *if their implied claim to be speaking in their academic capacity is reasonable*. This is not to say that only those who have a professional interest in a particular field should be "academically free" to comment on that field, while those who do not should not enjoy such freedom. In the case of comment on a piece of legislation, for example, the academic lawyer is hardly the only person with a professional interest: specialists in Political Science, Sociology or Education, to name but three disciplines, might clearly have ways of bringing their academic expertise to bear on a public or intra-institutional debate. But they should be expected to do so, if invoking their academic authority or position, according to the consensually agreed norms of academic activity and discourse – in effect, those principles of veracity, verifiability and accountability invoked earlier.

There is no formal code which specifies these norms, although entry into the academic *profession* for the most part requires minimum levels of *qualification,* which are generally conditional on achieving certain levels of scholarship – scholarship which, *inter alia*, will acknowledge high standards in relations to those three principles. Someone speaking from an academic position and/or with academic authority is thus expected to be telling the truth, and to be able to cite evidence or sources or other authorities for their conclusions. In short, again, there is a fundamental expectation of scholarship, even in cases of polemic. There is a moral dimension to academic freedom, which is extended to members of the academic profession because they are assumed to be speaking from a position which is neither narrowly self-interested nor demonstrably serving sectarian or partisan interests. The *political* justification for academic freedom, as distinct from the purely *practical* justification – that free enquiry is the best means to advance knowledge – is that academics do not shoot from the hip, nor are they alarmists, demagogues, or unreflective populists. In other words, although not infallible, they should inspire trust.

It is, at least, our adherence to these views that puts us in the unusual position of having to agree with the Vice-Chancellor at the time of the arrests, whose leadership of the institution we have otherwise consistently censured as reactionary, authoritarian and self-serving. His rebuttal of the accusations made against the University by its own academics was published in the following letter to the press:

> I was interested in your article "The Nottingham Two and the War on Terror: which of us will be next?" (5 June) but surprised by the interpretation of events that was offered.
>
> Inevitably, any arrests of individuals on campus stimulate conjecture and speculation. For that reason, I authorised release of factually accurate statements of relevant events to the entire university community (including to the authors of the article) on 27 May and 3 June.
>
> The second statement provided as full an account of events as was possible, given that some matters were (and still are) subject to legal process. Your readers can access the full statement entitled "Arrests on Campus" at **http:// my.nottingham.ac.uk/**.
>
> No amount of scenario analysis of what might have been, aimed at reinterpreting events as an "academic freedom" issue (for whatever reason) can alter what actually happened. The incident was triggered by the discovery of an al-Qaeda training manual on the computer of an individual who was neither an academic member of staff nor a student and in a school where one would not expect to find such material being used for research purposes. We became concerned. The university had to make a risk assessment – no panic, no hysteria, just a straightforward risk assessment. Our responsibility to university students and staff, and our public duty to the wider community, led us to the conclusion that there needed to be an investigation. So our concerns were conveyed to the police as the appropriate body to investigate (no judgment was made by us). The matter has now been properly investigated and outstanding issues are before the courts of the land.
>
> Much has been said on the matter of academic freedom. The University of Nottingham has always fully embraced this principle and continues to do so. Claims to the contrary in the Nottingham Two article are freely expressed and unconstrained. But they are careless, entirely false and bear little relation to the facts.[15]

---

[15] Colin Campbell, letter to *Times Higher Education*, 19 June 2008

This is an odd but telling performance, utterly in character in its clenched legalism and absolute self-confidence. The Vice-Chancellor does not state that academic freedom does not apply to students or administrators. Rather, he acknowledges and affirms the principle of academic freedom but reveals that it was *never even in question* in the assessment of the original situation, which had primary regard to the safety and security of the University – the community of students and staff. Whether or not one agrees with the decision taken in these specific circumstances, this *account* of the decision is reasonable. If one believes, on the information available, that there may be a risk to safety and security, and if there are no ostensible reasons why one should consider matters like academic freedom to apply, the decision to call in the police would seem straightforward.

The statutory obligations of senior management of institutions of Higher Education are embodied not only in law but in guidance given by the relevant Minister. Four months before the Nottingham arrests, in January 2008, the Minister of State for Higher and Further Education and Lifelong Learning had issued renewed guidance to Universities on how to "to protect all their students and staff from those who seek to exploit the freedom that Higher Education provides in order to promote violence, incite hatred, intimidate or bully others".[16] The advice, first issued in 2006,[17] struggles to maintain the difficult balance between freedom of expression/association and concerns for civil safety/security, and a full reading of the revised document does indeed give the impression that it remains effectively a charter for informally policing Islamic students and student groups, a matter which has been widely criticised, particularly in the light of the precipitate recent arrest – and subsequent release without charge – of eleven Pakistani students now

(http://www.timeshighereducation.co.uk/story.asp?sectioncode=26 &storycode=402458, accessed 19 June 2008).

[16] Bill Rammell, "Foreword", *Promoting good campus relations, fostering shared values and preventing violent extremism in Universities and Higher Education Colleges* (Department for Innovation, Universities and Skills, 2008), p. 3.

[17] *Promoting Good Campus Relations: Working With Staff And Students To Build Community Cohesion And Tackle Violent Extremism In The Name Of Islam At Universities And Colleges* (Department for Education and Skills, 2006).

themselves facing possible deportation.[18]

A chapter in this publication entitled "Scenarios and Responses",[19] offers "issues to consider" in relation to six concretely described campus scenarios. The first of these scenarios is as follows:

> A member of teaching staff has raised concerns with university authorities about some literature that was left lying around in a university room in which she took a tutorial group. Some leaflets were written in English, and others appeared to be in Arabic. She reported that the literature in English had titles such as "Who is a legitimate target?" and "From Jihad to a new world order". One of the students in the tutorial group reported that she had seen lots of the pamphlets lying around other places in the university earlier in the day, and a number of students walking around with bundles of them.

The first "issue to consider" in respect of this scenario is: "The leaflets may constitute a criminal offence under terrorism or racial and religious hatred legislation."

The third scenario, perhaps even more pertinently, is also quick to invoke the law:

Example Three – Inappropriate Student Use Of The Internet
College library staff have reported that a student has approached them expressing concerns at images she had seen fellow students looking at on computers in an IT room. She reported that two males were looking at some kind of home-made images of other men dressed in military and civilian clothing holding guns. The two men were joined by two others and she could see that they were watching shots being fired and explosions on the computer. The images then appeared to show somebody making a home made explosive device.

Issues to consider
• The dissemination of terrorist publications is an offence under

[18] See, for example, "No charges after anti-terror raid" (**http://news.bbc. co.uk/2/hi/uk_news/8011341.stm**, accessed 17 May 2009).
[19] *Promoting good campus relations* (2008), pp. 13-16. All quotations from this publication henceforth are from this chapter.

section 2 of the Terrorism Act 2006.

• The HE institution should have a policy on internet use and internet security as staff and students may need to access material of this sort as part of legitimate research. If it is alleged that these policies are breached then what is the process for sensitively investigating allegations, and if necessary who should decide whether to inform the police?

In other words, in discussion of these analogous scenarios, Rammell enjoins University authorities to decide on their course of action in a context-specific manner, but insists on the possibility that the scenarios are criminal and that therefore police involvement may always be on the agenda. He said as much when asked by *The Guardian* to comment on the specific Nottingham case: "'I want as much academic freedom and debate as possible, but there are going to be circumstances in which there are legitimate concerns about individuals and universities are going to report those to the police,' he said."[20]

Although decisions like these are inevitably made in real time, it does not seem to us that the Nottingham decision would be any less defensible retrospectively, even *had* subsequent information come to light that made the matter indisputably also a matter of academic freedom. What seemed to happen instead was that the issue was *made into* one of academic freedom so that the legitimate and widespread frustrations and anxieties at illiberal legislation could better be mobilised in support of a case and campaign which were, by this time, in reality *solely* concerned with immigration issues. This was, in the short term, a demagogically astute decision. But the demagogue, as we have intimated, is the enemy of the academic. The two are not compatible. Ultimately, the cause of the administrator and the reputation of the academics involved in the campaign were ill-served. More depressingly, not only did the reputation of the academic profession suffer a further blow, but resistance to illiberal legislation was compromised by association with – indeed exploitation by – a campaign which insisted on concealing the specific detail of the

---

[20] Anthea Lipsett, "Academic Freedom: Rammel stands by extremism guide", *The Guardian*, 5 June 2008 (http://education. guardian.co.uk/higher/ news/story/0,,2283885,00.html, accessed 14 July 2008).

case (immigration irregularity) behind banners and headlines loudly proclaiming threats to academic freedom. This is not a reactionary position: we strongly agree that academics have duties as public intellectuals, but they take part in public debate *as academics*, and should be mindful of the fact that it is their status and qualifications which permit them such a platform. (We might add that we argued directly with a large number of activists in the campaign about precisely these issues, and were repeatedly told that not only was academic freedom of central concern, but that the administrator himself was, by their own capacious definition, an academic.)

There is no doubt about the repressive nature of the relevant laws. The Terrorism Act (2006), for example, deals in particular with "Dissemination of Terrorist Publications" in the following manner:

(1) A person commits an offence if he engages in conduct falling within subsection (2) and, at the time he does so –
(a) he intends an effect of his conduct to be a direct or indirect encouragement or other inducement to the commission, preparation or instigation of acts of terrorism;
(b) he intends an effect of his conduct to be the provision of assistance in the commission or preparation of such acts; or
(c) he is reckless as to whether his conduct has an effect mentioned in paragraph (a) or (b).
(2) For the purposes of this section a person engages in conduct falling within this subsection if he –
(a) distributes or circulates a terrorist publication;
(b) gives, sells or lends such a publication;
(c) offers such a publication for sale or loan;
(d) provides a service to others that enables them to obtain, read, listen to or look at such a publication, or to acquire it by means of a gift, sale or loan;
(e) transmits the contents of such a publication electronically; or
(f) has such a publication in his possession with a view to its becoming the subject of conduct falling within any of paragraphs (a) to (e).[21]

---

[21] Section 2. The entire section is quite astonishing in its detailed definition of the manifold relations one may have to terrorist publications.

The Nottingham arrestees engaged in activity falling within subsection (2). The student transmitted the contents of a terrorist publication (as defined in the same section of the Act) electronically, and the administrator provided (or intended to provide) a service to the student enabling him to read the publication. But neither was charged with an offence under the Act because neither at the same time met the conditions in subsection (1).

The fact that the law was applied properly does not make it an ethically good law. And we would expect academics – in particular academics whose specialism involves textual study, or historians with an eye to precedents, or moral philosophers who might cast doubt upon the idea that merely to look at such a publication should be a criterion with similar weighting to reading it – to have something to say, with authority, as to the wisdom of treating citizens so summarily. In liberal democracies, a person is usually subject to arrest for possession and/or transfer of things like weapons, illicit drugs, stolen property and child pornography. One has not for many years been ordinarily subject to *arrest* for the possession of a mere *document*, and to most academics, whose entire endeavour in both research and teaching depends upon the free circulation of documents and an almost entirely permissive spirit in respect of the contents of documents, the idea of banned books and censorship and other forms of interference in relation to texts is anathema. The ethical acceptability or unacceptability of the two Terrorism Acts – not whether academic freedom was or was not observed – was the real dilemma *initially* forced into articulation by arrests like those of the "Nottingham Two", and on such questions we should hope that some academics will have something specific to say in answer. What we would not expect them to do would be to bring their own University and profession into disrepute by creating the straw monster of despoiled academic freedom. We would not have expected so many of our colleagues, in the then Vice-Chancellor's words, to utter statements which are "careless, entirely false and bear little relation to the facts".

The campaign

The campaign, co-ordinated through its own website, [22] which was

---

[22] The website **http://freehicham.co.uk/**, although self-evidently partisan,

mobilised from late May 2008 onwards within the University of Nottingham, first sought to secure the release from custody, where he was held on immigration charges, of the administrator. The centrepiece of this campaign was a mass demonstration and rally held on the University campus on 28 May 2008. "Originally called to voice outrage and concern over the threat to academic freedom, illustrated by the recent arrest of two innocent people on campus", a campaign press release of 27 May explained, "the focus has now widened to include support and solidarity for one of the arrested, Hicham Yezza, who is now facing imminent deportation."[23]

Hicham Yezza was the 30-year old Algerian administrator, who had previously studied at the University for an undergraduate Computer Science and Management degree (which he completed, gaining a third class B.Sc., in 2000) and a postgraduate research degree in Engineering (which he did not complete. He was excluded from the course after some two years of study either, according to his own account, because of funding difficulties due to problems back in Algeria, or, by his Department's account, because his funding body was not satisfied, on the basis of supervisory reports, with his progress). During his time at the University he was also a prominent student journalist and activist on behalf of several political causes, and was elected as a student representative on the University Senate. He was permanently employed from February 2007 as full-time personal assistant to the Head of the School of Modern Languages and Cultures. The British Pakistani student was 22-year old Rizwaan Sabir, enrolled on a Masters programme in the School of Politics.

By the time of the 28 May demonstration, stories reporting that the University of Nottingham had failed to defend academic freedom had spread considerably beyond the dense jungle of national coverage – as far as the *International Herald Tribune* (25 May), *The Washington Times*

remains the best single resource for links to the copious press and media articles on the affair. The site is no longer (May 2009) available at its original address, **http://www.wordpress.freehichyezza.com**, but that site had a hit counter which by 13 July 2008 registered over 58,000 – if accurate, an average of well over 1,000 hits per day since its inception.

[23]   See   **http://freehichamyezza.wordpress.com/2008/05/27/press-release-270508//**.

(26 May), *Der Spiegel* (27 May) and the *Taipei Times* (27 May). These articles, like most of the domestic coverage, quoted academics from Nottingham's School of Politics and International Relations openly suggesting that there had been, in particular, a breach of Rizwaan Sabir's academic freedom.[24] Much of this coverage also echoed the campaign's press release of 24 May 2008, which included the following quotation from Hicham Yezza: "The Home Office operates with a Gestapo mentality. They have no respect for human dignity and human life. They treat foreign nationals as disposable goods – the recklessness and the cavalier approach they have belongs to a totalitarian state. I thank everyone for their support – it's been extremely heartening and humbling. I'm grateful to everyone who has come to my aid and stood with me in solidarity, from students to Members of Parliament. I think this really reflects the spirit of the generous, inclusive Britain we know – and not the faceless, brutal, draconian tactics of the Home Office."[25] Two familiar binary oppositions were reiterated: (a) staff and students rallying against the University in defence of academic freedom; and (b) the "generous, inclusive Britain we know" rallying against "the Gestapo" of the Home Office.

We had by this time received a number of requests from members and colleagues to involve the local association of the UCU. However, neither

[24] There was a further article in *Le Monde*, 7 June 2008 (**http://www.lemonde.fr/cgi-bin/ACHATS/acheter.cgi?offre=ARCHIVES&type _item=ART_ARCH_30J&objet_id=1039081**, accessed 13 July 2008). Knowing the vagaries of quotation by the press, we have opted largely to ignore what the press said our colleagues said, and to rely more on sources in which it is clear that they are speaking for themselves. It is, for example, difficult to imagine that Bettina Renz actually told *The Guardian*, as it said she did, "Any kind of guidelines that require us to ask for permission before we research something I would find very worrying" (**http://education.guardian.co.uk/higher/news/story/0,,2282932,00.html**, accessed 17 June 2008) when her own School has a Research Ethics Committee: "A sub-committee of the School Research Committee, its remit is to consider the ethical implications of all research that is undertaken within the School of Politics and International Relations, whether by staff or post-graduate research students" (**http://www.nottingham.ac.uk/politics/Research/ResearchEthics.php**, accessed 18 June 2008).

[25] See **http://freehichamyezza.wordpress.com/2008/05/24/press release/** (accessed 13 July 2008).

of the arrestees was a member of UCU, nor were they eligible to be. The campaign had admitted, in its press release of 24 May, that there was "confusion over his [Yezza's] visa documentation":[26] an immigration case seemed a matter for the law rather than a trades union. In the end, the local association limited itself to a non-partisan statement to its members on 24 May, and a motion to UCU Congress – passed unanimously on 28 May – calling for normal procedures to be applied to Yezza's immigration case. [27] On the same day – the day of the demonstration – UCU persuaded the University to make public the fact that the Vice-Chancellor had also written in similar terms to the Home Secretary.

At this juncture the Home Office stood accused of threatening to "fast track" Yezza through deportation rather than press charges and wait for an ensuing trial. The campaign press releases of 24 and 26 May were insistent:

Hicham Yezza, a popular, respected and valued former Ph.D student and current employee of the University of Nottingham faces deportation to Algeria on Sunday 1st June. This follows his unjust arrest under the Terrorism Act 2000 on Wednesday 14th May [...][28]

Hicham Yezza, a popular and active member of the academic community at the University of Nottingham, was recently arrested along with another student. After six days of detention, both were released without charge. Hicham was re-arrested on immigration grounds. He now faces imminent deportation to Algeria without due process.[29]

The idea that "fast tracking" someone through deportation is doing so "without due process" is, in point of fact, quite untrue. It is simply that

---

[26] See **http://freehichamyezza.wordpress.com/2008/05/24/pressrel ease/** (accessed 13 July 2008).

[27] The two authors were party to drafting both the statement and the motion.

[28] See **http://freehichamyezza.wordpress.com/2008/05/24/pressrel ease/** (accessed 13 July 2008).

[29] See **http://freehichamyezza.wordpress.com/2008/05/26/press-rel ease-26th-may/** (accessed 13 July 2008).

the "due process" is not one of which, for this case, the campaign approved. The process that applies in "fast tracking" is known as "administrative removal" under powers conferred by Schedule 2 of the Immigration Act (1971). The decision to remove is taken, in the light of the available evidence (the passports, permits and relevant immigration documents of the individual concerned) by an Immigration Officer with the authority of a Chief Immigration Officer or Immigration Inspector. There is no court order and the decision is not ordinarily subject to a right of appeal or further legal scrutiny. Again, it is not, perhaps, a savoury piece of legislation, but all countries have something similar: these are the powers under which people are refused entry at any border control in the world if they do not have appropriate papers; they also extend, everywhere in the world, to persons who have entered a country who are *subsequently* shown to be in breach of immigration law. The claim that something irregular or indeed unlawful ("without due process") was being done to Hicham Yezza was untrue. In the event, however, the Home Office bowed to public pressure, and agreed to allow Hicham Yezza the day in court his supporters demanded – a grim irony that only his subsequent conviction made apparent. Had Hicham Yezza accepted the judgement of the Immigration Officer, which was effectively endorsed by the Court, he would not have gone to prison.

In the first quotation above, Hicham Yezza is a "former Ph.D[.] student and current employee" of the University. The press release goes on to say that Yezza "is an active member of debating societies, a prominent member of an arts and theatre group, and has written for, and edited, *Ceasefire*, the Nottingham Student Peace Movement magazine for the last five years. He [...] has established himself as a voracious reader and an authority on literature and music. An application for British citizenship was under way, and he had been planning to make his yearly trip to Wales for the Hay Festival when he was suddenly arrested." The rhetorical pressure here is to highlight Hicham Yezza's erudition, culture and good character. That his qualifications were in Engineering and that his employment in the University was administrative rather than academic is elided. In the second quotation, however, Hicham Yezza has become a "member of the academic community", which was simply not true, and Rizwaan Sabir is referred to as "another student", implying that Hicham Yezza was *also* currently a student, which was again false. This latter release goes on to tell the press that, "During this time at Nottingham, Hicham has served as a member of the Students' Union Executive Committee, and on the University Senate. He was President of the Arabic Society, and was the Editor of the influential *Voice* magazine for international students. He was a prominent member of the music and dance group 'Al-Zaytouna'". His essential rôle in the University – the reason he was now there at all – is studiously not mentioned in the press release. Instead, one of his fellow *Ceasefire* editors goes into the following raptures: "Hich is a wealth of knowledge and understanding. His perspectives and humanity shine through in his work and all that he does. His vision and resolve have been integral to the functioning and success of *Ceasefire*." This was the first of many personal eulogies which were to sound a mildly cultish keynote throughout the remainder of the campaign. The campaign website clearly gives the impression that Hicham Yezza was a student or an academic. One blogger wrote, "The way this eloquent scholar has been treated is a disgrace and shames Britain."[30] *Le Monde* simply referred to him as "un étudiant".[31]

These misleading statements, insinuating that Hicham Yezza was really a student or an academic rather than an administrator (though, by this time, the problem, which perhaps only Hicham Yezza then knew, was that, having been dismissed, he was none of these at all) were obviously necessary if the "academic freedom" argument was to be sustained. In our view, academic colleagues at this point abandoned their own intellectual and professional obligations. There duly emerged a number of internal emails (sent, we should say, to hundreds of people at a time) from Hicham Yezza's supporters which implied or insisted on the novel idea that it was Hicham Yezza's, not Rizwaan Sabir's, academic freedom that had been ignored.

Hicham Yezza was cast, in effect, as everything *but* an administrator about whose visa there was "confusion" and of whom his employer was unable to confirm he had a legal right to live and work in the country. On the day of the demonstration, a spokesman for the University was reported as saying, "As an overseas national he has failed to produce

[30] See **http://questionthat.me.uk/2008/05/university-clerk-threatened-with.html**, accessed 13 July 2008.
[31] See **http://www.lemonde.fr/cgi-bin/ACHATS/acheter.cgi?offre=ARCHIVES&type_item=ART_ARCH_30J&objet_id=1039081**.

evidence of his eligibility to work in the United Kingdom. The university is no different from other employers and is prevented in law from employing foreign nationals who do not have permission to work here. The institution has contacted him, and his defence team, to request any information which contradicts evidence that he was working at the university whilst ineligible for employment." [32] The problem for the campaign was that Hicham Yezza was indeed, at this point, an illegal immigrant with no right to work *even if* he technically satisfied the criteria for gaining indefinite leave to stay. Drawing attention to his victimhood (denied the freedom he would have had had he actually been an academic), and emphasising his contribution to the community were thus the strategic manoeuvres in a campaign which then necessarily obscured the legal and procedural realities of the situation. The apotheosis of this scheme was in Hicham Yezza's own comments (he was by this point at liberty), during a podcast produced by Riseup! Radio on 1 July 2008, in which, with seeming candour, he referred to himself as "an academic".

It is beyond doubt that this tactic was successful in terms of recruiting students, non-academic and academic staff in Nottingham (and further afield) to the campaign, and in getting them to donate money to it. [33] The two Facebook sites devoted to the cause, for example, soon claimed 850 (local Nottingham group) and 3,794 (global group) adherents. [34] The campaign was given an enormous boost by the unconditional support of the constituency M.P., Alan Simpson, who gave a powerful speech to the assembled crowd of hundreds at the demonstration before taping up his

---

[32] See Anthea Lipsett, "UCU aids university worker threatened with deportation", *The Guardian*, 28 May 2008 (**http://education.guardian. co.uk/higher/ news/story/0,,2282482,00.html**, accessed 14 July 2008). We shall return to this matter of Yezza's failure to provide evidence of his right to work, and to the University's culpability for it, in due course.

[33] The campaign press release of 24 May announced the establishment of a fund to meet Yezza's legal costs. Further information was published at **http:// freehichamyezza.wordpress.com/what-can-we-do/** (accessed 13 July 2008).

[34] The Facebook Groups were called "Global Support to Stop The Deporation [*sic*] of Hicham Yezza" (**http://www.facebook.com/group.php?gid=1966250 8427**) and "Stop The Deporation [*sic*] of Hicham Yezza!" (**http://www. facebook.com/group. php? gid=15205386383**).

mouth (in which pose he was publicly photographed)[35] and setting off with the others for a march and silent vigil:

> Alan Simpson, MP for Nottingham South attended to show his support for the demonstration. He described the arrests as a "dreadful cock-up". Addressing the university authorities he said, "How ashamed you should be of yourselves. How ashamed that you cannot come to the defence of one of your staff." Speaking on the terror legislation Simpson said, "we would live in a society where we fear each other and that is what the treatment of Hicham and Rizwaan actually demonstrates."
>
> The protestors then marched across campus to Trent Building, the administrative centre of the university. A silent protest was held in the building courtyard, with protestors standing still and silent, symbolically gagged in the pouring rain. Hicham was called and addressed the protestors from detention. Hicham said, "I am humbled and buoyed by all the support I have received, and my spirits are high. Thank you everyone, you are a credit to Nottingham."[36]

One wonders whose enforced silence it was that the gagging was meant to symbolise: Simpson was certainly free with his words and, thanks to modern technology, even Hicham Yezza's physical absence was no impediment to his addressing the crowd, and no one had been stopped from saying pretty much anything they liked for two weeks. Paradoxically, the entire period will be remembered, above all, as one in which so many exercised their freedom of speech, so publicly.

The momentum of the campaign was inexorable: those who stood against it were castigated as illiberal and inhumane. By 29 May, the day after the demonstration, a "Letter From Concerned Employees Of The University Regarding The Deportation Of Hicham Yezza" had been subscribed to by 67 academic and non-academic signatories. The letter

---

[35] E.g., in *Times Higher Education* (print edition only), 5 June 2008, pp. 12-13.
[36] Campaign press release, 29 May 2008 (**http://freehichamyezza.word press.com/2008/05/28/press-release-290508/**, accessed 13 July 2008). A full transcript of Alan Simpson's speech to the demonstration is available at **http://freehicham.co.ukwp-content/alan-simpson-address.pdf** (accessed 17 May 2009).

was a relatively restrained request for the University to intervene by all means possible to help ensure that Yezza received "a fair trial", but it also nailed its colours to the mast of "academic freedom": "We hope and expect the University will develop in consultation with its employees guidelines designed to avoid such unnecessary arrests and invasions into academic freedom in the future." [37] Two days later, *The Guardian* reported that Hicham Yezza was "a martyr to academic freedom in the eyes of a growing campaign group of lecturers and students". [38] The strategy had succeeded.

It was at this point that we wrote to *Times Higher Education* to protest at the conduct of the campaign. The print version having gone to press, our letter appeared as an online comment on the magazine's website. This letter was picked up by the *Nottingham Evening Post*, which contacted us for comment, and ran a story based on it. [39] We received a number of private communications from colleagues thanking us for articulating our position. We anticipated, and received, critical responses from colleagues associated with the campaign, as well as much personal abuse. We should put on record that Sean Matthews engaged in a lengthy correspondence with Hicham Yezza himself at this point, a correspondence which was courteous, detailed and direct. However, the campaign continued along its course regardless. On 3 June 2008, for example, 131 academics and students from the Universities of Sussex and Brighton sent a wild letter, replete with error and exaggeration, to both

---

[37] See **http://freehichamyezza.wordpress.com/2008/05/29/letter-fr om-concerned-employees-of-the-university-regarding-the-deport ati on-of-hicham-yezza/** (accessed 13 July 2008).

[38] Polly Curtis and Andrea Lipsett, "'This is not the way I should have been treated in a country I love'", *The Guardian*, 31 May 2008 (**http://ed ucation.guardian.co.uk/higher/news/story/0,,2283183,00.html**, accessed 13 July 2008).

[39] Macdonald Daly and Sean Matthews, "Open Letter from two University of Nottingham employees concerning the Hicham Yezza case", 2 June 2008 (**http://www.timeshighereducation.co.uk/story.sp?sectioncode=26& storycode=402188&c=1**, accessed 17 October 2008). For the *Nottingham Evening Post* coverage (4 June 2008), see **http://www.thisisnottingham. co.uk/displayNode.jsp?nodeId=133965&command=displayContent& sourceNode=133948&contentPK=20786400&moduleName=Interna lSearch&formname=sidebarsearch**.

the Vice-Chancellor and Liam Byrne M.P., Minister of State for Borders and Immigration.[40]

The affair took a dramatic turn, on 5 June 2008, when three academic members of Nottingham's School of Politics and International Relations themselves published a substantial opinion piece in *Times Higher Education* (already quoted: see footnote 13, above). This article shuttled between two positions, one of them untenable, the other persuasive. The first (untenable) was that academic freedom had been breached in the Nottingham case; the second (persuasive, but not relevant in the circumstances) was that "UK universities should stand up and defend academic freedom in the face of the potentially draconian ramifications of anti-terror legislation".[41] This strategic conflation of liberal concern about the terror legislation with issues of academic freedom and Hicham Yezza's immigration case by now amounted to an orthodoxy. The Head of the School of Politics, Simon Tormey, did make a formal apology for the actions of his academic colleagues to the University Senate on 11 June 2008, less than a week later.[42] Following the Vice-Chancellor's response to the article (quoted above), a rejoinder to it by Rizwaan Sabir's M.A. dissertation supervisor, Rod Thornton, was published in the same correspondence columns.

Thornton pointed out that he had himself been questioned for several hours by the police shortly after the arrests and that he had, early on, composed a "four-page rebuttal" to the "factually accurate statements" which the Vice-Chancellor claimed the University had issued. He defended his colleagues further thus:

A number of us who have been involved in, and affected by, this affair have been concerned that senior management will not discuss the issue with us. Since they are not open to discussion, and since they do not have all the details at their disposal, they have been prone to

[40] See **http://www.facebook.com/topic.php?uid=19662508427&top ic =4806**.

[41] Nilsen, Pupavac and Renz, p. 26.

[42] The minutes of the Senate meeting (document not publicly available) diplomatically do not record this apology: they simply state laconically under the heading "Recent police investigation" that Senate "ENDORSED actions taken by the University in connection with this investigation".

making maladroit statements. A brief meeting would have cleared up much of the misunderstanding. But instead of talking to those involved, Sir Colin has aired his views in public in the letters pages of *Times Higher Education*. I believe this to have been impolitic at this juncture.[43]

The tone of this letter was refreshingly sober, and its author genuinely seemed interested in the truth rather than in grinding axes, having largely stayed above the media melée.[44] Nonetheless, his argument that senior management was not in possession of the facts, and therefore that it should not say anything in public, was unconvincing.

We were, in particular, baffled by the suggestion that senior management would not discuss the issues, or that it was not in possession of the essential facts. We had been able to discuss the issues with University senior management since virtually day one, and had found them to be quite forthcoming with information, of which they had a great deal, much of it potentially damaging to the campaign's credibility and, in particular, Hicham Yezza's good name – which was *precisely*, quite apart from the issues around confidentiality mentioned earlier, why we felt justified in suggesting that senior management's responses had been restrained. Whenever we asked senior management for information – even information that did not show the University itself in entirely the best light (as we shall see) – we were never denied it. It was perhaps naïve of Rod Thornton to forward his analysis of the situation to a general enquiries email address, rather than to seek out the relevant managers personally; it was certainly surprising that he should expect those managers to come looking for him.

So, for example, when we requested a copy of Rod Thornton's letter, we received it within a day. As this was never intended to be a public

---

[43] Rod Thornton, letter to *Times Higher Education*, 26 June 2008 (**http:// www.timeshighereducation.co.uk/story.asp?sectioncode=26&storyc ode=402543**, accessed 13 July 2008).

[44] He had been cited, but only factually, in an Associated Press syndicated article which appeared as "Terrorism arrests on British university campus raises questions over academic freedom", *International Herald Tribune*, 25 May 2008 (**http://www.iht.com/bin/printfriendly.php?id=13195285**, accessed 18 June 2008).

domain document, we have refrained from quoting it. It is not a headline-grabbing stunt or a quotable verbal display. It is a serious and sincere attempt to help clarify a situation which everyone agrees was of justified and widespread institutional concern, by someone who very clearly had the interests and welfare of a particular student in mind.

The immigration case

The University of Nottingham is, of course, not blameless in this affair, even if its fault was not the violation of academic freedom. It is clear that it conducted itself illegally by employing Hicham Yezza in February 2007 and in continuing to employ him for a further *fifteen months* until his arrest *without obtaining from him the basic documentation which might verify his right to work*. This was a matter on which we questioned senior management and on which we found them wholly candid. The University cannot provide a statutory defence against the charge, if brought, that its employment of Hicham Yezza was illegal.[45] The University's failure to ensure that it was in line with the law could hardly be argued, however, to have done any harm at all to Hicham Yezza, as his employment aided him in what was, after all, his express wish to remain in the country.[46]

---

[45] Employers violating the law in this respect face a potentially unlimited fine. The legal framework for employers concerning illegal working was revised on 29 February 2008 (employers are now also potentially liable to imprisonment, among other changes), but the law as it applies in Yezza's case, given that he was employed in February 2007, is best summarised in *Comprehensive guidance for United Kingdom employers on changes to the law on preventing illegal working* (Home Office, 2004) (available at **http://www.ukba.homeoffice.gov.uk/ sitecontent/documents/employersandsponsors/preventingillegalwo rking/previousguidanceandcodes/comprehensiveguidance2004.pdf ?view=Binary**), a document which informs employers what they need to do by way of formal checks to provide a statutory defence against any charge of illegally employing.

[46] The authors wrote jointly to the Chief Constable of Nottinghamshire Police and to the Chair of the Nottinghamshire Police Authority on 30 July 2008 asking what steps the police would be taking to investigate this situation. We secured a belated reply (by telephone) from the Detective Superintendent who had been in charge of the initial anti-terror operation. He explained that issues relating to immigration had been passed to the appropriate department. He further pointed out that there is never an automatic obligation upon the police to recommend prosecution, but that a meeting had taken place with the University's

The University had agreed with Hicham Yezza that outstanding fees from his period as a doctoral student should be deducted from his salary, but in the course of making the administrative arrangements for these deductions someone, somewhere, seems to have noticed the legal deficiencies in his other documents. A number of letters requesting that he supply the necessary paperwork had gone unanswered. It is fair to say that, for Hicham Yezza, the immigration game was nearly up even before his arrest.

The University, in the event, has paid a heavier price for employing someone illegally than any to which it would have been liable under the law: the damage to its reputation from the campaign, as well the harm done internally by the internecine strife to which it gave rise, are incalculable. For a period of over two months, many students and staff, often exploiting their own University's facilities, engaged in or lent their weight to a vociferous campaign against their own institution, and against the government (the two neatly aligned as representative of the repressive State), to protect the academic freedom and other rights of a man who was neither an academic, nor legally entitled to be in the country. One suspects that the practical moral of the case, for any Vice-Chancellor, would hardly be to take a bold and radically dissident stance on the Terrorism Acts, as the campaigners wished, but, more prosaically, to ensure that those without an automatic right to employment (including those already employed by the institution) are ever more rigorously screened to ensure full compliance with immigration law. There will also be closer scrutiny of the *bona fides* of students requiring visas for the purposes of study. We doubt if these were the desired objectives of the campaigners, but we suspect it is the most by way of change they shall have achieved.

Conclusion

On 13 February 2009, Hicham Yezza was found guilty at Northampton Crown Court of securing avoidance of enforcement action by deceptive

management with a view to ensuring future compliance. The authors made a Freedom of Information enquiry to the University and were informed that no notification of prosecution for employing an illegal immigrant had been received by the University (email from Theresa Pollard to Macdonald Daly, 26 March 2009).

means. He had been illegally resident in the U.K. since January 2003. On 6 March 2009 he was sentenced to nine months in prison.

No reasonable person could feel anything but sadness faced with this story of an intelligent, gifted, peaceable, young man having his life so turned upside down. The saddest thing is how avoidable it all seems. It could have been avoided had the University of Nottingham's Department of Human Resources exercised the institution's statutory duty to check the legality of Hicham Yezza's residency: instead, it allowed him to continue in its employment for fifteen months. His imprisonment could have been prevented had Hicham Yezza been administratively removed or had he left the country without trial in the summer of 2008, an offer that was made to him but which he rejected, perhaps persuaded by the very violence of the campaign on his behalf that the tissue of untruth and assertion would actually exculpate him. It might not have happened had thousands of people and a Member of Parliament who is not standing for re-election desisted from encouraging a person already under acute stress into enduring a legal trial which he was, it would appear, almost bound to lose. It might not have happened had *The Guardian* not made Hicham Yezza its human rights poster-boy for fifteen minutes (needless to say the paper *never even reported* his trial and conviction, if ever further proof were needed of the dangerous imbalance of its reporting), and/or had *Times Higher Education* curtailed the excesses of its coverage of his case earlier than it did. And, of course, none of this would have happened had Rizwaan Sabir been prepared to pay for his own printing, or had his supervisors been alert to their responsibilities in respect of his handling of potentially inflammatory materials – ironically, issues which later became the very topic of this young man's Ph.D.

The Vice-Chancellor of the University of Nottingham left his post at the end of September 2008. The events related in this essay occurred in what he already knew to be the last six months of his tenure. One might imagine that a departing Vice-Chancellor, particularly one who is also a prominent public figure, might among his valedictory activities, in the twilight of his career, say or do something of moment to encourage those over whom he has had stewardship. But the note sounded as he prepared to leave the University of Nottingham was more minatory than heartening. On 17 July 2008 *Times Higher Education* reported a statement he had issued to University staff which included these words on academic freedom: "There is no 'right' to access and research terrorist materials. Those who do so run the risk of being investigated and prosecuted on terrorism charges. Equally, there is no 'prohibition' on accessing terrorist materials for the purpose of research. Those who do so are likely to be able to offer a defence to charges (although they may be held in custody for some time while the matter is investigated). This is the law and applies to all universities."[47]

One can see how superficially clever this is: in effect, it exonerates Rizwaan Sabir and Hicham Yezza (because it suggests they had ultimately been able to offer an acceptable defence to potential terrorist charges) but also exonerates the authorities (because it acknowledges their right to investigate and detain). And on this occasion, the Vice-Chancellor seemed to be implying, the system had worked: no one was unjustly harmed, and all's right with the world. But what is frightening, and revealing, is the diffidence shown in the face of the possibility of one's employees or students being arrested and held in custody while their possessions are seized and relatives questioned. What is absent from the statement is any kind of acknowledgment that a university has any rôle in this potentially difficult and compromising relation between researcher and police which, also as a matter of law, it surely does.

The University is meant to be a guarantor of academic freedom for those who fulfil their contractual obligations to it by conducting research. It is meant to have procedures and policies in place to ensure that researchers can confidently, within the law, "put forward new ideas and controversial or unpopular opinions, without placing themselves in jeopardy of losing their jobs or privileges".[48] This statement fails to communicate any sense of a responsibility to ensure that legitimate researchers do *not* work and live under the threat of being arrested and put in custody *until* they can demonstrate their credentials as researchers rather than as suspected terrorists. This is not to suggest that a university could have the power to *prevent* the police from arresting an innocent

---

[47] Melanie Newman, "Researchers have no 'right' to study terrorist materials", *Times Higher Education*, 17 July 2008 (**http://www.timeshigheredu cation.co.uk/story.asp?sectioncode=26&storycode=402844**, accessed 27 April 2009).
[48] See **http://www.nottingham.ac.uk/registrar/calendar/statutes/stat ute-35.pdf**, accessed 17 June 2008.

member of its staff. It is simply to say that a university must make every effort, in its own internal organisation, and in its relations with external authorities, to minimise such a possibility. What would be morally questionable, in this event, would be to strike the pose of Pontius Pilate: such a stance can give legitimate researchers no confidence at all, and is only likely to lead to controversial lines of research being avoided out of the basest fear.

It is not so much, then, that this statement is incorrect as a factual description of what might happen in any given scenario. But it is *inadequate* as a description of what usually should be the case. And this suggests the real damage done to the idea of the university in the course of these events. The Vice-Chancellor himself, after all, had long since abandoned academic work. He had not been an academic researcher for the preceding two decades and there is little evidence that he valued academic research any longer in its own right. Instead, he concentrated, very successfully, on making the University of Nottingham commercially competitive and business-friendly, to the extent, as the University's public affairs website still records, of calling, in September 1999, "for the effective privatisation of universities, saying that what is good for telephone companies, railways and airlines must be good for academia, too".[49] Although always a conventional and establishment figure, his earlier career as a Professor of Law encompassed areas of interest that might surprise those who later contemplated the man at close quarters. In 1980, for example, he edited a volume entitled *Do We Need a Bill of Rights?*,[50] a question to which his answer was, surprisingly, *perhaps we do.* By July 2008, however, his talk was, neutrally, of the rights researchers did *not* have.

One of the first public actions of the new Vice-Chancellor, David Greenaway, was to record a video interview for the University of Nottingham website in which he restated his own continued personal commitment to teaching and research, implying an understanding of the considerable benefit to a university of a Vice-Chancellor who continues

---

[49] See **http://www.nott.ac.uk/public-affairs/pressreleases/press-up. phtml?menu=pressuparchive&sub=153** (*International Herald Tribune* entry, 1/9).

[50] C. M. Campbell (ed.), *Do We Need a Bill of Rights?* (London: Temple Smith, 1980).

with active academic work.[51] Outsiders seemed to notice an immediately perceptible change of style: a *Nottingham Evening Post* reporter who interviewed the new Vice-Chancellor could not help but record, "The first sign of a new broom are [*sic*] the changes to the vice-chancellor's office. Gone is the Regency-style wallpaper and the green leather armchairs. The walls are painted plain grey and modern furniture has been introduced." [52] Furnishing choices are unlikely to bolster academic freedom, but we suspect a Vice-Chancellor who is himself an active researcher is likely to have such freedom higher on his agenda than one who is not.

Our conclusion is that, in the case of Hicham Yezza and Rizwaan Sabir, the University of Nottingham did not abandon its publicly stated commitment to academic freedom. Put in its most legalistic form, neither man had a claim to academic freedom because neither was an academic member of staff. Reviewing events in the most sympathetic light, one still has to acknowledge that Hicham Yezza's very presence in the country, and his employment at the University of Nottingham, were illegitimate, and Rizwaan Sabir's forwarding of the document was, at root, what initiated his friend's undoing. To criticise the University for the personally catastrophic results is perverse.

The most distressing aspect of the case, however, has not been the revelation of new threats to academic freedom, which continue to take the form of the insidious managerialism, craven instrumentalism and creeping commercialisation which characterise the reality of life in a twenty-first century university rather than any Big Brother bogey, but the nature of the Hicham Yezza campaign and, still more surprisingly, the liberal media's embrace of it. The strategic misrepresentation of Hicham Yezza's status, the mobilisation of widespread public concern about both immigration and terror legislation on his behalf, might be excusable (if not by us) on the grounds of efficacy – *had* they been successful, but of

---

[51] The video is available at **http://vc.nottingham.ac.uk/An-interview-with-the-Vice-Chancellor.html** (accessed 30 April 2009).

[52] Richard Tressider, "Inside man takes over at the helm", *Nottingham Evening Post*, 3 March 2009 (**http://www.thisisnottingham.co.uk/news/Inside-man-takes-helm/article-738454-detail/article.html**, accessed 29 April 2009). Note for the fastidious: the previous Vice-Chancellor's upholstery was actually dark blue.

course, with tragical and real personal consequences for Hicham Yezza if not for his idealistic supporters, they were not. The involvement of so many academics in the cause, colleagues who appear to have failed to assure themselves of the most basic truths of the case, in no small part because of their own *trust in the academic status and responsibility* of *other* colleagues, was a cause of genuine shock. Equally surprising was the convergence of conventional media and journalism (particularly in *The Guardian* and *Times Higher Education* but also, as we have shown, in publications around the world) with the blogosphere and "independent" media in the reporting – or rather promotion – of the campaign. There has been, in fact, little or nothing in the way of real investigative journalism, and much in the way of the simple trumpeting of a new orthodoxy of enlightenment. It would be simplistic to reduce the moral of these events to the level of the boy who cried wolf: the exposure of what we can only consider a significant *trahison des clercs*, alongside the overwhelming evidence of supine and rebarbative conduct on the part of independent and mainstream media, however, can only make one fearful for the health and vitality of our ever more necessary contemporary cultures of dissent.

2009

OTHER BOOKS BY MACDONALD DALY

AUTHORED OR CO-AUTHORED

A Primer in Marxist Aesthetics

Crackpot Texts: Absurd Explorations in Modern and Postmodern Literature

Engels on Video

Reading Radio 4: A Programme-by-Programme Analysis of Britain's Most Important Radio Station

EDITED OR CO-EDITED

Margaret Thatcher in Her Own Words

The Invisible Man by H. G. Wells

Mary Barton by Elizabeth Gaskell

Sons and Lovers by D. H. Lawrence

Kangaroo by D. H. Lawrence

Four Tales by John Herdman

Silviano Santiago in Conversation

Karl Marx and Frederick Engels on Literature and Art

Dead Iraqis: Selected Short Stories of Ellis Sharp

The Genres of Post-Conflict Testimonies

"Black and Whites" and other new short stories from Malaysia

Labyrinths: The Electronic Journal of Literary Postmodernism

www.ingramcontent.com/pod-product-compliance
Lightning Source LLC
Chambersburg PA
CBHW032036080426
42733CB000006B/96